The American
Political Scandal

Communication, Media, and Politics
Series Editor: Robert E. Denton, Jr., Virginia Tech

This series features a range of work dealing with the role and function of communication in the realm of politics, broadly defined. Including general academic books and texts for use in graduate and advanced undergraduate courses, the series encompasses humanistic, critical, historical, and empirical studies in political communication in the United States. Primary subject areas include campaigns and elections, media, and political institutions. *Communication, Media, and Politics* books will be of interest to students, teachers, and scholars of political communication from the disciplines of communication, rhetorical studies, political science, journalism, and political sociology.

The 2004 Presidential Campaign: A Communication Perspective
  Edited by Robert E. Denton, Jr.
Transforming Conflict: Communication and Ethnopolitical Conflict
  Donald G. Ellis
Bush's War: Media Bias and Justifications for War in a Terrorist Age
  Jim A. Kuypers
Center Stage: Media and the Performance of American Politics
  Gary C. Woodward
Message Control: How News Is Made on the Campaign Trail
  Elizabeth A. Skewes
Tag Teaming the Press: How Bill and Hillary Clinton Work Together to Handle the Media
  James E. Mueller
The 2008 Presidential Campaign: A Communication Perspective
  Edited by Robert E. Denton, Jr.
The 2012 Presidential Campaign: A Communication Perspective
  Edited by Robert E. Denton, Jr.
Last Man Standing: Media, Framing, and the 2012 Republican Primaries
  Danielle Sarver Coombs
Partisan Journalism: A History of Media Bias in the United States
  Jim A. Kuypers
The American Political Scandal: Free Speech, Public Discourse, and Democracy
  David R. Dewberry
Political Campaign Communication: Principles and Practices, Eighth Edition
  Judith S. Trent, Robert V. Friedenberg, and Robert E. Denton, Jr.

The American Political Scandal

Free Speech, Public Discourse, and Democracy

David R. Dewberry

ROWMAN & LITTLEFIELD
Lanham • Boulder • New York • London

Published by Rowman & Littlefield
A wholly owned subsidiary of The Rowman & Littlefield Publishing Group, Inc.
4501 Forbes Boulevard, Suite 200, Lanham, Maryland 20706
www.rowman.com

Unit A, Whitacre Mews, 26-34 Stannary Street, London SE11 4AB, United Kingdom

British Library Cataloguing in Publication Information Available

Library of Congress Cataloging-in-Publication Data
Dewberry, David R., 1977–
    The American political scandal : free speech, public discourse, and democracy / David R. Dewberry.
    pages cm. — (Communication, media, and politics)
    Includes bibliographical references and index.
    ISBN 978-1-4422-4291-3 (cloth : alk. paper) — ISBN 978-1-4422-4292-0 (electronic)
    1. Communication in politics—United States. 2. Scandals—United States. 3. Misconduct in office—United States. 4. Political culture—United States. I. Title.
    JK2249.D48 2015
    320.973—dc23

                                                                                    2015014725

∞™ The paper used in this publication meets the minimum requirements of American National Standard for Information Sciences—Permanence of Paper for Printed Library Materials, ANSI/NISO Z39.48-1992.

Printed in the United States of America

Contents

Preface

One of the most pervasive and perplexing forms of contemporary political communication is the scandal. While there are many books that address political scandals, *The American Political Scandal: Free Speech, Public Discourse, and Democracy* hopes to make a unique contribution in offering a holistic explanation and critique, not just a mere description, of the entire political scandal from start to finish.

The American Political Scandal answers questions such as, What is (and is not) a scandal? What are the conditions that bring about a scandal? Is freedom of the press as great as we hope in scandals? How are seemingly innocuous actions turned into major scandals to further political ends? How do the accused's actions at the end of the scandal affect the nature of democracy?

The answers to these questions provide the basis for the overarching argument of the book: that the government that creates the scandal is the very same government that rectifies the scandal. This closed system has severe implications for the study and practice of free speech, rhetoric, and democracy, which are discussed in each chapter.

ACKNOWLEDGMENTS

This book has been seven years in the making. It began with a question about political scandals posed by Dr. Christina Foust at the University of Denver. Her guidance and love of rhetoric has stayed with me to this day.

I am thankful for all the good people, friends, and my lovely wife who have helped me along the way with their continuous support. I appreciate the guidance of Leanne Silverman at Rowman & Littlefield and Dr. Robert Denton, who helped make this book possible. I am especially thankful for all those who have offered ideas and insights, including the peer reviewers for Rowman & Littlefield. All that is good with this book is because of them.

Chapter One

Scandalous State of the Union

The American political landscape is and has been littered with scandals. Once president, Obama quickly faced scandals due to three of his cabinet nominations.[1] Former senator Tom Daschle withdrew his nomination for secretary of health and human services after allegations that he had over $140,000 in unpaid taxes. Nancy Killefer was nominated to be President Obama's budget chief, but she also withdrew her nomination due to a tax scandal. Bill Richardson was Obama's nominee for secretary of commerce, but he withdrew due to allegations of accepting kickbacks during his tenure as governor of New Mexico.

Congress has had its fair share of scandals as well. U.S. senator John Ensign resigned in 2011 after a Senate Ethics Committee determined that he had tried to cover up an extramarital affair with one of his aides, who was also married to another one of Ensign's top aides.[2] Rep. Charles Rangel was censured by the House of Representatives for breaching the public trust in a number of violations ranging from soliciting donations from those who had matters before the Ways and Means Committee, which he chaired, to not paying taxes on his Caribbean home and not properly reporting over $600,000 in income and assets.[3] Rep. Tom DeLay was convicted and sentenced to three years in prison for money laundering in relation to another scandal involving Jack Abramoff, who himself engaged in a number of illegal lobbying practices.[4] Rep. Bob Ney was also involved in the Abramoff scandal and was sentenced to a thirty-month prison sentence.[5]

Not to be outdone by their legislative counterparts, the judicial branch has also had its share of scandals. Federal Judge G. Thomas Porteous was unanimously impeached and convicted for receiving cash and favors from lawyers, using false names to elude creditors, and intentionally misleading Congress during his confirmation hearing.[6] Another federal judge, Samuel Kent, was sentenced to thirty-three months for obstructing justice in regard to claims that he had sexually harassed his secretary and case manager.[7]

Even governors get into the mix. Illinois governor Rod Blagojevich attempted to sell President Obama's vacant Senate seat to the highest bidder, which is just one of the many controversies the former governor turned inmate has faced.[8] In fact, Blagojevich is just one of a handful of Illinois governors who have served time in prison for actions taken in office. As of the writing of the book, four of the last seven Illinois governors have been sentenced to prison for some form of chicanery.

President Bush also had his share of scandal-ridden cabinet nominees. Bush's nomination for secretary of labor in 2001, Linda Chavez, employed a live-in illegal alien.[9] One of Bush's top candidates for secretary of the treasury and secretary of energy, Kenneth Lay, who was also part of Bush's transition team into office, committed accounting fraud for years, which later resulted in the collapse of Enron.[10] In early 2005, *USA Today* and the *New York Times* reported that the Bush administration had paid columnists Armstrong Williams, Maggie Gallagher, and Michael McManus for their endorsement of the administration's policies.[11]

In addition, the Bush administration's firing of eight U.S. attorneys in March 2007 became a scandal after it was determined that the firings were politically motivated and not based on their performance. The purported political motivations for the firings were that some attorneys refused to investigate voter fraud after the 2006 elections, and others had successfully prosecuted Republican congressional representatives for bribery and fraud.[12]

Clinton's administration also had its share of scandals. Clinton's national security advisor, Samuel Berger, pleaded guilty in 2005 to removing classified documents regarding terrorist attacks from the National Archives in 2003 and cutting them up with scissors in his office before throwing them in the trash.[13] Berger initially claimed that removal of the documents—which he stuffed in his briefcase, jacket, and pants—as well as copies of notes in his own handwriting, was "an honest mistake."[14]

This list of scandals is in no way complete. There are innumerable scandals at the national, state, and local levels, and they occur in the executive, legislative, and judicial branches. What this list shows is that the political environment in the United States is riddled with scandals. The result is twofold. The presence of a scandal reveals that people in the government are up to no good. However, the system has worked. The wrongdoing has been revealed and addressed.

SEEING SCANDALS IN A NEW LIGHT

Political scandals demonstrate the worst and, paradoxically, the best of democratic ideals. On one hand, there is the accused politician, who has allegedly gone astray and transgressed the line between what is deemed appropriate and inappropriate. On the other hand, it is a vigorous press corps, protected by the First Amendment, that publicizes the alleged transgression.[15] Then there is an investigation by the government and, if warranted, a trial. Ultimately, the accused is either redeemed or punished. Often the punishment is removal from office by force of law or via resignation. The expunging of the accused demonstrates how the democratic system is fallible but able to redeem itself. In essence, the system that creates the conditions for scandals is the very same system that rectifies scandals. It is the government's ability to promote a democratic ideology while sustaining itself in the context of scandal that is the focus of this book.

Specifically, the book argues that a political scandal allows a democratic government to demonstrate its potential for self-sustainment, which limits the agency of the people. The scandal allows a democratic ideology to emerge at the beginning, middle, and end of the process. In the beginning, there is the appearance of a truly independent and vigorous press corps. In the middle, there are official investigations that follow the rule of law. In the end, there are the punishment (or vindication) and redemption of the accused that allow for the rebirth of power. However, the four major scandals examined here challenge this democratic ideology. Teapot Dome, Watergate, Iran-Contra, and Clinton/Lewinsky all demonstrate that the press is not as independent from the government as we might believe, that official investigations blur the line between judicial and congressional inquiry, and that allowing the accused to serve as his or her own redeemer severely limits the agency of the people.

In making these arguments, the book makes three main contributions. First, it offers a theoretical framework that can be used to describe and interpret political scandals. Many scholars address scandals topically or historically, and these treatments can be beneficial. However, addressing scandals topically misses the narrative structure of scandal, which, as will be shown, is instrumental in establishing a democratic ideology. Historical accounts do offer a narrative account of the scandal, but they only offer that and little to no theoretical or critical commentary. Consequently, the purpose of this book is to provide a holistic and in-depth understanding and explanation of political scandals.

The second contribution this book offers is a method of analysis to evaluate political scandals. Certainly, addressing scandals from the point of view of history reveals all the hidden aspects that were not known while the scandal was playing out. But we experience scandals as they happen, not in the rearview mirror of history. Consequently, it is beneficial to examine scandals as they were experienced at the time.

Third, this book uses four critical cases to explore this method of analysis. They are Teapot Dome, Watergate, Iran-Contra, and Clinton/Lewinsky. Furthermore, these examples provide a vocabulary for talking and thinking about scandals, they show how scandals enact democratic ideologies, and they suggest ways to address future scandals, which, if history repeats itself, will certainly be coming. In later chapters, the book addresses a few congressional and state-level scandals, scandals that just faded away, and some that are not really scandals at all. There are two reasons for including these smaller examples. First, they provide nuance and detail to some finer points of the political scandal that the major examples do not provide. Second, some of the smaller examples are more contemporary than the critical cases. These contemporary scandals provide examples that demonstrate the heuristic value of the ideas presented in chapters 2 through 5. But before examining the scandals themselves, we must first address what is (and is not) a scandal. Subsequently, we will review the conditions that allow scandals to come to light and preview the major scandals that are discussed in this book.

CONCEPTUALIZING SCANDAL

The earlier review of contemporary scandals demonstrates two fundamental aspects of a scandal that scholars have noted. First, a public person is perceived to have transgressed some legal, ethical, moral, or public standard.[16] In a political scandal, these actions or behaviors may or may not be related to the position of being a public person. For example, the perceived transgression could be sexual, financial, or power based.[17] Importantly, the perceived transgressions must be specific and cannot be broad-brush criticisms, general incompetence, or unpopular policies.[18] The public person can be an elected officeholder, a person seeking political office, or generally an individual appointed to or seeking a position of the public's trust.

Second, the public must know of the alleged misconduct, which the accused individual or others working on the individual's behalf must have actively attempted to suppress from public view.[19] As such, scandals originate in the relationship between attempted secrecy and the eventual publicity of some transgression. This aspect of covering up the crime, even if the crime is not a crime in the strictest sense, is what creates a scandal.

Secrecy and Publicity

This cover-up must be distinguished to some degree from the secrecy of the alleged transgression. For example, breaking into an office building at night and disguising oneself or hiding one's face may be seen as an attempt at concealment. However, for concealment to reach the level of scandal, the cover-up must be different and separate from the crime itself. Continuing the example, if one were to break into an office building and then parties affiliated with the break-in tried to cover it up or the burglar later tried to cover up the incident, then this would reach the level of secrecy and cover-up required to be properly considered a scandal. The degree of concealment can certainly affect the level of severity of the scandal in the public's mind.

In this conceptualization, it is important to note that the initial transgression may seem particularly pernicious, but the act does not make a scandal. Once the cover-up is revealed, then there is scandal. Before a series of events earns the title of scandal, some may use the term loosely to describe what is happening or call it a controversy or misconduct.

Thus, a political scandal is when a politician or other individual in government, who is perceived to have transgressed some legal, ethical, moral, or public standard, attempts (or someone on their behalf attempts) to conceal the action, which ultimately proves unsuccessful.[20] Defining a scandal in terms of the public's perception of an action as well as the attempted secrecy and resulting publicity makes scandal a rhetorical phenomenon.

This secrecy-publicity conceptualization follows Thompson's definition of scandal.[21] Thompson defines scandal as "actions or events involving certain kinds of transgression which become known to others and are sufficiently serious to elicit a public response."[22] In his explication of this definition, Thompson clarifies that there is some element of secrecy or concealment to the transgressions, which can be a "'second-order transgression' where attention is shifted from the original offense to a series of subsequent actions, which are aimed at concealing the offence."[23] This part of Thompson's definition is most useful. There is the popular cliché that the "cover-up is worse than the crime," but for the purposes here, the cover-up and the crime make the scandal. Thus, the second-order element of a scandal should not be considered ancillary to the first-order transgression; rather they are both required to reach the level of full scandal.

The aspects of secrecy and publicity regarding perceived misconduct distinguish the scandal from an ethics violation. Scandals arise from the publicity of an ethics violation. Scandals involve, as shown to this point, public officials or public persons—people in positions of public trust—who are expected to perform to a higher standard than society as a whole.[24] Typically, the scandal arises when there is widely disseminated knowledge about the behavior of public people and the public's expectations to which such people are accountable. Thus, one of the main aspects of the scandal is not the "conduct itself but its relation to a public role, and the attendant expectations of that role."[25] In other words, scandals differ from ethics violations in that scandals arise not from the misconduct itself but in the publicity of political or personal misconduct, which, prior to the publicity, has been actively suppressed or withheld from the public.

The aspect of receiving publicity also differentiates scandals from corruption. Corruption can be simply defined as an unknown (or widespread) scandal. As such, "scandal is corruption revealed."[26] For example, a repressive dictatorship may be completely corrupt and have no scandals whatsoever. However, corruption in a democracy has the ability to be uncovered by a vibrant free press, thereby becoming a scandal.

There are numerous competing definitions of scandal, and I have attempted to work from those definitions. Nevertheless, one could certainly point to a scandal that would not be classified as such according to my or others' definitions. I would caution, however, that there are many examples in which a political pundit labels some action as a scandal, but those events or actions may not truly be considered a scandal. In situations like this, the term "scandal" is used vernacularly. Thus, there are scandals and there are nonscandals.

Scandals and Nonscandals

The term "scandal" is used rather loosely in everyday discourse. Consequently, it is useful to not only define what a scandal is but also provide examples of what is and is not a scandal. Immediately, we can say that if a politician transgresses some standard and no one ever learns about it, then it is not a scandal. Like a tree falling in the middle of empty woods, if a politician engages in some malfeasance and no one is there to see or hear it, it did not happen. This is the obvious reason why people would attempt to conceal their actions.

Sen. Bob Packwood was accused of sexual harassment and abuse of women after having served in Congress for twenty-five years. In the resulting investigation, Packwood's diary was subpoenaed. He eventually turned part of the diary over, but it was soon discovered that he had altered information in the diary.[27] There was an attempt, perhaps minor, to conceal and suppress, but an attempt nonetheless. Thus Packwood transgressed a moral and public standard which holds that sexual harassment is to be avoided, and he attempted a cover-up by concealing his actions, which ultimately proved unsuccessful.

There are politicians who transgress some boundary and do not attempt, to any degree, to cover up their actions, and these therefore should not be considered a scandal. For example, Sen. Mike Crapo, a Mormon from Idaho, had one too many drinks at his home and went for a drive around the nation's capital and surrounding suburbs just a few days before Christmas in 2012. He ran a red light and was quickly stopped and arrested for drinking and driving. Did he cross a boundary? Yes. He committed an illegal action, and his drinking violated his and his Mormon constituents' values. Did he in any way attempt to suppress his actions? No. With no suppression or concealment, this type of action, while egregious, is not a scandal.

Since there must be an attempt to keep the misconduct from the public, the actions of Trent Lott and George Allen are not scandals because neither attempted to cover up their actions. Republican senator Trent Lott resigned his position as Senate majority leader because of comments he made in 2002 at the one hundredth birthday party of Strom Thurmond, who ran for president in 1948. Sen. Lott suggested that if Thurmond had won the election, there would be fewer problems facing the country today. The concern was that Thurmond ran for president primarily as a segregationist. While Lott's comments were certainly shocking and inappropriate and could be called scandalous, the resulting turmoil was not a scandal because there was no attempt at secrecy. Lott went on to be reelected in 2006 and became the minority whip in the Senate.

Republican senator George Allen was not so lucky, as he lost his reelection bid in 2006. During the election, Allen referred to one of his opponents' staff members with a racial slur. Moreover, Allen had also used various racial slurs throughout his college career. While these examples are not scandals per se, they often do "trigger a series of questions about the conduct of politicians."[28] When politicians are unwilling or incapable of answering such questions, the result is more and more questions. These questions might result in the discovery of a scandal (i.e., some perceived misconduct in Allen's past that he attempted to suppress); nevertheless, using inappropriate language or holding controversial beliefs is not a scandal. When Nixon's tapes were released, people were shocked by the president's foul language, which was omitted in the transcripts as "expletive deleted," but the real scandal had to do with the words that addressed the cover-up.

Another example of behavior that might raise eyebrows but is not considered a scandal is from the Texas lieutenant governor David Dewhurst. Dewhurst's relative was arrested for shoplifting at a grocery store. Dewhurst called the police department and asked the on-duty sergeant what he had to do to get his relative out of jail. Dewhurst explained how he was constantly highly ranked by Texas law enforcement agencies and repeatedly said that he wanted to do what was proper and did not want to circumvent any procedures. Some may claim that this is an attempt to use power to help a relative, but the police department released a statement that said they receive many such calls from relatives. Furthermore, there was no attempt to cover up the fact that the call had taken place. In fact, the police did not alter the tapes in any way. Dewhurst was on hold for two minutes during the call, and that entire time was not edited out. The police only edited out the lieutenant governor when he provided his personal cell phone number. Certainly it would have been very easy to cut out the two minutes, but the inclusion of it suggests that the rest of the recording has been unedited, save for the clearly reasonable edits to protect Dewhurst's private information.

There are cases where it is unclear whether there is a cover-up. For example, Sen. Larry Craig was arrested for lewd conduct in an airport restroom. Craig allegedly attempted to solicit an undercover police officer for sex. Craig disagreed with the arresting officer's characterization of his actions during his interrogation immediately after his arrest. Craig claimed that he was not signaling with his foot and hand under the restroom stall divider; rather he was a "fairly wide guy."[29] Much was made out of this response, and it became shortened to "wide stance."

The question here is whether Craig's characterization is a cover-up. One could argue that the wide stance defense was an attempt at a cover-up. However, this assumes that Craig was, in fact, soliciting sex. Giving Craig the benefit of the doubt, he may have been telling the truth. If the officer mischaracterized Craig's action, then what seemed like a cover-up is, in actuality, the truth. Again, this is giving him the benefit of the doubt.[30] If we do not give him that benefit, it would seem that the wide stance defense was an attempted cover-up. Whether one believes his statements are a cover-up or not, his remarks did not stop the accusations.

Craig later pled guilty to a lesser charge of disorderly conduct. He later said, "I chose to plead guilty to a lesser charge in hopes of making it go away."[31] Craig's comments could be taken as he did not want the information to get out, which is the point of a cover-up. If so, it was not successful, as the incident gained international attention. However, trying to make the charges go away could be interpreted as just that, avoiding them. That is, Craig was not trying to hide his actions from the public. He just wanted to avoid the issue and put it behind him, which is not a cover-up per se, at least compared to other more prominent scandals. Nevertheless, the Craig example demonstrates that cover-ups are based on perception. What one person believes is a cover-up may not necessarily be what another sees.

Sex, Money, and Power

From the previous examples, we can underscore two other important aspects of scandals. First, the basis for scandals can be virtually anything, but scandals typically arise from issues related to sex, money, and power. A comprehensive list of presidential and congressional scandals just from 2000 to the present would provide too many examples of scandals arising from the pursuit of money and power. Typically, congressional scandals involve money, and presidential scandals involve power. However, congressional representatives and presidents have both been involved in sex scandals. Newt Gingrich, who was the Speaker of the House during Clinton's impeachment for lying about a sexual relationship, was also engaged in an extramarital affair at the time. Before becoming vice president, Sen. Lyndon Johnson chased down and threatened the life of the Capitol Hill police officer who had inadvertently walked in on him and a female staffer late one night.[32]

While sex, money, and power scandals are all omnipresent in American politics, sex scandals are a bit different for two reasons. First, sex scandals do not necessarily involve abuse of power. Second, sex scandals are not politically motivated but do have political consequences. That is, "they are political scandals by accident, not in essence."[33] For example, Clinton's relationships had nothing to do with his executive leadership, as the numerous opinion polls stated, but did have indirect effects on his moral leadership.

The attempt to cover up misconduct is also present in sex scandals. While both Clinton and Gingrich had extramarital relations in the late 1990s, Clinton's was exposed in the 1990s, despite his attempts to cover up his actions by (in)famously debating what "is" means. Gingrich admitted his affair years later in 2007. Gingrich claimed that he did not attempt to cover up his actions but just chose not to reveal the information.

There are also sexting scandals. Sexting scandals do not involve physical sexual activities but are sexual in nature. U.S. representative Anthony Weiner repeatedly sent lewd and explicit pictures of himself to young females. Weiner's scandal will serve as the contemporary case study in chapter 6.

Rep. Mark Foley was also involved in a sexting controversy. Foley had contacted young congressional pages, who were high school juniors, with sexually suggestive e-mails and instant messages. There were reports that he had sexual relationships with two former pages. Such actions by a member of Congress, who was the chairman of the House Caucus on Missing and Exploited Children, certainly crossed a boundary.

But was there a cover-up, thereby making it a scandal? It depends on whom you believe. Again, perception is at play. Democrats insisted that the Republicans were covering up their own, whereas Republicans said there was clear and egregious wrongdoing but no cover-up. However, the Republican characterization is questionable. Republican Speaker of the House Dennis Hastert gave contrasting details about what he knew and when. At first the Speaker claimed he learned of Foley's actions when the story broke in the news. Then Republican representative Thomas Reynolds announced that he had informed Hastert's top aides about the messages as early as fall 2005. Republican majority leader John Boehner said he personally told Hastert about Foley months before the scandal broke; Hastert, according to Boehner, replied, "We're taking care of it."[34] Hastert did not disagree with these accounts; he just did not remember them taking place.

Eventually the matter was turned over to three representatives who oversaw the page program. Two were Republicans and one was a Democrat, who stated,

"I was never informed of the allegations about Mr. Foley's inappropriate communications with a House page, and I was never involved in any inquiry into this matter."[35] Although it is unclear whether any attempt at secrecy was actually made, the facts strongly suggest that there was, so we could properly label this a scandal.

Presidential and Congressional Scandals

While the conceptualization of the scandal presented here has used presidential and congressional scandals interchangeably, the presidential scandal is of primary concern for two reasons. First, "unlike members of Congress, who represent special constituencies, the president represents *all* the people."[36] When the president is involved in a scandal, it becomes an issue for everyone. A scandal-plagued senator in New Jersey may have no impact on the people in the great state of Arkansas. Second, the presidential scandal involves the "extra-constitutional powers of subverting the democratic process."[37] Therefore, next to the president, who "is charged with ensuring that the laws are faithfully executed, in terms of political profile, no other individual in government has more to lose through allegation of participation in corrupt, unwise or illegal activities."[38] This makes the president the prime target for scandalous accusations.

Moreover, presidential scandals are more severe compared to congressional scandals. Congress is able to mitigate the public fallout of their own scandals and exacerbate the damage of presidential scandals because "not only does Congress itself choose what scandals to investigate but it also appoints its own investigators."[39] Furthermore, the ethical violations that occur in Congress often never make it to the light of day. In the past, Capitol Hill police officers have often been disciplined by their superiors for stopping members of Congress for drinking and driving, and in several cases they have been told to let them go and never speak of the matter.[40] That is, the overseeing agent in congressional scandals is Congress itself, whereas the executive branch's self-investigation is typically met with skepticism. For example, five investigations of the Watergate break-in were ordered by the Nixon administration, and all found no wrongdoing on behalf of the president; external investigations, not surprisingly, came to different conclusions.

When Scandals Fizzle

There are big scandals, like Watergate, and there are shorter and smaller scandals. Then there are scandals that start and just fizzle out. One such example involved Janet Rehnquist, daughter of former Supreme Court chief justice William Rehnquist.

President Bush appointed Janet Rehnquist as the inspector general of the Department of Health and Human Services in 2001. After a rather uneventful start, there was some concern in late 2002. Two members of Congress, one Republican and one Democrat, quickly called for a review of her actions after it was discovered that she forced Clinton-era staffers out of the department and kept an unauthorized gun with no safety lock in her desk.

About two weeks after Rehnquist's questionable actions were first brought to light, she and the president's brother, Florida governor Jeb Bush, shared the scandalous spotlight. Apparently, Gov. Bush had asked Janet Rehnquist to delay a federal audit of the state's retirement funds, which the governor oversaw. Rehnquist willingly delayed the investigation, claiming there were staff issues, and started the investigation at a point when the audit would be completed after the November 2002 elections, which the governor won by a landslide.

Shortly after these revelations, speculation of wrongdoing increased as her office shredded documents after receiving notice that it was being investigated. Rehnquist claimed that her office routinely shredded documents to prevent the release of individuals' personal and health information. In response to three governmental investigations, Rehnquist resigned in June 2003.

With clear wrongdoing and actions that seemed like a cover-up—given an ongoing investigation—the ordeal was a scandal. But given that Rehnquist resigned and that Gov. Bush won his reelection by a landslide, which suggests that whatever help the delayed investigation provided, it was not necessarily needed, the scandal began to fizzle out.

In response to her resignation, a spokesman from the congressional investigation said that he was unsure if the inquiry into her actions would continue. Nevertheless, an investigation found that Rehnquist had created an "atmosphere of anxiety and distrust" and had repeated lapses in judgment.[41] Another investigation, however, found that Florida had overcharged the federal government. Despite the fact that the job of making sure the federal government was not being overcharged in such situations belonged to Rehnquist, nothing more came of this microscandal, and it faded from the news.

Another example of a scandal fizzling out involves Sen. Ted Stevens and the prosecutors who went after him. Ted Stevens, who was one of the longest-serving senators of all time, was found guilty of corruption in October 2008, which in part contributed to his losing his reelection bid in November and caused Republicans to lose control of the Senate. Stevens had failed to disclose numerous gifts he had received. Stevens claimed the omissions were due to sloppy bookkeeping and not criminal actions.

The gifts included remodeling and doubling the size of his home by workers from the VECO Corporation, an oil company in Alaska. This was not the first time VECO was in the news. In 2007, VECO executives were found guilty of bribing Alaskan state legislators. On a cursory view of the facts, it seems there was wrongdoing (i.e., receiving gifts from an oil company, with a questionable past, in an oil-rich state) and an attempt to keep things secret (i.e., failing to disclose). Such actions merit the title of scandal in the eyes of the public; however, that title was soon revoked.

The guilty verdict was overturned before sentencing due to prosecutorial misconduct. The prosecutor failed to share exculpatory evidence with the defense. The judge believed it to be one of the worst cases of judicial misconduct. A *Wall Street Journal* editorial stated, "Mr. Stevens deserved a fair trial and the full protection of the law. He got neither here, and that's a larger scandal than anything he was charged with."[42] In response, newly appointed attorney general Eric Holder stated, "In consideration of the totality of the circumstances of this particular case, I have determined that it is in the interest of justice to dismiss the indictment and not proceed with a new trial."[43]

The scandal that was, was no more, at least in terms of Stevens. The final report was completed in 2011, but some of the prosecutors who were under investigation attempted to keep the report from being released to the public. The report was eventually made public, but it did not get much attention as the senator was killed in a plane accident in 2010.

With a better understanding of what a scandal is, we can now turn to addressing the conditions that foster a scandal-ridden government.

THE CONTEXTS FOR SCANDAL

One of the major reasons there are so many scandals throughout the American political landscape is that the conditions of our political and governmental system allow it. While there may be several contextual factors that allow for political scandals, none is more important than the democratic ideals of our country. Scandals arise in the context of democratic governments with free speech and a careful and oftentimes zealous free press as a means of political accountability.

Free Speech

Free speech, protected in the United States by the First Amendment, allows citizens to criticize the government and thereby bring the scandal into being. Specifically, the nature and relationship between free speech and democracy in the United States make it an ideal location for examining scandals in the executive branch. As the example of the Zenger trial will suggest and all the previous examples confirm, "the United States has long enjoyed a reputation as a global leader in the political scandal."[44]

One of the major philosophical underpinnings of the First Amendment of the U.S. Constitution is the checking value of free speech.[45] In early eighteenth-century England, two British writers, John Trenchard and Thomas Gordon, used the pseudonym "Cato" to write essays criticizing the malfeasant English government. One of Cato's letters was *Of Freedom of Speech*, which argued that Roman and English history demonstrates that free speech presents no threat to enlightened rulers and was only harmful to tyrannical oppressors. Another writer was John Wilkes, who was a member of the House of Commons and published his own journal, the *North Briton*. In response to a speech by King George III, Wilkes viciously responded, which led to a charge of seditious libel, removal from Parliament, and having his personal office raided and his papers burned. He fled to France and sent several public letters back to England supporting his position. In one such letter, Wilkes wrote, "The liberty of the press . . . has been the terror of all bad ministers; for their dark and dangerous designs, or their weaknesses, inability, and duplicity, have thus been detected and shewn to the public."[46] A handful of other writers in England also used pseudonyms to argue on behalf of Wilkes. While such attitudes were not representative of the majority of English subjects, in the colonies this oppositional posture was "devoured" by the colonists.[47]

The proponent of the checking value of free speech, law professor Vincent Blasi, used the case of John Peter Zenger as a point of departure from the English conceptions of free speech to what would become the First Amendment. In 1730, Zenger worked as a printer for the *New York Weekly Journal*, which was the first politically independent newspaper in North America and was the first paper to openly criticize colonial governments.[48] Zenger published a critique of New York governor William Cosby, whom he called "a petty, tyrannical sycophant."[49] Although Zenger did not write the critique, he did print it. Like Wilkes, henchmen raided his office and burned his papers. The authorities charged Zenger with seditious libel in 1735. Zenger attained the counsel of Andrew Hamilton, who argued at the trial, in part, that truth is a defense. In just a matter of minutes, the jury returned a not guilty verdict, which garnered "loud cheers in the courtroom and has ever since been celebrated as one of the great events in the history of freedom of the press."[50]

The acceptance of truth as a defense altered the concept of free speech in the American colonies from that of England. That is, in England, seditious libel comprised "any false news or tales" that prompted any discord "between the king and his people."[51] True seditious libel would often create greater dissonance between the king and the people, for the criticism—

being true—could not be "defused by disproof," which prompted the "oft-quoted maxim after 1606 that 'the greater the truth, the greater the libel.'"[52]

It is the nature of the free press to investigate and publish the good, bad, and scandalous, that allows the publicity element of the scandal to exist. If there were no free press to reveal the transgression, then the cover-up and the underlying initial transgression would never be revealed. The tales of Zenger and Cato's letters provide the beginning of a long tale of journalists vanquishing tyrants, not with the sword, but with the word.

But the free press and freedom of speech are not the sole means of oversight. Judges and juries provide oversight, but their purpose differs from the press. While the press may be driven to increase circulation and disseminate the news, judges and juries seek to dispense justice. Mediating these two views are presidential commissions and independent counsels. Presidential commissions are research or investigative committees that are initiated by an act of the president. Examples of these include the Warren Commission, which investigated the Kennedy assassination; the Rogers Commission, which investigated the space shuttle *Challenger* accident; the Watkins Commission, which investigated the HIV epidemic in the 1980s; and the recent 9/11 Commission. Independent counsels, who are special prosecutors, investigate misconduct in the federal branch. One of the most famous recent examples is the independent counsel led by Kenneth Starr who investigated President Clinton. Presidential commissions and independent counsels do seek truth as the courts do, but they also widely publicize their findings—often in the form of written reports and verbal reports to Congress or, as Starr did, with numerous press leaks, which reaffirms the need for a free press to criticize our political leaders.[53]

Democracy

The context and ideals of democracy also allow for a scandal-rich environment. While most popular conceptualizations of democracy are as a procedural form of government with the driving principle that the people rule, this book also relies on a conceptualization of democracy as a civil religion. The idea of democracy as a civil religion has been the source of considerable debate ever since Robert Bellah introduced it in 1967. Although Bellah eventually came to abandon the idea, despite continuing to imply it in his later works, the idea still serves as a useful concept.[54] It is useful here because it drives the perspective taken, as will be shown, on the conclusion of the scandal.

Bellah argued, "There actually exists alongside of and rather clearly differentiated from the churches an elaborate and well-institutionalized civil religion in America."[55] While Bellah noted that America's civil religion was inspired by Christianity, it is "clearly not Christianity itself"; moreover, God is on the "austere side, much more related to order, law, and right than to salvation and love . . . and is actively interested and involved in history, with a special concern for America."[56] As such, America's civil religion is a manifestation of the archetypes in the Bible: "Europe is Egypt; America is the promised land. God has led his people to establish a new sort of social order that shall be a light unto all the nations."[57] The Americanized manifestations of these archetypes continue at the conclusion of the scandal.

There is no holy scripture of America's civil religion; rather it is a pastiche of sources including political speeches and writings that constitute the American scripture. If America's civil religion does arise from any one text, it is Thomas Jefferson's Declaration of Independence, which, beginning in 1787, local officials customarily read publicly on Independence Day. The day "constituted something of a 'religious observance,'" on which people would gather and listen to the reading as if it were a sermon.[58] At the time, people said that America was "destined to be the political redeemers of mankind!" and "Liberty descended from Heaven on the 4th of July, 1776."[59] The Fourth was seen as even more divinely inspired when Thomas Jefferson and his political opponent turned friend, President John Adams, both died on July 4, 1826—fifty years to the day.[60]

These notions of independence perpetuate values which stress that when the government or parts of the government become an impediment to democratic ends, they are to be removed or overcome. These same values are present at the end of a scandal. The accused, confirmed of wrongdoing, is detrimental to the ends of a democratic system, and there must be, not a revolution or rebellion, but a rebirth of leadership and power.

Bellah's notion of civil religion finds its basis in presidential rhetoric that invokes, in one fashion or another, God in the context of democracy. In fact, Bellah points out that all presidents have invoked God in their inaugural addresses, and many presidents invoke God in speeches on solemn occasions. The invocations of God or the Almighty do not point to any specific incarnation such as Christ, although civil religion heavily reflects a Protestant Christian theme. As such, the conclusion of the scandal almost necessitates a sacrifice for a rebirth of authority.

While the president is seen as the "high priest of American civil religion" and the Founding Fathers as the ones who ordained it, there is a question about the opposing evil.[61] Bellah's conceptualization of democracy as a civil religion asks, "Does American civil religion need a satanic image in order to exist?"[62] The majority of scholarship on the subject has found that the invocation of civil religion is for the purpose of war, from the Civil War to the Iraq

War and even the War on Poverty, thereby demonstrating that the military enemy of the United States is evil.

However, since America's civil religion is based on a decidedly Protestant Christian ethic, our civil religion includes themes such as the covenant, death, and a ritual calendar, as well as resurrection and rebirth. Bellah does recognize that civil religion can be "a cloak for petty interests and ugly passions," which reflects politicians' attempts to cover up their misconduct and their covenants with financial campaign contributors, which are renewed on a ritualistic calendar.[63] This suggests that the politician also has a unique opportunity for resurrection and rebirth in a scandal: resignation from public life to private life. We can see this renewal in each of the four major examples: Teapot Dome, Watergate, Iran-Contra, and Clinton/Lewinsky.

THE SCANDALS FOR SCRUTINY

Each chapter theorizes about and critiques key stages and elements of the scandal. As such, each chapter focuses on a specific moment in the scandal. This section offers a brief introduction for each scandal. However, before discussing the cases, I want to address why these scandals were chosen.

I have relied on critical case sampling, which provides a few key examples to examine. Focusing on a small number of critical cases permits "logical generalization and maximum application of information to other cases because if it is true of this one case, it's likely to be true of all other cases."[64] In other words, these four scandals are the yardstick by which all other scandals are measured. Watergate is at the top of any list of scandals; its importance in American political history is unquestioned. The suffix "-gate" is virtually synonymous with the term "scandal." Before Watergate, Teapot Dome held the top spot. The Iran-Contra and Clinton/Lewinsky scandals did not knock Watergate from its place (and it is difficult to imagine what it would take to do so); nevertheless, they were major in their own right, as both had a significant impact on the presidency. In short, these four scandals were chosen because whenever anything resembling a scandal occurs, it is or has been directly or indirectly compared to these four major scandals.

Teapot Dome

The first example is the Teapot Dome scandal, which is named for a rock formation resembling a teapot in a Wyoming oil field. President Harding appointed a nearly bankrupt senator from New Mexico, Albert Fall, as the secretary of the interior. Fall, it seems, made the most of his new position to remedy his financial problems. Fall was able to convince the secretary of the navy to release control of the Wyoming (and California) oil fields to him. Fall, an anticonservationist, then discreetly leased the drilling rights to two wealthy oilmen, Harry Sinclair and Edward Doheny, who both happened to be Fall's friends.

Fall's actions were motivated by a desire to protect the government's resources and the nation. Specifically, Fall and others believed that the government's oil might be tapped and drained by neighboring wells. Nearby companies could drill into the government's oil and siphon it all away. Moreover, the oil might flow under both the companies' and the government's land; since the government was only holding oil and not drilling for it, the company could simply drain all the oil from their own land, leaving the government with none. These were not abstract concerns. The government was actively losing oil in California to neighbors who were siphoning the navy's oil. This fear is what motivated Congress to move the control of the oil lands from the navy to Fall.[65] The secretary of the navy and other high-ranking naval officers, who all fully supported Fall, were eager to conserve the resources, for they were "nervous about possible trouble with Japan" and wanted oil ready for the fleet at Pearl Harbor and other strategic locations.[66]

Once the scheme was revealed, politicians assailed the reversal of President Theodore Roosevelt's policy of conservation and the clandestine transfer of the oil lands from the navy to Fall. Oilmen resented the fact that they did not get the oil lands that were leased to Fall's friends. While pockets of opposition were to be expected, the attacks on Fall became much more serious when it was discovered that one of the oilmen had loaned him around $385,000, thereby fixing Fall's financial troubles.

After a lengthy congressional investigation and numerous court cases, it was determined that Fall had in fact been bribed in exchange for leasing the oil fields. Fall became the first cabinet official to ever be sentenced to jail. Strangely, the oil executives, who supposedly bribed Fall, received no punishment for the offense. Thus, a politician was found guilty of receiving a bribe that no one was found guilty of giving. Furthermore, when Fall was unable to repay the loan, which the courts called a bribe, the oilmen foreclosed on Fall's house. Given these aspects, Fall maintained his innocence throughout the ordeal and unsuccessfully requested a presidential pardon. His only option was to appeal to the Supreme Court, which refused to hear his case.

The Teapot Dome scandal "came to epitomize all the evil in what is usually regarded as the worst of all presidential administrations. . . . It also became the darkest stain of corruption on a political party in the twentieth century, until Watergate in the 1970s."[67] President Harding gave his cabinet members relatively free rein over the departments. When Harding died three years after his election, it became evident that he "had presided unwittingly over one of the most corrupt administrations in history."[68]

The Teapot Dome scandal became a major election issue in 1924, and for every presidential election for the next fifty years.[69] The Teapot Dome scandal's popularity has become an allusion that permeates scandals up to relatively recent history. "Newspaper writers like[d] to say things like 'the worst scandal since Teapot Dome.' Watergate and more have come along since, but Teapot Dome still has some resonance."[70] In 1924, an eleven-year-old boy became so enraged about the Teapot Dome scandal that he told his mother, "When I get big I'll be a lawyer they can't bribe."[71] Many years later, the young boy, Richard Nixon, became president.

Watergate

The second example is Watergate. During the 1972 presidential election, five burglars broke into the Democratic National Committee's office in the Watergate Hotel in Washington, D.C. The burglary itself was anything but well orchestrated, but neither were the actions of two young metropolitan reporters, Bob Woodward and Carl Bernstein, who were assigned to the local break-in because it was initially considered politically insignificant. Nixon was able to overcome the accusations in the 1972 election. The politically experienced Nixon effectively characterized the Democratic opposition, including presidential candidate George McGovern, as willing to engage in partisan rhetoric to gain control of the government.

Nevertheless, Woodward and Bernstein pursued the caper wholeheartedly and found a connection between the burglars and high-level Republican leaders. Due to the reporters' work and a major congressional investigation, it became clear that those involved with the break-in (and numerous other instances of political espionage) were linked to the White House and the president.

When members of the White House administration realized they might be sacrificed for the sake of the president, they turned on Nixon. When the investigations learned of a secret recording system in the Oval Office, they sought out the tapes. Nixon refused to turn them over and offered edited transcripts. After a tumultuous battle over the tapes, Nixon eventually handed over the evidence that unofficially confirmed his own guilt. But before any official declaration of guilt was made, Nixon became the first president to resign. Nixon's vice president turned president, Gerald Ford, would later pardon Nixon.

The importance of this scandal is unquestioned. The suffix "-gate" became a moniker for many scandals that followed it: Koreagate[72] (congressional bribery in lobbying), Rubbergate[73] (congressional check bouncing), Irangate[74] (Iran-Contra), Billygate[75] (in reference to Jimmy Carter's brother), Lawyergate[76] or Attorneygate[77] (the firing of eight U.S. attorneys), Plamegate[78] (the name of a CIA operative outed by journalist Robert Novak), Nannygate[79] (the nomination of Linda Chavez for secretary of labor), and Troopergate, Travelgate, Filegate, and Christmas-card-gate,[80] which all refer to scandals uncovered during Clinton's administration.

Watergate, like Teapot Dome, influenced many legal and political minds, including a young University of Arkansas law professor, who proclaimed that there is "no question that an admission of making false statements to government officials and interfering with the FBI and the CIA is an impeachable offense."[81] Many years later, that law professor, Bill Clinton, became president.

Iran-Contra

The third example is the Iran-Contra scandal. At the heart of Iran-Contra was President Reagan's desire to protect the American people, especially those who had been captured overseas in hostile territory, as well as his desire to export American democracy abroad. These tenets of Reagan's political philosophy were driven by his greatest asset, which also turned out to be his greatest weakness: management by delegation. While it is unclear whether Reagan did or did not order the foreign policy initiatives at the center of the Iran-Contra scandal, it is clear that his desires were well understood by the members of his administration who carried them out.

Specifically, Reagan wanted the return of American hostages in Iran, and he also wanted to support the "freedom fighters" in Nicaragua, who were known as the Contras. Members of the National Security Council, who worked closely with the president on national security and foreign issues, enacted a policy that would directly and indirectly (through Israel) sell U.S. arms to Iran, which was engaged in a bloody war against Iraq. In return, hostages would be released, and the arms, which were sold at an inflated price, would create a monetary surplus. That surplus, then, was shifted to an unrelated foreign policy initiative in Central America. The surplus of money funded those who opposed (hence the name Contras) the Nicaraguan government. On its face, it was a simple solution; it solved one problem with another. However, such actions violated federal law and kept Congress in the dark. In a system of checks and balances, such a unilateral action did not go unnoticed once the ordeal was exposed in the foreign press, which was nearly as shocking as the scandal itself. Ultimately, Reagan claimed he did not know of the plan; a young marine officer, Oliver North, was fired; and his boss resigned.

Iran-Contra was a major scandal, although its timing might question its status as such. Iran-Contra occurred in the shadow of Watergate, which was a tough act to follow. Then, shortly after Iran-Contra, the Whitewater investigation of Bill Clinton, which would eventually morph into impeachment, began. Despite being bookended by other major scandals with major consequences for the presidency, Iran-Contra holds its own as a major U.S. scandal.

What makes Iran-Contra different from its predecessor and successor is that we know with some degree of certainty the role of Fall, Clinton, and Nixon (at least in terms of the cover-up) in their scandals. What we do not know is Reagan's and Vice President Bush's involvement. Reagan himself boldly asserted to the American public that his "heart and best intentions" told him that he did not trade weapons for hostages despite the "facts and evidence" pointing to the cold reality that the United States did, in fact, trade arms for hostages, which ran contrary to the official position of the United States when dealing with terrorists. Besides making deals with terrorists, Reagan ran afoul of several laws about funding the Contras. Bush publicly stated that he was not in the loop but privately confessed that he was one of the few who knew what was going on. Iran-Contra was a clear and major breach of the law and the Constitution; however, virtually no one was punished. Those involved were either granted immunity or pardoned. This sets Iran-Contra apart from other scandals and further establishes it as a major scandal.

In the end, the astonishing aspect of the scandal was that relatively low-level military officers ran U.S. foreign policy without the president's knowledge or official approval (unless Reagan did approve the policy). Yet, if the president did know, then the seriousness of the scandal is all the greater in that Reagan effectively engaged in duplicitous conduct and faced no punishment while his underlings were able to fall on their swords and through some legal maneuvering escape any substantive punishment themselves.

Clinton/Lewinsky

The fourth example was a scandal within a scandal. An independent counsel investigated President Clinton's business dealings—Whitewater, sometimes known as Whitewater-gate—during his tenure as governor of Arkansas. The initial investigations focused on the accusation that Hillary and Bill Clinton exploited their governmental positions in Arkansas to make money, which arose during the 1996 presidential election when an Arkansas jury convicted Clinton's former partners, Susan and James McDougal, and Clinton's gubernatorial successor in Arkansas, Jim Guy Tucker. Republicans used this occasion as a means to make Clinton's public character one of the predominant campaign issues in 1996. To be clear, Bob Dole, the Republican candidate for president, did not make Clinton's personal character a campaign issue, for Dole himself was involved in extramarital affairs. Other Republicans, however, did.

The intimate relationship between President Bill Clinton and Monica Lewinsky was the major scandal of the president's two-term tenure. The *Newsweek* reporter who uncovered the scandal claimed it was not Watergate, but it was the biggest scandal in twenty-five years—not necessarily just because of Clinton's actions but also the political fallout: Clinton became the second president in U.S. history to be impeached and then acquitted by the Senate.

In late January 1998, a *Newsweek* reporter had long been investigating Independent Counsel Kenneth Starr's intention to examine President Clinton's alleged infidelity. *Newsweek* editors, however, decided to hold off on publication due to the sensitive nature of the allegations against the private individuals involved. Nevertheless, a young Internet blogger, Matt Drudge, published the reports online. Soon the relationship was a matter of gossip not just among Washington insiders but to the entire nation as well.

Drudge soon identified the young intern as Monica Lewinsky, who coincidentally lived at the Watergate complex, the scene of a break-in some twenty-five years prior. Lewinsky testified before Starr in a sexual harassment case brought against the president by Paula Jones. When asked if she had a relationship with Clinton, Lewinsky denied any intimate contact. With the nation's interest awakened, President Clinton publicly denied the allegations numerous times and uttered what would soon be a political catchphrase: "I did not have sexual relations with that woman." Despite his forcefulness, much of the public did not believe him, but that did not seem to matter, for there was prosperity at home and abroad.

Republicans officially opted not to accuse or attack the president for several reasons. One of the primary reasons was that the United States was prospering on both foreign and domestic fronts. Another reason was that Clinton was politically strong, and any bombastic political rhetoric was certainly doomed to fail. Furthermore, there was an independent counsel, who was ostensibly free of any Democratic or Republican connection, investigating the president. However, the apparently judicial Kenneth Starr was far from apolitical. Constantly leaking information and engaging in a rampant inquiry into the president's private—not political—life, Starr gave the Clinton administration plenty of substance with which to fight back.

Starr nevertheless soon found himself with damaging information against Clinton. Starr offered immunity to Lewinsky for her truthful testimony. Lewinsky also turned over a blue dress which had evidence that proved there was a sexual encounter between the president and Lewinsky. Clinton found himself in a situation not unlike Albert Fall and Richard Nixon were in during the Teapot Dome and Watergate scandals. Clinton, however, did something neither Fall nor Nixon did. Clinton participated in the inquiry against him. Moreover, Clinton publicly admitted his deception and even at one point claimed he was sorry. With two apologies, one on August 17 and the other on September 11, 1998, the public generally ceased to have any interest in the scandal. While the public largely felt that the apologies ended the scandal, Clinton soon found himself facing impeachment, which resulted from a personal affair, and it arguably became the greatest scandal since Watergate.

While it may be argued that Clinton did wrong, the main difference between Clinton and Fall, Nixon, and Reagan was that their acts were politically relevant acts, while Clinton's transgression was a private, personal act with political implications. Craig Allen Smith argued that the charges of impeachment at the end of Clinton's second term were not considered politically significant because the first thing most voters knew about Clinton in 1992 consisted of allegations of a twelve-year affair with Gennifer Flowers, of marijuana use, of dodging the draft, and of engaging in war protests. Allen concludes, "Whatever the voters' reasons for preferring Clinton in 1992, the purity of his character was surely not the foremost among them."[82]

THE TEXTS OF SCANDAL

In the spirit of understanding the scandals as they happened, I use data that was publicly available to the people and citizens at the time of the scandal, such as newspaper and other journalistic reports concerning the scandals, as well as speeches and press releases from the executive branch (e.g., the president, cabinet members). First, for the Teapot Dome scandal, I rely on numerous reporters. Saint Louis journalist Paul Y. Anderson was the predominant reporter in that he was the only journalist present at the Senate investigation committees.[83] Moreover, Anderson continued to investigate the story even after Fall's imprisonment, which work earned him the Pulitzer Prize in 1929.

Second, I rely predominately on the *Washington Post*'s Carl Bernstein and Bob Woodward's reporting of Watergate. With the help of a confidential informant, Deep Throat, who turned out to be the FBI's second in command, Woodward and Bernstein brought the Pulitzer Prize home to the *Washington Post* in 1973. Woodward and Bernstein also wrote two best-selling books on the scandal, one of which was made into a movie.

Third, unlike Teapot Dome and Watergate, there is no journalistic protagonist in the Iran-Contra scandal; in fact, the foreign press broke the story even though the U.S. press had known about the U.S.-Iran arms deal four years before the scandal hit the front pages. Moreover, President Reagan quickly called for investigations, which spurred Congress to start their own investigations. Thus, the newspaper accounts, which reported the findings of the governmental investigation, provide the source of information for Iran-Contra.

Finally, like Iran-Contra, the Clinton/Lewinsky affair had no major journalistic protagonist but involved a major shift in the media scene. Therefore, this final scandal will rely on a variety of news sources from the new media (i.e., Internet, cable, etc.) to the traditional old media (i.e., print and the big three of televised news), as well as speeches from Bill Clinton and Hillary Rodham Clinton.

THE NARRATIVE FLOW

There are many popular books that recount the who, what, and when of the scandals presented here. The purpose of *this* book is not to repeat what is already known about these scandals. Rather, I use these specific examples to provide a holistic understanding of scandal at a theoretical and critical level. This book also strives to address the scandals as they were experienced by the public by presenting their evolution from beginning to end.

Scholars have noted that while scandals have a mono-narrative pattern, "allegation, denial, exposure, inquiry, cover-up, fresh allegations, further inquiries and sometimes even a conclusion . . . no two scandals are exactly similar and they occur in different political contexts"; but the focus here is on the general similarities across the four case examples.[84] The Teapot Dome, Watergate, Iran-Contra, and Clinton/Lewinsky scandals play out similarly. They begin in a political context of relative prosperity that is shattered by the press's publicity of misconduct. Politicians then engage in partisan rhetoric that depicts the charges as politically inspired attacks. Shocking evidence and testimony then reinvigorate the public's attention, but the heightened attention is lost as the scandal often goes to the courts, where it receives sporadic news coverage and results in little comment by those involved, as well as a lack of full participation by the accused. Finally, the scandal concludes with the confirmation or vindication of wrongdoing or in abdication. The book follows this narrative pattern and offers a critique of the issues presented at each stage in terms of free speech, political rhetoric, and democracy. These implications help us to understand how a scandal can perpetuate a democratic ideology.

Chapter 2, "The Role of Journalism," addresses the scandalous revelations. As the scandal begins and reveals the alleged misconduct of an entrusted politician, the people may find some solace in that the press, who, in accordance with their role as watchdogs of democracy, check the government. That is, in the beginning of a scandal, it is the journalistic hero who triumphantly expresses the wrongdoing of those in political authority. However, a close reading of the journalistic hero myth in press history shows that the American press has not performed as heroically as we would like to think.

Chapter 3, "Partisan Discourse Prior to the Smoking Gun," addresses the political nature of scandalous accusations. As the scandal unfolds, a battle for meaning commences. On the one hand, there is the accused, who engages in several forms of *apologia* to defend him- or herself against the allegations. On the other hand, there is the accuser, who attempts to legitimize and officialize the accusations to raise them above the characterization of political rancor. The battle goes back and forth and thereby creates a crisis of meaning, which is typically settled by a smoking gun, which is the focus of the next chapter.

Chapter 4, "From Smoking Gun to Impeachment," argues that the smoking gun allows for the redefinition of the original misconduct into a major political scandal. The smoking gun, in essence, demonstrates that the accusations are true, but, more importantly, the smoking gun also proves that the accused has lied. To the official investigators, the main issue of the scandal is not the original misconduct, which may not necessarily be illegal. The main focus is the lie. A lie is obstruction of justice, which is an impeachable offense. Redefining the lie rather than the original misconduct as the major scandal issue allows for an impeachment. Impeachment therefore empowers Congress, which otherwise would have very little punishment power over the original misconduct, to take action against the president.

Chapter 5, "Political Martyrdom," addresses the culmination of the scandal. In the end, there is a hero: the accused politician who redeems the political order through mortification (i.e., resignation) or becoming a scapegoat (tried and/or convicted) by the government of which he is a part. Members of the electorate, who are normally agents in democracy, have their agency limited in the scandal as the government is able to contend with the accused politician.

Chapter 6, "Contemporary Issues and Scandals," offers an analysis of a contemporary case study of Anthony Weiner's sexting scandal. The chapter also makes use of several minor scandals and controversies to demonstrate additional nuances and subtleties to various elements of the scandal narrative.

Chapter 7, "Yesterday, Today, and Tomorrow," addresses how those who were involved in Teapot Dome, Watergate, Iran-Contra, and Clinton/Lewinsky understood the events that were unfolding around them. This understanding comes from the very scandal narrative. The book concludes with an ongoing political scandal that has not yet ended. Readers are free to use the ideas in this book to speculate on what will happen next.

CONCLUSION

There are innumerable scandals in the U.S. democracy. Politicians often take great liberty by assuming authority beyond the power afforded them by the Constitution. Other politicians take freedom in their business and personal lives far beyond what the public expects of its elected officials. When a politician unsuccessfully attempts to hide these actions, the result is scandal. We may be disappointed in our public officials and proud of our free press for catching the scoundrel, but, as this book will demonstrate, there is much more to the political scandal.

My hope is that after reading this book, the reader will have a better understanding of what a scandal is, how scandals unfold, and why scandals perpetuate democratic ideologies. Furthermore, I hope this book provides the reader with the means and ideas to critically examine future scandals as well as a fresh perspective to think about old scandals.

Chapter Two

The Role of Journalism

In retrospect, when all or most of the information has been uncovered, scandals often have a nebulous beginning. Teapot Dome was just one, albeit the most extreme, example of the scandals that erupted during Warren G. Harding's presidency. Teapot Dome's beginnings can be found in any number of shady backroom discussions and deals that helped propel Harding into the White House. Similarly, Watergate's origins are unclear. Was it a single and distinct effort by Nixon's men, or was it just one in a series of acts of political espionage? Despite nebulous beginnings, we can point to a single instance when all scandals begin in the eyes of the public: political scandals begin when the news first breaks. It may break in the newspapers, magazines, television news, or online. If the scandal seems especially juicy, it could break on all simultaneously. Regardless of the medium, behind each and every story stands a journalist, digging up and delivering the latest politicians-gone-awry news.

In American political culture, it is the journalist who seeks the truth, rights the wrongs, and shines a light on all manner of nefarious behavior. There are, to be sure, many examples of this characterization. But in four major American political scandals of the twentieth century—Teapot Dome, Watergate, Iran-Contra, and Clinton/Lewinsky—the idea of crusading journalists making their way through the political muck to bring the story to the masses is a bit off the mark.

This chapter first explores two popular conceptions of journalists with respect to scandals. The first relies on Blasi's checking value theory of the First Amendment. The second involves two instances of heroic journalism from popular memory. After exploring these two popular conceptions, the chapter provides an alternative conception of the journalist during a scandal. This alternative conception does not necessarily suggest that journalists are of no value in the scandal; rather, we must be careful not to heroize their efforts, as journalists are part of a larger ensemble cast. By failing to accurately understand the role of journalists in scandals, we play a part in perpetuating a strong and vibrant democratic ideology when the foundations of governmental and political institutions and processes are questioned, shaken, and upended. To challenge this journalist-as-hero conceptualization, this chapter makes use of an informing metaphor to better understand the role of the journalist in scandal.

POPULAR CONCEPTIONS OF THE JOURNALIST

The Watchdogs of Democracy

The notion of a heroic press has grounding in First Amendment theory. Americans have a natural distrust of authority and a seemingly natural instinct to call those authorities out on any potential transgression they might commit. There are two primary entities that enact this opposition: the opposing political party and the press. Between these two, there is a clear choice: the American press, the fourth estate, the watchdogs of democracy, who serve as what law professor and constitutional scholar Vincent Blasi labeled the "checking value" on government.

Blasi's checking value theory has received considerable praise since its introduction in 1977. A journalist historian has stated, "The strongest argument by a press law theorist for an aggressive press came from legal scholar Vincent Blasi, whose 'checking value' theory of the First Amendment directly assigns a role for the press as watchdog of government."[1] The checking value theory is not a new idea; Blasi draws support for it from as far back as the John Peter Zenger trial and from the writings of James Madison and Thomas Jefferson, but his explanation helped to give the idea some "contemporary currency."[2]

The idea of the checking value is simple: a free press is the means by which a free society can check public officials' abuse of power. While we hope there is no abuse of power, the government has the ability to exercise great harm (e.g., fines, restraint, detention); thus, the potential fallout from any abuse of power, however slight it might be, can have serious and lasting consequences. Therefore, for Blasi, it is imperative to check the government more so than to check private citizens or organizations. As Blasi writes, "No private party—not Lockheed, not United Fruit, not the Mafia—could ever have done what our government did to the Vietnamese people and the Vietnamese land."[3]

While freedom of speech and of assembly can serve as a means for checking the abuse of power, it is the free press that is paramount. This prioritization of the press is based on two points. First, since the majority of voters have elected those in office, there is a tendency for the majority of people to trust that their choice is on the up-and-up. The second reason is more pragmatic. Federal and state governments are too large and too complex to be navigated by the average person. Thus, there is a need for "well-organized, well-financed, professional critics . . . [who are] capable of acquiring enough information to pass judgment on the actions of government, and also capable of disseminating their information and judgments to the general public."[4] Here Blasi suggests that the journalist has special abilities and access that the average protestor or amateur investigator does not have. It should therefore be no surprise that journalists have frequently been overheroized, for they are guardians of democracy with truth on their side.

The Journalist as Hero

If the politician is a dealer of lies and contempt, then the press is the revealer of truth. When the press does its job, an unknown and underhanded activity is publicized, thereby creating the basis for scandal. Quite simply, with no publicity of wrongdoing, there is no wrongdoing.[5] Therefore, the dogged journalist is an integral part in the democratic process. In the beginning of a scandal, it is the journalistic hero who triumphantly exposes the wrongdoing of politicians to the people. This is called the free press myth.

The free press myth is the "sustaining myth of journalism [which holds] that every great government scandal is revealed through the work of enterprising reporters who by one means or another pierce the official veil of secrecy."[6] The press are the fighters of freedom armed with the mightier-than-the-sword pen and a tenacious unrelenting drive for the truth.

Here, "myths" are not false tales but rather are "long-enduring stories, often anonymously created, that dramatize a culture's deepest beliefs and dilemmas."[7] Myths, therefore, allow us to examine how archetypes are consciously or unconsciously appropriated in response to "historical and political contingencies."[8]

Myths can be found in any culture—including that of journalists. Slotkin claims that the free press myth provides "a genuine and usable national consensus."[9] In line with the notion of a civil religion, McChesney and Scott explain that the free press myth is not anonymously created but "is thought to be ordained by the Founding Fathers as the engine of participatory self-government."[10] The supporting ideals of the free press myth can further be found in the history and popular culture of the United States.

John Peter Zenger

The narrative of John Peter Zenger reached legendary status almost immediately after the judge's gavel signaled the end of the case on August 4, 1735.[11] The account of the trial was dutifully written and published shortly after Zenger was acquitted for sedition and libel against the English governor of New York, William Cosby. Cosby was not well liked by his "subjects" in the colonies, who saw themselves more as free men, and Cosby seemed to do very little to help improve his image.

One particular incident drew great ire. There was an election for the county representative to the Provincial Assembly. The campaign was between the anti-Cosby William Forster and the pro-Cosby Lewis Morris. Forster won the election, but the very unhappy governor demanded a reelection, which would be run by the local sheriff, who was appointed and controlled by none other than Cosby himself. The sheriff turned away many supporters of Forster and even persuaded those who were ineligible to vote to swear that they were entitled to vote, which they did, for Morris. Not surprisingly, the reelection resulted in a victory for Morris. This galvanized the opposition, who then sought to spread the word of Cosby's antics. Those who opposed Cosby soon found a willing printer, John Peter Zenger. One week after the convoluted election, the first edition of the *Weekly Journal* appeared.

Zenger published long-standing and well-known criticisms about Cosby. This point is worthy of note. Zenger did not write any of the critiques himself. The attacks were anonymous, but Zenger's name appeared as publisher. There was tremendous speculation that most of the attacks came from James Alexander and William Smith, who would later defend Zenger in court. Nevertheless, these criticisms did not sit well with Gov. Cosby. Since only Zenger could be identified, he became the prime target of Cosby's wrath.

In response, Cosby sought a number of ways to stop the *Weekly Journal*. A grand jury was convened twice to bring charges against Zenger, and twice the attempt failed. The Governor's Council then sought a petition to have copies of the *Weekly Journal* burned by the local hangman. That petition was also unsuccessful. Cosby then petitioned a court to force the burning. The court refused. Finally, Cosby's sheriff ordered his slave to burn the papers, and Zenger was arrested on November 17, 1734, for false and seditious writing.

Zenger languished in jail for nine months. Nevertheless, the *Journal* still published a paper every week—only missing one week. When the trial started, Alexander and Smith originally defended Zenger, but there was a last-minute change of counsel for Zenger.

Andrew Hamilton informed the Cosby-appointed judge that he was now representing Zenger. By virtually all accounts, Hamilton was eloquent and persuasive. Hamilton argued that, yes, Zenger did publish the attacks, which was enough to convict him, but that the content of the accusations was true and that punishing someone for telling the truth was absurd.

Since Hamilton freely admitted his client's role in publishing the attacks, which was the primary charge, Zenger could have easily been found guilty.

But Hamilton's defense appealed not to the law or the facts but to popular anti-Cosby sentiment in New York. The jury was swayed by Hamilton's arguments and took only ten minutes to find Zenger not guilty of publishing the criticisms, for they were true. The not guilty verdict garnered several rounds of cheers from within the courtroom. The next day, as Hamilton left New York to return to Philadelphia, he received a gun salute from ships anchored in the harbor.

Copies of *A Brief Narrative of the Case and Trial of John Peter Zenger* were subsequently distributed whenever times of government opposition of the press appeared, such as the enactment of the Sedition Act of 1798, which outlawed scandalous and malicious writings about the government. Consequently, the Zenger case became a point in which true criticisms of the government were recognized as being valuable to a healthy political society.

The Heroes of Watergate

The free press myth is undoubtedly present in Watergate. The scandal was exposed when Bob Woodward and Carl Bernstein first reported about the arraignment of five burglars who were caught breaking into the Democratic National Committee offices at the Watergate office building. When Woodward and Bernstein were done, they had "generated enough damaging publicity about 'Watergate' to cause the White House to vilify them and the *Washington Post*, and thus elevate them to the status of journalistic martyr-heroes."[12] "No other story in American history," Schudson claims, "features the press in so prominent and heroic of a role."[13]

Popular conception holds Woodward and Bernstein as the modern-day equivalent of John Peter Zenger, with Nixon as the tyrant who stymied the press not overtly in court like Cosby did but covertly through inclusion in Nixon's infamous enemies list, which contained celebrities, politicians, and journalists who all, Nixon believed, posed a threat to him. Up to 1973, journalists "had been spied on, intimidated, tax harassed—and they feared the worst" from Nixon and his administration, but in true heroic spirit, the journalists pushed back by defending themselves with a relentless spirit at all costs.[14] Journalists were "defending far more than the news system. [They were] defending the rights of all Americans; if individual reporters and newspapers and TV outlets were not safe, then no one was safe from the same search and seizure, harassment, tax menace, and reprisal to which the news system felt itself subject."[15] Here the journalist as hero is exceeding their checking role by not only preventing and containing government abuse and crime but also safeguarding citizens' basic rights.

At the vanguard of this counterattack were Woodward and Bernstein, who amended the dictum in American folklore that any boy can grow up to be president to include that any boy can "grow up to topple a corrupt president."[16] This new perspective was strongly influenced by the best-selling book and then widely successful film, *All the President's Men*, which was a dramatized documentary of the two reporters' efforts, but the film does much more than that. According to Schudson, "The film, even more than the book, ennobled investigative reporting and made of journalists modern heroes. A mythology of the press in Watergate developed into a significant national myth."[17]

The film *All the President's Men* resonates with cultural ideologies of American politics and the heroic press. As the film begins, the first shot "produces an almost bearable tension. It's held for eighteen seconds before there's any action, a key stroke, its impact resounding like cannon fire."[18] Quite plainly, while there is a battle between the press and president, it is not a blood battle; rather, it is a hallmark of democracy where the pen or, in this case, the typewriter is mightier than the sword.

The film ends with Nixon's second inaugural in which there is actual cannon fire, ostensibly showing the real danger faced not only by journalists but by democracy as well. But the thunderous volleys of cannon fire are overpowered by the precision speed and sound of the Teletype announcing the guilt of the president's men and ultimately Nixon's resignation, which firmly reinforces the film's residual message that journalists with perseverance and truth on their side can overcome corrupt power.[19] This "legend of the heroic and indispensable role of the press in foiling [Nixon became] the accepted version of what had happened."[20]

Woodward and Bernstein wrote *All the President's Men*, which was then adapted to film by William Goldman, who puzzled over the question of how to present a story that everyone was familiar with and some were even sick of. He came to the conclusion that he had to tell the story behind the story—the view of journalism in Watergate, the efforts of the reporters, who, as the film portrays, brought down Nixon.[21] The journalist is portrayed as the dogged, selfless worker who is motivated to maintain the ideals of democracy. They were outsiders with nothing to lose and everything to gain, and they were hungry, which makes a great American story.[22] Woodward and Bernstein seem to portray that heroic ideal.

But Woodward himself said that the book and film leave "the false impression . . . [that] the authors Carl Bernstein and Bob Woodward, not the FBI, solved the Watergate case."[23] Others have echoed this sentiment.[24] For example, Epstein claims, "It was not the press which exposed Watergate; it was agencies of government itself."[25] Epstein here is saying that the government did the investigation, but the press was the means by which the government's findings were relayed, or "exposed," to the public. Thus, as Feeny states, "the press was the cavalry that rode to glory while the infantry slogged the way to victory."[26]

HEROIC PROBLEMS

The examples of Zenger and *All the President's Men* show how historical and popular culture influence and maintain the image of a powerful and ever-vigilant free press with respect to scandal. But there are more details to each of these stories. These details do not destroy the idea of a free press, but they do question the overly heroic status of journalism in scandals. Moreover, they suggest that we need a more appropriate conceptualization of the press in scandal.

Zenger

Zenger's triumph in the courtroom certainly was a cause for celebration, but the verdict, it seems, was the only cause for celebration. Zenger has been described as "unassuming and unheroic" and as a "poorly educated tradesman," who served as a "mouthpiece for the chief opposition" against Gov. Cosby.[27] In other words, Zenger was not a crusading journalist. He had limited journalism experience but was a capable printer who, as stated earlier, did not actually write the criticisms of Gov. Cosby but only printed (i.e., reproduced) them. Moreover, it is difficult to say that the circulation of the *Weekly Journal* spread the criticisms, for most of them were already widely known.

It is also important to question whether the trial was about freedom of the press or was an expression of anti-Cosby sentiment. The jury was charged to determine if Zenger published the attacks. The evidence directly confirmed Zenger's guilt: his name was clearly on the *Weekly Journal* as publisher. Moreover, Zenger's chief defender, the renowned Philadelphia lawyer Andrew Hamilton, even admitted in court that Zenger published the attacks. Despite this very condemning evidence and admission, Zenger went free. This is because the case was a jury trial. Zenger was not so much innocent as the jury was anti-Cosby (as were many in the area). In other words, releasing Zenger was more about sending a message of disapproval to and about Cosby rather than a notion of the freedom of the press.[28] This also explains why Zenger avoided so many grand jury indictments.

To further support this notion that the Zenger case has had a less significant impact than popularly imagined, it is important to note the legal impact of the case. The case "did not directly further the development either of political liberty or of freedom of the press."[29] The case never changed common law and was not seriously cited in English courts. Even in 1804, a U.S. judge refused the argument that truth was a defense in a New York case where Harry Croswell defamed President Thomas Jefferson. Furthermore, a few years earlier, the Adams administration successfully prosecuted Congressman Matthew

Lyons and political pamphleteer James Callender under the Sedition Act of 1798. They both criticized Adams with nothing more than "political slanging."[30] To the Adams administration, this was sedition, for which Lyons and Callender both served time in jail.

The Zenger incident was about immediate political gain—to oppose the unpopular Gov. Cosby. Not surprisingly, when Cosby died in 1736, the *Weekly Journal* stopped attacking the administration. What is surprising is that when an anti-Cosby administration took over, Zenger's press received contracts for official printing, and his *Weekly Journal* sided with the government. Thus, while the Zenger case demonstrates a change of thinking in the colonies about the free press, we must be careful not to over-romanticize or overestimate its influence. Close attention to the Zenger case shows that it was more about the realpolitiks of the time than about ideological notions of a free press. The same could be said of Watergate.

Watergate

In the book *All the President's Men*, Woodward and Bernstein recount the rather unpleasant invitation to attend Judge Sirica's packed courtroom. The duo had earlier approached members of the grand jury for information. Sirica, who was known for his seriousness, praised the members of the jury for their silence and informed the entire courtroom full of reporters that such actions by anyone would not be tolerated. Only the judge and the two reporters knew specifically whom he was addressing. Other reporters speculated on the intended audience. Woodward and Bernstein, writing in the third person, said, "They had not broken the law when they visited the grand jurors [but] they had chosen expediency over principle."[31] Like Zenger, this particular incident was not about high-value notions of freedom of the press and democracy. Rather it was simply about getting the information. Woodward and Bernstein continued in the third person: "They had dodged, evaded, misrepresented, suggested and intimidated, even if they had not lied outright."[32]

Nevertheless, "at its broadest," the journalistic myth in Watergate "asserts that journalism, in particular two young *Washington Post* reporters, brought down the president of the United States."[33] While the facts do not seem necessarily to destroy this narrative, they do strongly question the David and Goliath account of journalism in Watergate. Would Watergate have been the major scandal it was without the two reporters? We can never know, but what we do know is that journalism was not the sole contributor to Watergate's finale but rather was part of a large ensemble cast including Judge Sirica, the Ervin Congressional Committee, John Dean, Alexander Butterfield, and others, including a great number of sources rather than just Deep Throat.

Despite the roles played by this large ensemble, there are some who claim that the *Washington Post* deserves special credit, for they kept attention on the scandal until others joined the inquiry. While this argument has its merits, it nevertheless undercuts the efforts of democratic presidential candidate George McGovern, who repeatedly mentioned the break-in throughout the 1972 election; the General Accounting Office's reports; the Democratic National Committee and its lawsuit against the Nixon campaign; and the *Los Angeles Times'* October 1972 interview with Alfred Baldwin, the lookout poised across the street during the break-in, which all forced disclosures that did their fair share of publicizing the Watergate story early on. Nevertheless, the journalistic myth of Watergate continues in that Woodward and Bernstein were able not only to endure but also to overcome the hugely intimidating and powerful Nixon administration with only truth on their side. But, in truth, Woodward and Bernstein greatly benefited from some luck.

Both Woodward and Bernstein were unexpectedly single at the time of the Watergate burglary, which gave them a great deal of time to work relentlessly on the story. But this was not the only advantage the reporters had. While Woodward served in the U.S. Navy, he delivered top-secret communications to the White House as an aide to the chairman of the Joint Chiefs of Staff.[34] He frequently found himself waiting in the hallways and would strike up conversations with others. One of those others happened to be the second in command at the FBI, Mark W. Felt, who would later serve as Woodward's super-source, Deep Throat. Deep Throat appeared as "the shadowy, even mythical figure who played a crucial role in bringing down the Nixon Presidency" in *All the President's Men.*[35] Examining the relationship between sources and journalists and their respective outlets gives us a better understanding and conceptualization of journalism during major political scandals.

JOURNALISTS AS SHAMANS

While the popular narratives of Zenger and Woodward and Bernstein are overly heroized, it would be misleading and inaccurate to say that journalists have had no role whatsoever in scandals. The truth, as is often the case, is found between two extremes. The press has played an important role in major political scandals, but it is important to be accurate with our history and how it is presented, for these are the tales that support our most cherished liberties in a free society. The question is, if journalists are not superheroes and are more than do-nothings, then what is their role in a scandal? We can turn to an "informing metaphor," which compares journalists to shamans, to help answer this question.[36]

Shamans and journalists are alike in that they are both mediums.[37] Shamans are a medium in that they "gain power from a supernatural [which could be the over- or under-] world that allows them travel to and from that world and accords them control over its spirits in the realization of some social task."[38] Journalists are mediums in that they "collect certain ongoing happenings in the field and narrate them for society within a recognized mass media framework set up to realize some social aim."[39] Simply put, journalists and shamans are "empowered to go where others cannot and return with stories" that not only help and inform individuals but also address social problems.[40]

The journalist and shaman's degree of access constitutes their identities, for they are nothing if all others could see what they see and hear what they hear. Zelizer offers a thought experiment to understand this idea: "Consider the possibly different outcome of Watergate had Woodward and Bernstein shared the identity of Deep Throat."[41] The answer is uncertain, but by concealing the identity of Deep Throat, Woodward had an unshared vision. The unshared vision is the hallmark of Washington news, for it "is valued precisely because it is an insider's conversation."[42]

Watergate

Watergate is the ideal example of journalist as shaman. Woodward described his super-source as a "backdrop or second source of information and conclusions gathered elsewhere. He could steer toward what was right, or towards a fruitful line of inquiry."[43] But Deep Throat claimed he would never give original FBI information. This motivation perhaps served as a means to protect his anonymity; after all, being the second in command at the FBI gave Felt access to information very few others had. Thus it might be very easy for investigators to narrow down the pool of suspects who might be leaking information that was known to a select few. But even if this was the case, Woodward later lashed out at Felt during one of their 2 a.m. secret, underground meetings in a parking garage. Woodward told Felt that they were "playing a degrading chickenshit game pretending that [Felt] was not passing original, new information to me."[44]

Bernstein described the relationship similarly: "What Deep Throat did more than anything was confirm information for us that we obtained elsewhere. There's a couple exceptions to that [i.e., Felt gave original information]. That's basically what Felt did. It was hugely helpful because it gave us a solidity we knew we were right."[45] Here, Bernstein supports Woodward's assertion that Felt confirmed what the reporters had already found. Felt may not have given much original information—he did by Bernstein's quote—but he also approved information the reporters had found by themselves. In the world of journalism, unconfirmed or uncertain information is not credible information. The substantiation of information, especially from the second in command at the FBI, gave substantial credibility, direction, and faith to Woodward and Bernstein.

The nature of this shamanistic relationship between the reporters and Felt was depicted in *All the President's Men*. The journalistic shaman descends to the dark and frightening parking garage underworld to meet the divinely knowledgeable Deep Throat, only to return to the brightly illuminated *Washington Post* offices to reveal the truth to all. Without such aid, as Woodward later believed, the *Post*'s coverage of the scandal would have been "handicapped."[46]

Arguably, Woodward and Bernstein's reporting could have happened without Deep Throat, but perhaps not as effectively. With the numerous sources and tenacity of the two reporters, it is possible, since the reporters had other inside sources. Woodward, for example, helped an old acquaintance, Scott Armstrong, get on Sen. Erwin's Watergate Committee as an investigator, and "Armstrong did not forget his friends and benefactor."[47] Moreover, "even inside the Special Watergate Prosecutor's office, the most nearly leak proof of all the groups investigating Watergate, Woodward and Bernstein found lawyers they could befriend over dinner and convince to help them with confirmation of information the reporters first learned elsewhere."[48]

All of these sources just mentioned could be described as having special access to certain knowledge. These sources, for a number of reasons, were unwilling or unable to spread the word of what they know. Inversely, the journalist does not necessarily have direct access to information but has the ability to spread the word. In a partnership, the journalist can visit, so to speak, a hidden world and then return to spread the information. Thus, just as Woodward and Bernstein needed Deep Throat, Felt needed them. Felt could not reveal information to his newly appointed boss, the recently Nixon-appointed director of the FBI, L. Patrick Gray. It is often the case that the inside source, "who may, of course, be implicated in the wrongdoing or beholden to those who are,"[49] cannot give information to the prosecutor. And Gray, whose loyalties may have been too close to Nixon, was not the outlet Felt needed. Felt's top position at the FBI gave him a near omniscient view of the scandal, but that position also denied him the means to speak out publicly. He needed a messenger. And this shows us a less heroic, but more accurate shamanistic view of the press during Watergate.

Clinton/Lewinsky

The relationship between source and medium is not without problems. The journalist, like the shaman, can be controlled by his or her sources, which is the characterization of the relationship between journalist and source in the Clinton/Lewinsky scandal. While *Newsweek*'s Michael Isikoff, who was the primary investigative journalist of the scandal, "attracted criticism for his involvement with sources who arguably used him as much as he used them," the sources were ultimately in control.[50] When *Newsweek* and Isikoff did not serve as the willing conduit their sources wanted, those sources made the most of less reputable outlets, thereby creating a press scandal during a sex scandal.[51]

The scandal that began with an intimate relationship between a White House intern, Monica Lewinsky, and President Bill Clinton and ended with the president's impeachment was shocking for many reasons. One of them revolved around the initial publicizing of the scandal by Internet blogger Matt Drudge. Drudge got credit for breaking the scandal after *Newsweek* decided to hold off publishing Isikoff's investigations because the editors believed doing so would severely affect the lives of private citizens; out of respect and responsibility, the editors opted to wait for more information and confirmation.[52] Drudge, however, "placed no journalistic restrictions on the material he published on his Internet Web page. If the story was juicy, sexy, and eye-catching, he would run it."[53] So when he heard that the president was rumored to be having an illicit affair with an intern and that *Newsweek* was not publishing the story, he eagerly posted it. At best, Drudge revolutionized the traditional news media by publicly breaking the scandal online.[54] At worst, Drudge was, as NBC commentator Matt Lauer claimed, a "media gossip . . . known for below-the-Beltway reporting."[55]

Before Drudge broke the scandal online, there had been two unpublicized investigations of Bill Clinton. One was by Independent Counsel Kenneth Starr, and the other was by Isikoff. Initially, Isikoff and Starr did now know of each other's investigations; however, both Isikoff and Starr shared a common source—Linda Tripp, a longtime critic of Clinton.[56] Isikoff had long been following allegations about President Clinton's numerous affairs, including Paula Jones, when Tripp told him about the latest one involving her new friend, Monica Lewinsky. Tripp and her book agent, Lucianne Goldberg, worked out a plan to give a little information to Isikoff to "'titillate the public.' . . . Then Goldberg would hustle Tripp to a book publisher so she could cash in with a more complete version."[57] Isikoff, however, was not an easy pawn for Tripp, who, unbeknownst to the reporter, had also given Starr some key information about Lewinsky.[58]

Isikoff later received an anonymous tip that Lewinsky and Tripp were having lunch, and as part of Starr's inquiry, the FBI had wired Tripp for the meeting.[59] Isikoff was stunned that a special prosecutor was "launching a secret criminal investigation of the president—and targeting his supposed girlfriend in an effort to nail him."[60] Isikoff called one of Starr's prosecutors, Jackie Bennett, and said, "I know what you guys have been doing. I know everything."[61] Bennett realized that publicity of the investigation would hamper Starr's efforts, so he asked if Isikoff would delay publishing the story.[62] Isikoff did not want to interfere with Starr's investigation, but at the same time, Starr's inquiry into the president's relationship with Lewinsky was "breathtaking news."[63] Isikoff believed he had a shamanistic role to play as he said, "The only role I had here was as a reporter—the guy who tells the public what's going on."[64] But Isikoff said he would delay a few more days, and Bennett was grateful; it was this decision that resulted in Drudge breaking the story.

While Isikoff's willingness to wait benefited Bennett, it did not help Tripp. Tripp, Goldberg, and her lawyer, James Moody, all wanted the story out, as did a group of conservative lawyers, known as the "elves," who were secretly helping prosecutors in the Paula Jones sexual harassment suit against Clinton.[65] After speaking with Isikoff, a frustrated Moody called one of the elves, who e-mailed the "essence of what he knew about the *Newsweek* decision" to Drudge, who then confirmed the story with Goldberg (Drudge even called Isikoff to confirm the story, but Isikoff was asleep and his wife did not want to wake him).[66] Goldberg wanted the story to come out in a "reputable magazine," but when that failed, Goldberg claimed she would have given the story to anyone, and "the fact that Matt [Drudge] called me was everybody's dumb luck."[67]

While investigative reporters need their sources just as shamans need theirs, when there is one source and numerous outlets, the source is in a powerful position. While Isikoff was the "Hollywood" archetype of an investigative reporter—following up false leads and never relenting over months and years, which garnered comparisons to Woodward and Bernstein—he was outdone by a few quick phone calls and e-mails.[68] Quite simply, the Clinton/Lewinsky scandal shows us that just as water will follow the path of least resistance, the leak will do the same, thereby influencing how and when a scandal breaks.

While sources were more in control of breaking the Clinton/Lewinsky scandal than the reporter, Isikoff can still be considered a shaman. Isikoff did his job as investigative journalist—perhaps even more so than Woodward and Bernstein in that Isikoff was independent of government investigators. Moreover, even though Isikoff did not break the story, he did write extensively on the sex scandal as well as his role in the press scandal. Despite his efforts, it was the editors' decisions that stopped him from breaking the scandal. Consequently, "it is important to distinguish editorial decisions from decisions made by reporters. The revealers generally made contact with reporters, but it was the editor who decided whether the revelations would be made public."[69] Thus, not only were the sources in control of the journalist as shaman, but so were the *Newsweek* editors.

The Clinton/Lewinsky scandal demonstrates that journalists, like the sha-man, can be controlled by their sources, and such interpretations have been applied to Watergate in understanding why Felt helped Woodward. When Felt identified himself in 2005, the great mystery of "Who was Deep Throat?" then became "Why did Felt talk?" Years before Deep Throat revealed himself publicly, Woodward sought him out in his California home and asked him, but he did not recall the motivation behind his actions. Others argued that Felt, a longtime supporter of J. Edgar Hoover, used Woodward to retaliate against Nixon, who appointed Nixon supporter Patrick Gray to the top slot at the FBI after the sudden death of Hoover. Felt denied this, but admits he was unhappy, although not jealous and not out for retribution.

But the point remains that while investigative reporting needs inside sources, the journalist as shaman "is dangerous in part because high-powered journalists become enmeshed in the Washington establishment, their reputa-tions and stories dependent on privileged access to power-brokers."[70] Thus there is a concern about the press aligning too closely with government, though Woodward and Bernstein did not fall victim to this. They cannot be criticized for not relying on sources, for that is the very nature of investigative journalism. The investigative journalist's duty is to report (i.e., not "investi-gate" in the true sense of the word, but to "report"—to inform the public of the happenings in the supernatural world) "about a public affairs issue that reveals information someone or some entity has tried to keep secret or which was not readily available to the general public."[71]

This necessary relationship between government and press earns the press the title of the fourth estate, which is an often-invoked term that puts the press on equal footing with the other three estates of government. In England, where the term is believed to originate, the three estates were the monarch's clergy, the House of Lords, and the House of Commons.[72] In the United States, the fourth estate may be more appropriately titled the fourth branch as "it operates as a de facto quasi official fourth branch of government, its institutions no less impor-tant because they have been developed . . . haphazardly."[73] With such a label as the "fourth estate," the press undeniably must work with the other branches, but again the concern is being subsumed by and aligning too closely with the other branches, which is the fate of Teapot Dome journalist Paul Y. Anderson.

Teapot Dome

In various cultures, there are "individuals who profess to maintain relations with spirits whether they are possessed by them or control them."[74] The sources controlled the story in Clinton/Lewinsky, but the reporter controlled much more than the sources in Teapot Dome.

At the heart of the Teapot Dome scandal in the early 1920s was President Warren G. Harding's secretary of the interior, Albert Fall. Fall had leased oil fields in California and Wyoming (one of which was called Teapot Dome) to two oilmen, who were rumored to be Fall's good friends. These friends also just happened to have loaned Fall a great deal of money around the time they received the leases to drill the government's oil. With the untimely death of Harding in 1923 and a new administration in place, it was best to let "bygones be bygones," and the scandal quickly faded from the public's attention.[75]

In 1927, the Supreme Court ultimately ruled the leases invalid, but there was the question of what happened to all the ill-gotten profits, $3 million, made by Fall's oil friends from those years of drilling (1922–1927). Attorney General John G. Sargent had no interest in following the money, and key Democratic leaders were hesitant to start another congressional inquiry, which might have been characterized as political maneuvering for the upcoming presidential election against Republican Calvin Coolidge.[76] But Paul Y. Anderson, a highly motivated reporter from the *St. Louis Post Dispatch*, convinced a number of senators to reopen the Teapot Dome investigation.

After Attorney General Sargent expressed no desire to ascertain the status of the missing funds, Anderson then went to Democratic senator Thomas Walsh. Walsh was hesitant because he had been criticized for using his earlier investigations of Teapot Dome as political warfare against the incumbent Republican president. But Walsh mentioned he was willing to be part of another inquiry if someone else started it. Walsh suggested that Anderson speak with Sen. George Norris. Undeterred and full of energy, Anderson continued to form a congressional committee.

Anderson eventually persuaded Sen. Norris to introduce legislation to investigate the missing funds. Anderson also convinced other senators, including Republican senator Robert LaFollette, to join the inquiry. With a mix of both major parties, Sen. Walsh then joined the investigation. Anderson had, in effect, created a congressional investigation, not by using the front pages of the paper, but through aggressive lobbying.

Anderson did more than convene the committee; he was a de facto member of the investigation.[77] Anderson actually sat with the congressional investigators. As Sen. Walsh was casually questioning Robert Stewart, who was a partner of one of the oilmen, Anderson thought to himself, "Great God! They are letting him off without asking him just the things I wanted them to ask."[78] Anderson thought the oilman was being too sly and was going to get away. In response, Anderson quickly scribbled two questions on a scrap piece of paper and passed them to one of the senators. The two questions addressed Stewart's knowledge of who received the funds or if he discussed them with

Sinclair. After some failed attempts at evading the questions, he declined to answer both. Until that point, everything had been going smoothly for Stewart.[79]

Such antics were not uncommon for Anderson throughout the investigation. Anderson was the "quintessential participatory journalist of his day."[80] Moreover, "questioning by proxy was not an isolated practice for Anderson, but it was not the usual modus operandi of Washington correspondents."[81] It was his active participation that became part of his legacy.[82]

As Teapot Dome simmered, Paul Y. Anderson was credited with bringing the scandal to a conclusion. Anderson won a Pulitzer Prize in 1929 for his scandal reporting and worked so "persistently and with such telling effect that he was credited, as much as any single individual, with exposing the malefactors who had abused the public trust."[83]

Anderson was far different than many of his journalistic peers. President Harding owned and operated a newspaper in Ohio, so he was seen as one of them. Additionally, Harding "won the correspondents with warmth and an openly friendly feeling after hours."[84] As a result, he was "better protected by the press during his early days in the White House than any other President."[85] While this period of protection was short lived, it was a boon that served him well in the earliest days of his administration. Moreover, journalists also had limited information. Political journalists gathered news "through press releases and briefings," which made the Washington reporter "a fairly limited political animal" and made reporting "no more exciting than knitting."[86] All in all, "the White House was a dull news source."[87]

There was wrongdoing happening; it was just that favorable and controlling sources were unwilling to give out information, and these were the primary if not sole sources of information. Furthermore, editors cautioned reporters to make "their reports as favorable as possible" to Fall and other defendants.[88] Editors feared that muckraking would cause oil companies to pull their valued advertising. Here, not only is the journalist limited by receiving uninteresting and controlled information, but those who support the very business of journalism control the journalist. Thus, Paul Anderson was unique in that he was willing to go where even other journalists were unwilling to go and to risk more than they were willing to risk.

While Anderson was the seemingly heroic reporter of Teapot Dome, as a member of the fourth estate, he seems too closely aligned with one of the other branches of government. Critics claimed that Anderson was more investigator than reporter. Some claimed he was not a journalist but "an important ally" to LaFollette and Walsh and was "a fact finding agency in his own person."[89] Others challenged him as "possessing a 'prosecutorial complex.'"[90] Moreover, if Anderson was a reporter, some of his editorials focused on his own story, on what he did rather than what was going on with the actual scandal.[91] In other words, Anderson was more inquisitor than investigative journalist. Anderson actually sat with the congressional investigators and fed them questions during the second round of the Teapot Dome hearings. To return to Zelizer's shamanistic analogy, Anderson remained in the other world not as a witness but as an investigator. His unique role of staying in the other world would often be the focus of his reporting, as he often covered his own story of bringing about a congressional investigation.[92]

Woodward and Bernstein may have some similarities with Anderson in that they became heroes for their scandal coverage. But Woodward and Bernstein fulfilled their shamanistic role of bringing the public news from the other world where the people could not go. The public of the 1920s was not much interested in politics. Anderson, however, found a willing audience for the congressional investigations where it is extremely rare for reporters to be actual members of the investigating committee.

Iran-Contra

Out of the four scandals examined here, the journalist as shaman analogy does not hold up in the Iran-Contra example. Nor does journalism in Iran-Contra demonstrate the spirit of the checking value. To contextualize this argument, we must take into account the media during Reagan's presidency.

One of the main features of the 1980s news media was the addition of the twenty-four-hour news format introduced by CNN. The constant news cycle allowed CNN to provide the news as it happened.[93] Although CNN struggled financially in the 1980s, it succeeded in improving the "immediacy" of news coverage.[94] CNN was first on the scene of the attempted assassination of Pope John Paul II and was the only network providing live coverage of the ill-fated *Challenger* launch. Moreover, CNN allowed for "saturation coverage," which allowed for expanded reporting and, consequently, greater understanding.[95] Such abilities soon rectified the early financial difficulties of the network, but this came with a different type of cost. While the constant news format became popular for the type of coverage it offered, it later became apparent that "CNN generally had built its reputation on saturation coverage and *not on investigative journalism* [emphasis added]."[96]

Popularly known as the Great Communicator, Reagan benefited from the early new media that focused on saturation coverage but also from traditional television and print media. Mixing Hollywood and public relations, Reagan appeared in limited and controlled settings where his style was his great substance.[97] This led to one of Reagan's greatest attributes: his "like-ability."[98] Generally, Reagan was liked not necessarily for his agenda or policies but more so for his amiable presence, which made people—voters, politicians, and the media—want him to be a success.[99]

While the news media knew about the Reagan administration's dealings with Iran and the Contras well before the scandal erupted publicly, the press did not pursue the stories vigorously.[100] That is not to say that the press ignored the matter entirely. The press reported on the Reagan administration's activities. The *New York Times* and *Time* magazine, for example, mentioned that Israel had sold U.S. weapons to Iran as far back as 1982.[101] Coverage still continued, and one story appeared on the front page of the *New York Times*, but the "stories were not deemed worthy of vigorous pursuit, were not picked up throughout the rest of the news media, [and] were not accorded a sufficiently high profile to attract the attention of the American public."[102]

Instead, the focus was on domestic issues like the economic boom of the mid-1980s that brought about the Yuppie—the young, urban professional, or the young, upwardly mobile professional, who was enjoying the economic revival that Reagan had brought about. Domestic success, however, was overshadowed by the publication of an article in a small Lebanese weekly, *Al Shiraa*. *Al Shiraa* was a "Beirut publication that is usually well informed on Iranian affairs."[103] Consequently, it was no surprise when *Al Shiraa* revealed that one of Reagan's national security advisors, Robert McFarlane, had made a trip to Iran to talk about hostages. With only two years left in office, the Iran-Contra scandal was the first great threat to Reagan, who later called *Al Shiraa*, "that rag in Beirut."[104]

Al Shiraa was not the first Lebanese source to reveal McFarlane's trip. On October 15, 1986, "radical university students" distributed five million leaflets that detailed the trip complete with a picture of McFarlane.[105] Then a small paper in Baalbek, Lebanon, published a story on October 15 that would become the basis for the report in *Al Shiraa*.[106]

Al Shiraa ran the story, "Between Reasons of State and Reason of Revolution: What Happened in Tehran," on pages 24 to 26. The article reported on former national security advisor Robert McFarlane's trip to Teheran in May 1986. McFarlane, it was reported, was sent by the Reagan administration to secure the release of Americans involved in the Lebanon hostage crisis. The article, which was released on November 3, 1986, made one small but costly mistake: it referred to the trip "last month," which technically meant he was there in October, but McFarlane was in Iran in May. Based on this error, McFarlane "categorically" denied he was in Tehran "last month."[107] Moreover, Reagan's acting press secretary, Larry Speakes, claimed that the United States would continue its arms embargo against Iran and that any further comment might affect the lives of the remaining hostages.[108] Nevertheless, Ali Akbar Rafsanjani, the speaker of the Iranian Parliament, confirmed

McFarlane's trip the day after *Al Shiraa*'s report. With that, the Iran half of Iran-Contra became front-page news, and this time it would not go away.

Just two weeks after the *Al Shiraa* revelations, the *Washington Post* published the self-reflective "How the Newshounds Blew the Iran-Contra Story."[109] The article tried to answer two questions: "Why did the U.S. news media miss the biggest story of the Reagan administration?" and "How did such a big story tiptoe almost silently past the most powerful media establishment in the world?" The answers varied. First, the sources whom journalists frequently relied upon were the very same individuals who were responsible for the scandal. Second, the nature of the 1980s news media changed investigative reporting: "Reporters and editors are so busy focusing on the fast-breaking news that the important time-consuming stories can get away from them." Third, the story was complex. Randolph wrote, "Uncovering the Iran-Contra affair wouldn't have been easy—even for the best of journalists." The story was difficult and time consuming even for the likes of Bob Woodward, who was the assistant managing editor for investigative stories at the *Washington Post* during Iran-Contra. Woodward recounted, "Managing Editor Leonard Downie Jr. said, 'Let's get out and plow the fields on this story.' Woodward blames himself because 'I didn't get out and plow the fields.'" The *Washington Post*'s executive editor during Watergate and Iran-Contra said, "'Unlike Watergate, all newspapers were on to this story very quickly.' It was true, sort of. News organizations did get onto the Iran-Contra story quickly—but only after it was dropped into their laps, courtesy of the small Lebanese weekly *Al Shiraa* and the Reagan administration itself."[110]

IMPLICATIONS

The opening stages of a scandal have several implications, which focus on free speech, public discourse, and democracy, that help us understand how the American political scandal perpetuates a democratic ideology. Specifically, the popular conception of journalists as being heroic watchdogs, who are seemingly separate and distinct from the government they oversee, misses the mark. Popular culture and public memory mischaracterize the actual role of journalists in the four major scandals, which are the benchmark of all other scandals. Believing in a heroic press in such popular scandals perpetuates the belief that the press performs the checking value and a key democratic role. Consequently, when a scandal breaks, we are shocked, but that shock is abated by the notion that the free press caught the wrongdoer and is publicizing the details of the transgression. The upsetting but reassuring nature of the opening stages of the scandal perpetuates a democratic ideology in that, while things may go bad, the free press, a hallmark of democracy, is alive and well. However, the argument presented here is that while there is a press, there is a symbiotic relationship between it and the government that mitigates the pure normative ideals and values of a free press that are perpetuated in culture and history.

Free Speech

The First Amendment is revered in the United States. It protects the natural right of people to express their ideas. Those who are politically minded appreciate the First Amendment's protection of expression with regard to oversight and criticism of their government. This is an abstract high-value idea, which is reassuring. Abstract notions of free speech and a free press give comfort that, while public officials may do bad things, there will be the press there to report, comment, and critique those individuals.

The specific concrete reality, as evidenced by the four case studies used here, presents a less heroic role. These four cases demonstrate that the fourth estate and the government are too closely aligned, at least to warrant the idea of such a heroic independent free press. The government either provides the information or controls the sources of information; the reporter or investigative journalist, on the other hand, may push or drive a governmental investigation or turn a blind eye to some unpleasantness.

Abstract notions of a free press where the press is separate and distinct from the government mirrors that of the alleged separation of church and state. In reality, church and state can mix (provided that the government does not endorse one religion over another, etc.) as many religious rituals, such as prayers, are routinely conducted at government functions. Similarly, the press and the government may intertwine.

The newspaper business needs information to publish, and that information comes from a source, which might very well not have the ability to disseminate information. The relationship between publisher and source is a symbiotic one. Thus, it is not incorrect to say that the government and press should not be completely separate. But what is incorrect is to say that when a politician transgresses some boundary, and the ideals of our government are shaken, the free press is touted as being the virtuous redeemer to compensate for such political shenanigans. This is how a scandal perpetuates the democratic ideology. A heroic free press is seen as the counterbalance to our politicians gone astray. But in reality, the press is closely aligned with the government. In some instances, like Clinton/Lewinsky, within the political scandal is a journalism scandal in which there are debates about the relationship between traditional (*Washington Post* and *Newsweek*) and new media (online gossip reporters like Matt Drudge).

Public Discourse

The role of the journalist also impacts the public discourse of and about the role of the press in scandal. While the press is ultimately held as heroic for their efforts, the initial public discourse around the scandal often addresses the journalist, who has caused harm, not the accused politician. Specifically, in each scandal examined here, the press is criticized for disrupting the existing relative political prosperity. For example in Teapot Dome, when Albert Fall gained control of the oil lands from the secretary of the navy, the transfer, which many in Washington saw as suspicious, received very little attention in the media. The news coverage of the 1920s generally shied away from politics; people wanted a vacation from politics after enduring the Great War. People were more avid to read about "baseball players, prizefighters, gangsters, and silent film stars than politicians and diplomats." The *New York Times* gave six front-page columns to Jack Dempsey's latest boxing victory while, on the same day, one column was given to Germany's signing of the peace treaty. Reporters who criticized politicians and others were pejoratively labeled muckrakers, who were the political paparazzi of the time.

In the beginning of Watergate, the press was seen as disrupting the relative political prosperity with their early reports of the scandal. The prescandal political prosperity included the first visit by a U.S. president to communist China and the end of the hugely unpopular Vietnam War. Americans of the early 1970s wanted a break from Vietnam, just as the Americans of the 1920s wanted a break from the Great War. Just as Harding's platform of a "return to normalcy" from war earned him a landslide victory in 1920, Nixon's achievements contributed to his 1972 landslide victory, which was the largest victory until Reagan's in 1984, which was two years prior to Iran-Contra.

More specifically, many looked down on Woodward and Bernstein, as many did not believe their mysterious unnamed sources, which made the young inexperienced reporters easy targets for Nixon supporters. The two young reporters were challenging a hugely popular Nixon, who had just won reelection by a landslide. Consequently, Woodward and Bernstein initially brought consternation to the 1970s electorate much like the Teapot Dome muckrakers, who brought the disinterested public of the 1920s back to politics.

Iran-Contra and the Clinton/Lewinsky scandals both saw journalists initially attacked for disrupting the relative political prosperity. Iran-Contra began during an economic revival, and those who enjoyed and benefited from it had their own label: the Yuppie. Likewise, the accusations against Clinton came at a time of economic prosperity. Moreover, the allegations seemed no different from all the previous accusations of Clinton's personal misconduct. Among the first things that the voting public knew about Clinton were the allegations of his draft dodging, war protests, questionable drug use, and numerous allegations of sexual misconduct. Consequently, the fledgling scandal seemed like all the other accusations that followed Clinton before becoming president. Moreover, the press for the Clinton/Lewinsky scandal was different. The press was made up of a nonstop, virtually unregulated new media journalist, who, along with editorializing pundits of the traditional press, brought the scandal to public light. These individuals were seen as not operating akin to the *New York Times*'s famous motto, "All the News That's Fit to Print," but publishing anything to fill the twenty-four hours.

Despite these early characterizations, the press was eventually vindicated in these scandals, thereby contributing to their seemingly heroic status. Most notably, Paul Y. Anderson, Bob Woodward, and Carl Bernstein were awarded the Pulitzer Prize for their efforts. Matt Drudge seemingly validated the legitimacy of new media journalism. The press of Iran-Contra received no such accolades.

This initial assessment of the journalist as not necessarily heroic ultimately flips. For if there is anything more valued and intrinsic than calling out those in positions of authority, it is the struggle of the underdogs, who with all odds against them persevere, with truth on their side, to become the apparent true watchdogs. Such is the case with reporters, who seem to disrupt prosperity to show that not all is going well.

The evolution of journalists from disrupters of a relative political prosperity to heroic saviors of democracy perpetuates a democratic ideology. The politician who has been doing well is a sign of a strong democracy. The people have spoken and spoken well. The politician acts and acts well, at least until the scandalmongers in the press tarnish that image. The roles later flip when (or if) the politician is revealed to be a wrongdoer. We demonize the press for bringing us bad news, which threatens our democratic choices, but we celebrate the press for its part in expunging the threat to our democratic system. These dynamic and malleable characterizations always provide the means for the people to find an interpretation of the scandal where there is some redemption for democracy; consequently, the democratic ideology is perpetuated.

Democracy

Undeniably the press has a tremendous responsibility in a democracy, and it is no surprise that their efforts can be described as the stuff of heroes and myths. The high-level values attributed to the press by the trial of John Peter Zenger and the popular memory of Watergate perpetuate the ideology that a strong, independent press is in action. This popular memory is partly due to the book and film versions of *All the President's Men*, which was publicized by telling the "whole behind-the-scenes drama the way it happened."[111] Critics quickly pointed out that the "behind-the-scenes" perspective was not shown, as the movie did not explain how the government did the investigation."[112]

But the press did have a role to play. The film and book depicted some of the original investigation of Donald H. Segretti, who was part of Nixon's dirty tricks doctrine. Segretti was sent to prison for his role but was found to have no connection whatsoever to Watergate, as most of his work was done before the break-in.

But the real contribution of the press in Watergate was in their shamanistic role. The government did the investigation, and it was the press who went to governmental sources, including the FBI and Justice Department, and relayed that information to the public. Quite simply, the press "exposed" the wrong-doings that the government investigators had discovered. Epstein would claim that even this interpretation would be going too far in that the public would still be able to hear the information found by government investigators, not by leaks but when the cases came to trial.[113] Regardless, the press would still—as Woodward did when he was originally dispatched to the ar-raignment of the five burglars—serve a shamanistic role by going where few can (or in a cynical view, are willing to) go and spread the word, much like the messenger god Hermes. Zelizer's argument that journalists are similar to shamans implies that journalists are "gods" of a sort—much like Hermes, the messenger god of Greek antiquity.

Hermes was divine in that he was in contact with other Olympian gods and therefore was able to pass along information from the gods. But he also had contact with humans—often serving as a guide to the dark and dangerous underworld of Hades, which is not too distant from the politics of Watergate. Woodward and Bernstein were like Hermes, able to navigate people through the dark underworld of Watergate and allow democracy to emerge vindicated on the other side. The concern arises that the journalists and their reports can be controlled by their sources (and editors), as can be seen in the Clinton/Lewinsky scandal, and that the journalist may remain in the spirit world as was the case of Paul Y. Anderson, who, in Teapot Dome, arguably seemed to serve the investigators more than inform the people.

The real value of the press, then, as exemplified in Watergate, Clinton/Lewinsky, and Teapot Dome, is not in checking the government but in issu-ing a reunderstanding of the scandal from the view of the audience, of the people. Journalists as shamans serve the people by publicly airing informa-tion, whereas investigative branches of the government such as the FBI and Justice Department are primarily investigators.

But to be sure, both the press and the investigative arms of the government are capable of investigating and publicizing. Thus, one caveat should be clearly noted: there is undoubtedly value in an investigative press corps; there are too many examples of investigative journalism fulfilling their checking roles true to Blasi's ideas. Certainly one cannot be too careful when relying on government investigators, for those very investigators may be implicated in scandals, as was the case in Iran-Contra. But while "it is clear that the [Watergate press] myth, in its unadulterated form, is overblown . . . it remains a powerful force in the news media."[114] The free press myth perpetrates a democratic ideology in that it is the journalist who is seen as a hero in that they tip the scale back to the idea of democracy—of politicians being held accountable. However, the four case studies used here question that heroic portrayal.

CONCLUSION

This chapter argues that when a scandal threatens democracy, a hero is not only wanted but needed. We should not be worried when we see political scandals on the front page, for the presence of scandal suggests a vigorous investigative press corps. And any ill that results from the publication of scandalous behavior is far outweighed by the ultimate benefit that the public knows what their government is doing.[115] Such interpretations reign supreme, for the journalist has exposed the wrongdoing in the spirit of democracy.

Within this interpretation, we must be aware of the overheroization of journalists, especially as exemplified in Watergate. The free press myth states that journalists right the wrongs of politicians. But one must be careful of having an inflated sense of a virtuous checking press, for the sources, be they governmental as in Watergate or private as in Clinton/Lewinsky, often exert great control. While journalists may not be the most heroic players in a scandal, we must recognize the key role they do play: it is the journalist who dares go where others are incapable and returns to tell us the tale.

In telling the tale, the result is that the press is criticized for breaking the scandal but is then often rewarded for their work spreading the information. What this means is that the democratic value of a free press ebbs and flows during a scandal. When the press disrupts the relative political prosperity, their value to democracy is low; when the press is vindicated, their value to democracy is quite high, for it is, as we often over-romanticize, the press protected by the First Amendment and with truth on their side that rights the wrongs. But in reality the press is an extension of governmental investigations, which are embedded in the very system in which the political transgression has occurred.

Chapter Three

Partisan Discourse
Prior to the Smoking Gun

Once the scandal hits the front pages, the opposition does their best, as Richard Nixon once said, to make a "little thing" into a "big thing."[1] The little thing is the initial accusation of some transgression. The big thing is a full-fledged scandal. Following the allegations of misconduct, political discourse can be characterized as political contestation constituted in and through relatively unsubstantiated and speculated attacks and dismissive responses until a smoking gun, if it exists, is discovered. In this contestation is the attempt to make the alleged transgression a "big thing" by the accusers and an attempt to diminish the accusations into a "little thing" by the accused. This political contestation, especially the attacks, are often negative and vitriolic. Even the press, as the last chapter discussed, is initially characterized negatively for its attacks on the relative political prosperity. The accusations and attacks by political actors outside of the news media context, however, are seen as the typical mudslinging that is standard fare in politics.

Partisan discourse during scandals seems to offer little contribution to the political debate. Scandal rhetoric is, as Cass Sunstein writes, "low quality fare," which is nothing more than sensational entertainment to the masses.[2] While political speech has long been recognized as the most valuable speech, scandal rhetoric does not seem to hold such an esteemed status. Political speech deals with the issues and policies of a state, not necessarily attacking and attempting to discredit a political opponent. Accusations and denials of some transgression may not necessarily deal with matters of state, but they do have political implications. Thus, early scandal rhetoric may not be pure political speech, but it does carry political implications. And, as the future often reveals, these political implications are substantial and severe.

Consequently, this chapter argues that subsequent to accusations of some transgression, there is political contestation, which is characterized as low-value political rhetoric by the accused. However, there is value in this so-called low-quality rhetoric, as history clearly shows that what was once popularly believed to be just typical anti-Nixon or anti-Clinton partisan rhetoric was in fact accurate and therefore had real and substantial value to the political landscape in the United States.

To make this argument, this chapter first reviews the genres of scandal discourse in the wake of allegations and then argues how those genres are partisan in nature. Next, the chapter offers a reading of the partisan scandal rhetoric in each of the four case study scandals. The chapter then concludes by addressing the implications of the early scandal rhetoric for free speech, rhetoric, and democracy.

IN THE WAKE OF ALLEGATION

Scandal Rhetoric: Exigence

Before the presence of scandal rhetoric, there is an exigence that political rhetoric addresses.[3] An exigence is a pressing problem that must be attended to by rhetorical discourse. The first exigence for scandal rhetoric is the initial publicity of some transgression. The authority over leasing the Teapot Dome oil fields, the burglary at the Watergate, the downing of a U.S. military cargo plane in Nicaragua, and the reports of *Newsweek*'s decision not to publish a story about an affair were all exigences that required discourse.[4]

The exigence, however, need not be limited to just the initial publicity of misconduct by the press. Possible exigences also include the decision to investigate (by the executive, judicial, or legislative branch or by agencies such as the Federal Bureau of Investigation or the Government Accountability Office), testimony of key officials or participants, the discovery of incriminating evidence, or the release of official reports. In Watergate, for example, accusatory discourse followed numerous exigences, from the initial break-in to linking the burglars to Nixon's campaign staff and the White House, as well as the discovery and battle over the tapes, the Saturday Night Massacre, and the discovery of the smoking gun, to name just a few. Ultimately, the culmination of evidence led Nixon into a "rhetorical bind from which he could not escape."[5] Nixon, that is, had to respond.

While the Watergate example demonstrates that the exigence calls for a response, we can also understand the exigence as offering a rhetor an opportunity to speak.[6] In terms of scandal, virtually any exigence can provide an opportunity. That is, the possibility of an accusation is seemingly unlimited, as any potential political mileage that could be made from a wrongdoing will undoubtedly be followed up, especially given the importance of the high-level political context. Consequently, there will be a response to an exigence in the form of accusations of misconduct, which is what scholars label *kategoria*. Conceptually, *kategoria* is public discourse that attacks or critiques another; the accusatory discourse, in turn, calls for a response. That response is called *apologia*, which is public discourse that aims to defend oneself. Since the accusatory discourse calls for a response, scholars claim that it is appropriate to think of *kategoria* and *apologia* as a speech set.[7]

Scandal Rhetoric: *Kategoria*

In the *kategoria-apologia* speech set, the accuser is the "prime-mover . . . [who] perceived an evil [and] is motivated to expose it . . . through accusatory discourse."[8] As mentioned earlier, given the high-level political context of major scandals such as Teapot Dome, Watergate, Iran-Contra, and Clinton/Lewinsky, seemingly any exigence can and will be taken as an opportunity to besmirch a politician and the party he or she represents. This is undoubtedly true of the president. Next to the president, who "is charged with ensuring that the laws are faithfully executed, in terms of political profile, no other individual in government has more to lose through allegation of participation in corrupt, unwise or illegal activities."[9] Due to the innumerable attacks on presidents and their administrations, it is beyond the scope of this chapter to offer a complete enumeration of *kategoria* within each scandal. I do, however, want to briefly review the genres, sources, and timing of accusations, which suggest that accusatory scandal discourse is partisan and serves as a means of political warfare.

The *kategoria* themselves may come in many different genres. There are two primary forms of accusatory discourse: accusations against character or accusations against policy.[10] Accusations against Nixon (aka, "Tricky Dick") and Clinton (aka, "Slick Willie") were both attacks based on their character. Albert Fall was attacked based on his anticonservationist policies. Reagan's policies on the Nicaraguan Contras and arms for hostages and his management style were at the heart of the attacks during the Iran-Contra scandal. These examples are not meant to suggest that Clinton and Nixon were solely attacked on their character or that Reagan and Fall were solely attacked on their policies. But these examples demonstrate that attacks are the primary means of "political competition" with the purpose of besmirching the reputation or the policies of the accused.[11]

The *kategoria* may also come from a myriad of sources. Accusatory discourse may come from an individual source such as a politician (e.g., 1972 Democratic presidential nominee George McGovern), party official (e.g., 1972 Democratic National Committee chairman Lawrence F. O'Brien), or political pundit (e.g., Matt Drudge). If there is an absence of a single, formal accusation, there may also be, as Benoit observes, a "climate" of accusation; moreover, there can be a climate of accusations dotted with formal *kategoria*.[12] In Teapot Dome, for example, there were numerous voiced and printed rumors of Albert Fall's sudden increase of wealth as well as constant criticisms of Fall's anticonservationist policies by well-known conservationists throughout the United States.

It should be noted that the press, whether it be a lone reporter (e.g., Paul Y. Anderson in Teapot Dome), a newspaper (e.g., the *Washington Post* in Watergate), or a vast wave of media attention (e.g., converging media in the Clinton/Lewinsky scandal), may serve as a source of *kategoria*. One may rightfully claim that the press does not use accusatory discourse (as opposed to, for example, editorials and pundits), but this is to limit the heuristic potential of *kategoria*.

For example, recognizing the integral relationship of *kategoria* and *apologia*, one can identify a *kategoria* based on *apologia* (i.e., attacking the attacker). Nixon's responses to many of his political obstacles and defeats were based on the press—some of which attacked via editorials whereas others simply reported on the happenings, be they seen as positive or negative. One may feel that the press's coverage is a seemingly benign objective presentation, whereas another, who may attract unwanted attention from the coverage, may feel that the press's coverage is quite harmful. Such was the case with Nixon, who included many members of the press in his infamous enemies list. Consequently, depending on one's point of view, some information could be considered *kategoria*.

Several rhetorical critics note the importance of the timing of the *kategoria*.[13] The notion of timing is *kairos*, which is the timely response to a "passing instance" before it is overshadowed by another exigence, and the response should be delivered with enough "force if success is to be achieved."[14] Consequently, by examining the timing of the *kategoria*, we can gain insight into the nature of the accuser, for "the impact of scandal relies heavily on political opportunism and timing."[15]

The timing of each of the major scandals under discussion here might provide some insight. For example, Iran-Contra and the Clinton/Lewinsky scandal all played out within the last two years of a president in his second term; Watergate also played out in Nixon's second term, but he did not complete his second four-year term.[16] In this light, the *kategoria* seems to be a political weapon not necessarily to discredit a lame-duck president, but to discredit the president and his policies, his administration, and the political party he represents, which includes his party's nomination to become the next president.

The fallout of the scandals seems to show this. Notwithstanding President Clinton's accomplishments, his heir apparent, Al Gore, suffered from the scandals; Gerald Ford's election for a second term suffered greatly, if not exclusively, due to his pardon of Richard Nixon. George H. W. Bush's election was the result of many factors, and one can speculate that Bush's constant distancing of himself from the Iran-Contra episode surely did not hurt him, although many believe Bush was more involved than he admitted.

Teapot Dome was unique in that Harding had died, and his successor, Calvin Coolidge, was not implicated in the scandal, thereby making the political ramifications somewhat moot; moreover, Fall resigned as secretary of the interior. Nevertheless, and as if by clockwork, the second round of Teapot Dome investigations began in 1927, which was one year before the election of 1928. Herbert Hoover, who was secretary of commerce under Coolidge and Harding, won the 1928 election "only after the Democrats denounced him as a member of the Harding gang" who sat alongside Secretary of the Interior Fall in Harding's cabinet.[17]

Coupling *kairos* with *kategoria*, we can understand the accuser as "both the hunter and a maker of unique opportunities."[18] That is, the accuser not only can make the most of a situation when it appears but can then bring up the situation later for his or her advantage. Consequently, the timing and the nature of various forms of *kategoria* demonstrate a partisan aspect to allegations of misconduct.

Role and Context of Kategoria

The timing and nature of accusatory scandal rhetoric suggest elements of partisanship; however, the accusers often attempt to portray themselves in nonpartisan ways to give the perception of validity to the *kategoria*. In other words, the accusers "do not want to be viewed as mere vigilantes or political opportunists."[19] To appear as nonpartisan, accusers attempt to officialize the pursuit of transgressions as serious business. The accused, on the other hand, attempts to deofficialize the process to delegitimize the *kategoria*. Officialization is contingent on two factors: role and setting.[20]

First, to be official is to have "the attribution of 'role' and 'authority'" to indict individuals of wrongdoing.[21] McGovern's accusations over Watergate in the 1972 election, for example, were not officialized, as he was a political candidate. Moreover, he was a comparatively weaker candidate taking aim at the stronger incumbent. Consequently, his accusations regarding Watergate were ineffective, for "the voting public heavily discounts allegations of wrongdoing that appear to be the result of partisanship by the opposition party."[22] Independent counsels, however, have the office and statute to support their accusations. In other words, independent counsels operate from a more proper role with legally mandated authority.

Second, officialization requires "the employment of proper 'places' for waging the battle over such judgments."[23] Gronbeck claims that the settings of official accusation must be apart from the everyday routines of public discourse. The places must be grand with formal rules for conduct and "pomp and spectacle."[24] Thus, "not everyone can seriously accuse a public figure of corruption anywhere."[25] Gronbeck offers the example of the elevated platforms and flags during Sen. Ervin's Watergate committee as a prime example of the proper place.

During the attempts to officialize, the accused attempts to deofficialize the attacks and criticisms. This is achieved via *apologia*.

Scandal Rhetoric: *Apologia*

While the initial publicity of misconduct is an exigence, the *kategoria* itself can also be considered an exigence. That is, the accusation calls for a response from the accused person or a surrogate such as the president's press secretary or a campaign official. Scholars have examined *apologia* as a form of image restoration in response to *kategoria*.[26] While *apologia* can be found in numerous contexts, "presidential *apologia* studies have concerned themselves with three individuals: Richard Nixon, Ronald Reagan, and Bill Clinton," who have all dealt with a major scandal.[27] While several scholars have developed typologies of *apologia*, many of the rhetorical critics of presidential scandal *apologia* have relied upon Ware and Linkugel's typology, which includes denial, bolstering, differentiation, and transcendence. Each of these genres of *apologia* serves to deofficialize accusations.

First, the accused can offer a denial, which addresses whether the act occurred or states that the accused was not involved in the act and that others were responsible. Each denial comes in response to formal accusations or a climate of accusations regarding some misconduct. The denial typically appears early in the scandal. In Teapot Dome, Albert Fall claimed that he had never received "one cent on account of any oil lease or upon any account whatsoever" from Doheny and Sinclair.[28] In Watergate, Richard Nixon claimed, "The White House has had no involvement whatever in this particular incident." In Iran-Contra, Reagan claimed, "We did not, repeat, did not trade weapons or anything else for hostages, nor will we." In the Lewinsky scandal, Clinton stated, "I did not have sexual relations with that woman, Miss Lewinsky." On a side note, afterward, Clinton explained using the phrase "that woman" because, in his words, "I blanked out on her name."[29] This was nothing new to Lewinsky, who once reminded Clinton of her name because he called her "Kiddo."[30] Regardless, in each example, the denial eventually gains infamy in the popular political lexicon as subsequent events and revelations shatter the illusion of integrity and question the honesty of the accused. Until infamy is attained, the denial serves to quash the accusations by directly contradicting the attacks.

Second, the accused can engage in bolstering, which is when the accused assuages the accusations by presenting an image of him- or herself identifying "with something viewed more favorably by the audience."[31] Fall defended the secrecy of the bidding for the oil lands because it entailed matters of national security as the leases called for the production of military facilities at Pearl Harbor during a time when there were growing tensions over a conflict in the Pacific.[32] Nixon responded to accusations, albeit ineffectively, by stating that he had a mandate from the people through his 1972 landslide victory.[33] Reagan responded to criticism by claiming that his policy toward Iran was to build a stronger relationship between the countries, end the Iran-Iraq War, return the hostages, and eliminate state-sponsored terrorism.[34] Clinton, as well as Nixon and Reagan, responded by emphasizing his willingness to cooperate with the investigation. Such willingness suggested that the accused was open and honest, which is viewed more favorably than refusing to cooperate. Bolstering deofficializes the *kategoria* by marginalizing the accusations.

Third, the accused can engage in differentiation, which is when the accused compares the accusations to "similar but less desirable actions" thereby deofficializing the *kategoria* to be "less offensive."[35] Fall claimed that the bribe from oilmen was, in fact, a loan from friends. In response to criticisms about his role in the burglary during the campaign, Nixon differentiated "his direct management of his earlier campaign [in which he was not president] and his delegation of authority in this one [i.e., as president when he had to run the country]."[36] Reagan differentiated in that while he was negotiating, he was doing so with moderates, who were not extremists or terrorists.[37] Moreover, Reagan claimed that while he had shipped weapons to Iran, they were, according to Reagan, "a small amount of defensive weapons" rather than, as critics claimed, "presumably dangerous offensive weapons."[38] Clinton used this strategy only once; he differentiated his moral misconduct from legal misconduct.[39]

Fourth, the accused can engage in transcendence, which is when the act is placed into a larger and often high-value context. Fall, who claimed he would testify in court, did just the opposite; he did not speak at his criminal or civil trials. Fall preferred to exercise his constitutional right to protect himself from self-incrimination.[40] Nixon responded to accusations of not cooperating because he would not hand over the tapes by claiming that the constitutional doctrine of executive privilege was paramount.[41] Reagan had the possibility of "arguing for the transcendent importance of their [covert] mission," but his earlier rhetoric did not allow for the option.[42] We do, however, see transcendence in the form of the "patriotic defense" from Oliver North, who claimed that ignoring and misleading Congress was necessary in covert missions for national security.[43] Clinton transcended the allegations by stating, "I've got to go on with the work of the country. I got hired to help the rest of the American people."[44] Nixon also used this strategy claiming that while the scandal was bad, it was taking up far too much time that could be better spent on more pressing national obligations. Transcendence allows for deofficialization by characterizing the accusations as relatively unimportant in the big picture.

An additional form of *apologia* is to attack the accuser. By attacking the accuser, one can discredit the source, thereby weakening his or her accusations. The accused can attack the source of the original accusation or the press for giving undue attention to (as well as being the source of) the original accusation. For example, Fall explained that he would not comment on or testify during the Senate investigation, which he viewed as being a politically motivated attack upon him.[45] Nixon attacked John Dean several times for his then unsubstantiated testimony. Nixon claimed that Dean had "no evidence" for his accusations and that Dean was the only one out of thirty-five witnesses who implicated the president in a cover-up.[46] In Iran-Contra, Reagan attacked the credibility of the sources of information, as it was coming from unnamed sources from abroad and within his administration; Reagan responded, "Well, now you're going to hear the facts from a White House source, and you know my name."[47] President Clinton repeatedly attacked Kenneth Starr's investigation. Clinton questioned the nature of the inquiry into his "private business dealings 20 years ago."[48] Moreover, Clinton claimed the investigation went not only into his private life but into the lives of his staff and friends, which he called "the pursuit of personal destruction."[49] Clinton also noted that Starr's investigation was under investigation itself. Each of these examples demonstrates that the accused deofficializes the attackers as nothing more than partisan attackers.

Nixon, Reagan, and Clinton also accused the media of being responsible for the accusations. Nixon also often lashed out at the press, claiming that the media gave him "hell" when they disagreed with him and that journalists engaged in "outrageous, vicious, distorted reporting."[50] Nixon's press secretary, Ron Ziegler, also assaulted the press by claiming that their reports were "fiction," "shabby journalism," and "character assassination."[51] Reagan referred to *Al Shiraa*, which broke the Iran-Contra story, as "that rag in Beirut."[52] The *Chicago Tribune* reported, "Reagan blurted out an angry remark blaming the press for reporting false information. 'I've never heard such dissemination of misinformation since I've been here as has been going on in the last several days.'"[53] Teapot Dome was unique, for it was the press that attacked the politicians, who accused Fall of wrongdoing, for publicizing the scandal.[54]

CONTESTING MEANING

The exponential exigences and abundant attacks and responses result in a contestation in which meaning has not yet definitely emerged. Is the accuser, who is attempting to officialize *kategoria*, correct? Or is it the accused, who is attempting to deofficialize the attacks via *apologia*, who is correct? For the accuser to be successful, Gronbeck argues, he or she must make accusations with some degree of officialization. Important in Gronbeck's discussion is that guilt or vindication of the accused comes at the very end of scandal rhetoric, and up to that moment, the scandal is still a "battle."[55] That is, the key agents are in the "realm of accusation."[56] This contestation is enacted not only through *kategoria* but also through *apologia*.

Thus, if the *kategoria* is done with some form of officialization, then the *apologia* serves, in part, as a means of deofficialization in the wake of allegation. That is, in the rhetoric of defense against allegation(s), there is a direct or indirect attempt to stop or reverse the accusers from officializing, and this is called deofficialization. Deofficialization directly or indirectly characterizes the accusatory political discourse as expressions of partisan rancor and not the instrumental application of justice. Successful deofficialization, then, reduces the legitimacy of the accusation, creating a situation in which the accusation is not seen as a means of applying justice, which is what the accusers would prefer, but rather as the means for gaining political advantage by discrediting the accused. That is, the scandalous accusation is depicted as a political weapon used "to achieve victories over rivals who had defeated [the accusers] at the ballot box."[57] Hence, deofficialization is an attempt to politicize the officializer's accusations.

As stated earlier, one of the major sources of *kategoria* is the political opponents of the accused. The nature of competing in a party system creates "incentives to reveal the indiscretions of the opposition party or parties."[58] Thus, "one of the most powerful influences on public reaction hinges on whether or not one is a fellow partisan with the accused."[59] Moreover, given that there is no serious punishment or penalty for accusing those in public office, there are only incentives for one side to attack another. Consequently, "allegations are not proof, and the volume of allegations may be more an index of the strength of congressional opposition, or the zeal of critics and the austerity of their standards than of the culpability of the accused."[60]

The attempt to characterize accusations as political benefits the accused, for as the *apologia* strategies suggest, the characterization affords the accused the opportunity to show that the accused is not involved (e.g., denial and differentiation) or that the accusations are insignificant (e.g., bolstering and transcendence). As such, the accusations are not about punishment for a crime but are an attack based on the success or popularity of the accused. But on a larger scale, deofficialization benefits the accused by depicting attacks as being "played out on a political stage, doing little to enhance the political process or encourage popular confidence in the primary political institutions in Washington."[61]

Crisis in the Political Contestation

During the *kategoria* and *apologia* contestation over the meaning of the allegation, there is a crisis of meaning in which a shared meaning is difficult to achieve. To better understand this crisis of meaning, we can look at a criticism of crisis communication scholarship.

Two popular contexts for crisis communication scholarship are corporate crises and political image repair. Critiquing this scholarship, Heide claims, "A common feature in the greater part of the literature on crisis communication is the perception of a crisis as a result of some external threats in the surrounding environment. Thus, a crisis is normally understood as an objective and a 'real' thing 'out there.'"[62] In this characterization of a crisis as an "objective thing out there," there is an exigence that is a catalyst for accusation as well as response. While this characterization of a crisis may be accurate in some instances, it is certainly not accurate in all situations. Often, a politician or organization cannot deny that some event triggered a crisis. For example, an oil spill from a rig or ship run aground cannot be dismissed when the company's name is plainly visible on the rig or ship. Political transgressions are rarely based on such public circumstances. In these instances, the attribution of misconduct is not so readily apparent. Thus, there is a contestation of meaning.

This contestation is an opportunity, as stated above, to create meaning for those seeking to attribute responsibility as well as for those who claim there is no need for responsibility as they have not been involved in any wrongdoing or there is no misconduct. Given the high degree of seriousness of these political scandals, there is a tremendous incentive to define the meaning of the accusations. There is much at stake for both sides, and the importance of this contestation cannot be emphasized enough.[63] Those who are successful at attributing meaning in the wake of an allegation or misconduct are those who have "control[ed] the individual's relationship to reality."[64] Moreover, those who are able to create meaning benefit in that "the sheer proliferation of mediated forms of communication has helped to ensure that those who wish to use scandal as a political weapon are likely to find some media forum" that allows for further controlling others' relationship to reality.[65]

It should be noted that at this point in the drama, the apologist is not spinning.[66] Zaremba claims, "Spinning is a term that has become a metaphor for taking a reality and changing it."[67] Rather, this battle over meaning is enacted not because language mirrors reality but because communication constructs social and political reality.[68] Consequently, with political survivability at stake and the numerous media outlets, the contestation over meaning creates a situation in which the audience is bombarded with competing constructions of reality that result in a "crisis of meaning" in which there is much uncertainty.[69] The political contestation and uncertainty leads Busby to claim that "scandals appear to have become something of a political game, an ongoing duel between political elites, consisting of allegation and counter-allegation with no natural termination point."[70] We can see this play out in the Teapot Dome, Watergate, Iran-Contra, and Clinton/Lewinsky scandals.

SCANDAL RHETORIC

Teapot Dome

Albert Fall, the central protagonist of Teapot Dome, was infuriated with the initial murmurings about the leases. Fall criticized a conservationist in the Forest Service, who spoke out against Teapot Dome, for a "vicious and unwarranted attack upon the head of a coordinate department of the Government" and was "indignant at this blatant attack on his record as a public servant."[71] He spoke of this "impropriety" directly with President Harding, who publicly defended Fall.[72] Harding claimed he had "thoroughly" known about and supported the transfer and leasing. Harding also stated, "If Albert Fall isn't an honest man, I'm not fit to be President of the United States."[73] Harding ominously died shortly thereafter.

Yet, in November 1923, Fall's "reputation and integrity were still secure."[74] Like other Republican leaders, Fall assumed that Democratic senator Walsh's congressional investigation was only trying to "pin something on the Republicans."[75] Harry Sinclair called the inquiry "a political move and a case of American politics."[76]

The press and public reacted similarly with "the harshest condemnation" for "those [senators] who insisted on bringing the facts to light."[77] Senatorial inquisitors were called "the Montana scandal mongers," "mudgunners," "assassins of character," and even "socialists and communists," who were engaged in a "democratic lynching-bee" with "poison-tongued partisanship."[78]

One thing was "perfectly clear, namely the chief aim of the oil investigation [was] not the defense of the public's interest, but the besmirching of the other side."[79] In April 1924, five inquiries began looking into Teapot Dome, but each investigation waited "so that each could have front-page attention."[80] At the time, there were around twelve minor scandals and "a long list of others less known."[81] These were not major scandals "simply because there [was] no political advantage to be gained from them, since both parties might be equally besmirched."[82] The Teapot Dome inquiry ostensibly began because "Democrats reached for what seemed to be a winning issue."[83]

Democrats made much political mileage from Teapot Dome. Sen. Caraway egregiously equated Fall with Benedict Arnold.[84] The Democratic National Committee (DNC) defended the use of "pitiless publicity as a weapon of attack," which was effective in stopping financial corruption during President Taft's Republican administration.[85] Cordell Hull, chairman of the DNC, called Teapot Dome, which the press had not equated with any other previous or current scandal, "the greatest political scandal of this or any other generation."[86] Although the scandal occurred under Harding, Hull also attacked Coolidge who, as Harding's vice president, unofficially sat in on cabinet meetings and knew of the transfer and leasing. "Silent Cal" Coolidge was known for his reticence, but Hull was particularly appalled that Coolidge had been president for six months before commenting on Teapot Dome publicly.

With shocking testimony in early 1924 from one of the oilmen, Edward Doheny, who had loaned Fall money, Democrats had "political dynamite" for the approaching presidential election, which they hoped would put Democratic favorite William McAdoo into the White House.[87] Even Republicans who sought the White House began questioning whether President Coolidge should be the Republican candidate.[88]

Coolidge, however, took sudden action and had "subtly and cleverly stolen" the "Democratic thunder."[89] Immediately after Doheny's testimony about the loan, Coolidge announced his intention to investigate the affair. Coolidge claimed, "In this effort there will be no politics and no partisanship. . . . I am a Republican, but I can not on that account prosecute any one because he is a Democrat."[90] Democrats spoke out "about the 'politics'" of Coolidge's "midnight statement," which came the night before the Senate's anticipated similar announcement so that it "might make the front pages of Sunday morning's newspapers."[91] Democrats had hoped that Coolidge would be judged guilty by his Republican association, but people pictured "Mr. Coolidge as wielding the big stick to correct a situation, which was not his making."[92]

Democrats continued to lose their initiative in early February 1924. Doheny revealed that he had employed Thomas Gregory, the Democrat appointed by

Coolidge to investigate the scandal.[93] An even bigger shock came when Doheny testified that the Democrat's prime choice for the White House, William McAdoo, had also recently worked for him and earned around $250,000. Moreover, Doheny still kept McAdoo on retainer, paying him $50,000 a year. McAdoo's presidential ambitions were over despite no "proof of corruption" on his part—he did not take private money while in public office.[94] No matter how hard he tried, McAdoo could "not get an explanation, however frank and convincing it may be, into the minds of the voters" in an election year.[95] Even Democrats abandoned him. The Democratic National Committee either had to reshape their platform or lose the individual. By eliminating McAdoo, they hoped, the scandal would remain exclusively a Republican one.

Those hopes were soon lost. The *Springfield Republican*, a Massachusetts newspaper respected by both Democrats and Republicans for its bipartisan advocacy of conservation, claimed, "The Senate investigation became a 'gusher' and both Republicans and Democrats" were becoming covered with oil.[96] One editorial writer claimed that the "presidential campaign [is] devoted chiefly to proving that the pot is blacker than the kettle, or that it isn't," and that an inquiry with a nonpartisan spirit would be impossible.[97] Democrats were "ready to inject the partisan note into each successive disclosure," and Republicans banked "heavily upon the traditional inability of a public to remember the facts and keep interested. . . . [Republicans were] already venturing to assert this whole affair is merely a Democratic bombshell prepared for the election."[98] The result of such tactics was that "both parties [were] going to be thoroughly discredited in the minds of the public."[99] Independents reveled in the situation and gunned for both Republicans and Democrats, which gave a third party the first real chance at the White House since Roosevelt's Bull Moose campaign in 1912.[100]

The dominant political discourse was not on any actual wrongdoing but on highlighting what could be made to look malfeasant, which would create an "inflamed and indignant public."[101] The oil inquiry reached "the stage in which rumor [was] confounded with evidence."[102] One writer claimed, "The people will never get anything out of a political investigation of a political scandal."[103] That is, the people did not find justice in political investigations but only found each party attempting to discredit the other party. Editorialists noted that "during the first round of hearings, the strong tribal loyalties of the Senate were noticeably at work."[104] Even when the Senate voted to approve the final report, "they all voted their politics—and nothing else."[105] A Republican newspaper claimed that rather than "hearing tales of highly imaginative quality . . . the courts provide the best means for getting at the truth."[106] The *Washington Post* claimed that when public cases are tried in the newspapers, the accused are presumed guilty rather than innocent.

Press coverage over the Senate's findings, however, varied. Some claimed that the report, which was approved by Democratic senators and two "insurgent Republicans," was a "failure."[107] The report was, as one writer claimed, "as weak constructively as it is in its remedial aspect. . . . If this is all Senator Walsh had to recommend, we might not have undertaken the investigation at all."[108] Similarly, "the weeks and months spent listening to scores of witnesses of doubtful reputation were wholly wasted."[109] Some, on the other hand, praised Sen. Walsh's investigation as "the greatest public service rendered by any American since the Armistice."[110]

Soon after the release of the Senate's findings, Fall, Sinclair, and Doheny were indicted for conspiracy to defraud the United States and for giving and receiving bribes. Shortly thereafter, Teapot Dome slipped into obscurity.[111] New investigations were being planned, and campaigns began to address issues other than oil. While Democrats and Republicans were covered with oil, Republicans had one asset: the president. Coolidge had the "full trust of the Nation" during the drama and was elected in 1924.[112] In 1927, with the next election looming, the partisan rhetoric reappeared. Republican senator George Norris started a second round of investigations. But the public was uninterested as "the steady passage of time made the later investigation seem like a washing of very ancient dirty linen."[113]

Watergate

Nixon and his administration responded to the unproven allegations in two ways. First, the Nixon administration claimed that they were separate from and above the actions of a few malcontents. While Nixon was relatively silent on the matter initially, he and his administration did offer terse and pointed responses to the news of the break-in. This was done by dissociating themselves from those who planned and carried out the burglary. One of the first official comments came within forty-eight hours after the break-in. Press Secretary Ronald Ziegler claimed it was a "third rate burglary" and predicted the inevitable partisan rancor that would follow by adding, "Certain elements may try to stretch this beyond what it is."[114] Months later, John Mitchell, chairman of the Committee to Reelect the President (CRP), would echo this sentiment, as he told reporters that the "ridiculous caper . . . was blown out proportion" by the media, who as it seemed were just as guilty as the Democrats of attempting to tarnish Nixon.[115] Although Ziegler would later claim that certain information he gave was "inoperative" or no longer credible, immediately after the burglary, his initial denial "sounded quite credible."[116] Partisan players, after all, should be expected to make the most out of anything that can discredit the chief executive.

Initially, members of Nixon's administration issued denials of White House involvement in the break-in, but Nixon occasionally did take the opportunity to dissociate himself from any involvement with the matter.[117] Five days after the break-in, Nixon offered his first comments. He first acknowledged his vicarious approach: "Mr. Ziegler and also Mr. Mitchell, speaking for the campaign committee, have responded to questions on this in great detail. They have stated my position, and have also stated the facts accurately."[118] He added, "This kind of activity, as Mr. Ziegler has indicated, has no place whatever in our electoral process, or in our governmental process."[119] The political discourse was to be focused on the issues, not scandalmongering. Nixon continued more directly: "The White House has had no involvement whatever in this particular incident."[120] Nixon then remained silent due to possible criminal charges involved.

In later press conferences prior to the election, Nixon would continue to dissociate his administration from the burglary. In late August 1972, Nixon stated, "I can say categorically that his [i.e., Nixon's counsel, John Dean] investigation indicates that no one in the White House Staff, no one in this Administration, presently employed, was involved in this very bizarre incident."[121] Nixon then stated, "What really hurts in matters of this sort is not the fact that they occur, because overzealous people in campaigns do things that are wrong. What really hurts is if you try to cover it up."[122] Perhaps this was a bluff to further characterize his attackers as partisan, but his words were quite prophetic.

In his last press conference before the election, Nixon agreed with all the effort put into the investigation. He stated, "I wanted every lead carried out to the end because I wanted to be sure that no member of the White House Staff and no man or woman in a position of major responsibility in the Committee for the Re-Election had anything to do with this kind of reprehensible activity."[123]

Regardless of these public statements at the time, he saw the entire situation as nothing more than politics. Nixon stated in his memoirs, "I was handling in a pragmatic way what I perceived as an annoying and strictly political problem. I was looking for a way to deal with Watergate that would minimize the damage to me, my friends and my campaign. I saw Watergate as politics pure and simple."[124] The potential for damage came primarily from the Democratic presidential candidate, George McGovern.

George McGovern "was generally unknown" prior to the campaign.[125] According to his campaign director, Gary Hart, McGovern was a "long-shot candidate who had to do everything right and get almost all the breaks."[126] "President Nixon," Hart continued, "had to make a few mistakes, that is to say, he had to come out and campaign."[127] McGovern's slim chance for election made him an ideal candidate from the perspective of the Republican

Party. That is, in the Democratic primaries, Nixon wanted "to knock down [Hubert Humphrey] and build up McGovern."[128] With Humphrey, the stronger candidate, out of the race, Nixon would have a greater chance of victory in the election against the weaker McGovern.

While McGovern was a long shot, he was given a seemingly extraordinary break with the burglary, but early on, his campaign saw the incident as a "comic episode" and eventually became "divided over the value of Watergate."[129] McGovern's deputy campaign manager stated, "We were anxious to exploit it to the extent we could politically. I frankly think we made more political mileage out of the [Russian] wheat-sale scandal than we did out of Watergate."[130]

Nevertheless, McGovern did speak out on Watergate during the campaign. He constantly derided Nixon's secret $10 million fund and characterized the administration and CRP as scoundrels. Specifically, he claimed the break-in was "the kind of thing you expect under a person like Hitler."[131] Moreover, "history shows us it is but a single step from spying on the political opposition, to suppressing that opposition and imposing a one-party state in which the people's precious liberties are lost."[132] McGovern also said, "What first looked like a caper now appears to be a central part of the Republican strategy. . . . It now appears that the headquarters of one of the two major political parties of the United States was treated as if it were the headquarters of a foreign enemy."[133] Later, McGovern labeled the Republican tactics as "the shabbiest under-cover operations in the history of politics."[134]

At times, McGovern would speak off the cuff regarding the bugging. When a microphone was not working at a campaign stop, he apologized for the delay and humorously claimed, "We don't have as many wiring experts with us as President Nixon."[135]

McGovern was not the only Democrat to speak on Watergate. DNC chairman Jean Westwood called the Government Accounting Office's (GAO's) investigation "the bare outlines of the largest and possibly most corrupt set of financial misdealings in the history of American presidential politics."[136] DNC campaign chairman Lawrence O'Brien was the most outspoken Democrat and filed a lawsuit against CRP quickly after the burglary. He called the break-in a "cheap cloak-and-dagger intrigue at the national political level."[137] He would also call it an "incredible act of political espionage" with "a developing clear line to the White House."[138] O'Brien maintained that there was "a calculated Republican attempt to suppress and cover up the facts of the case [which] will turn out to be the biggest political blunder in Richard Nixon's career," and that the investigations where nothing more than a "whitewash."[139]

The Democratic attacks were "immediately denied and described as political libel and slander."[140] Republicans deemed McGovern's likening Nixon to

Hitler as "'character assassination' and political hyperbole."[141] Republicans depicted Watergate as a "peripheral issue."[142] Consequently, McGovern's remarks were, as one Republican representative said, "obviously politically motivated . . . the Watergate case is all McGovern has going for him."[143] Mitchell called O'Brien's lawsuit a "political stunt" and claimed it was "another example of sheer demagoguery on the part of Mr. O'Brien."[144] Republicans then filed a countersuit against the Democrats for "creat[ing] political headlines for partisan ends."[145]

In response to the GAO's findings, Republican National Committee (RNC) chairman Bob Dole retorted by hinting at "devious" cover-ups by the DNC, which he claimed should also be investigated.[146] The Nixon administration called a Banking Committee investigation, lead by a Democratic representative, a "'scurrilous political tract' and an attempt 'to rescue the sinking political campaign of George McGovern.'"[147] Then, with the indictments of the burglars, Nixon's campaign manager, Clark McGregor, asked for public apologies from all those who attempted to link the burglary with CRP. Dole expected "McGovern to stop trying to make a political issue out of the matter."[148] Republican Senate minority leader Hugh Scott added that the investigation would not be appropriate "unless we keep it out of the political arena" by starting it after the election.[149]

Iran-Contra

While Watergate was over a decade old, it was fresh in the minds of the public and members of Congress. In fact, some members of Congress who participated in the Watergate investigation were still in office during the Iran-Contra scandal. Consequently, Watergate became an important benchmark for discussing and framing the public discourse of Iran-Contra. The comparison between the two scandals showed two different motives. Watergate was "an effort by the presidential inner circle to get the dirt on Democrats, thereby achieving the President's reelection. The motive [in Watergate] was narrow and self-serving."[150] In Iran-Contra, the motive was far less self-serving in terms of political party, which affected the partisan nature of the scandal rhetoric.

There were, however, self-serving motives of the executive versus the legislative branch. That is, in Watergate, much of the battle was between Democrats and Republicans. In Iran-Contra, much of the battle was between the president and Congress, for while Reagan's motives were less self-serving than Nixon's, his administration had still misled Congress.[151] Such a situation led Sen. Bob Dole, who was then the Senate majority leader, to state that Reagan's policy was "well motivated [but was] a little inept."[152] Both

Republicans and Democrats echoed similar sentiments early on and noted the inconsistency of Reagan's public declaration not to negotiate with terrorists and the recently uncovered arms-for-hostages deals.

Reagan faced the toughest criticism from within his own party and administration. For example, Republican senator William Cohen claimed that Reagan "took foreign policy underground," which allowed the president to bypass the system of checks and balances in the Constitution, and therefore cannot escape responsibility.[153] Cohen also stated, "I think that what is clear is that the president turned to amateurs for his advice on a major foreign policy initiative rather than listening to the sound and seasoned voices of the experts."[154] This was the strongest criticism of the president from a leading Republican in the four months since the Iran-Contra affair first broke in November.[155] Cohen, however, was not representative of the entire Republican Party. Rep. Dick Cheney responded to Cohen's attack on Reagan by admitting that the president was "responsible for what occurs on his watch . . . [but] I think it is premature for Republicans or anyone else to make judgments at this point."[156] Furthermore, former president Nixon cautioned Republicans not to "go on with their favorite sport of cannibalism," which could weaken the president in his last two years.[157]

Members of Reagan's administration also spoke out against him. Secretary of State George Shultz publicly stated that he opposed the shipment of arms to Iran. Shultz was asked if the administration would continue sending arms to Iran; he responded that the United States would not. Shultz was then asked, "Do you have the authority to speak for the entire Administration?" Shultz replied simply, "No."[158] The *New York Times* noted the discrepancy of the views and stated, "It is rare and potentially embarrassing for a Secretary of State to publicly advocate a course of action and then admit that his views are not necessarily those of the administration for which he is the chief foreign policy spokesman."[159]

Reagan also faced some criticism from Democrats. Former president Carter said that Reagan had "'made the worst mistake any president has made' by paying ransom to Iranian terrorists in the form of arms and trying to avoid responsibility."[160] Carter also believed that by trading arms for hostages, Reagan not only contradicted his 1980 campaign platform against such policies, but also, and more importantly, demonstrated to terrorists that the United States has "paid them to get the hostages back. This is a very serious mistake in how to handle a kidnapping or hostage-taking."[161] The 1984 democratic presidential candidate, Walter Mondale, argued that the "worst thing for the country and the [Democratic] party would be an all out attack on the president, who still remains popular despite his plummet in the approval ratings."[162] That is, Democrats had to be careful since Reagan might recover, and they would have to deal with an electoral backlash.[163] Moreover, Democrats were not offering any alternatives to Reagan's foreign policies; the *Nation* described such a posture as a "Democratic surrender on the political issues generated by the hearings."[164] Consequently, most congressional Democrats took a "statesmanlike approach" to the scandal.[165]

While there was partisan rhetoric, the amount was much less compared to other scandals. The lack of partisan rancor was due in part to the immediacy with which Reagan appointed the Tower Commission and to the calls for other investigations, which created a bipartisan atmosphere. When each house of Congress voted to approve investigative committees, Sen. Dole, for example, was "eager today to dispel any notion that he might be trying to exonerate President Reagan prematurely in the Iran-Contra affair."[166] Dole also stated, "It is necessary that we start off on a totally nonpartisan, bipartisan basis."[167] Sen. Robert Byrd said that he had "every faith" that the Senate investigation would be conducted "in a statesmanlike and bipartisan fashion."[168] Rep. Dick Cheney, who called himself "a very partisan Republican," said he had "every reason to expect" an impartial inquiry.[169]

Democrats, such as Sen. George Mitchell, also maintained that while the policies were flawed, the whole affair "should be put behind us."[170] Democratic House majority leader Rep. Foley also added that his party never "intended to make [Iran-Contra] a major campaign issue."[171]

Clinton/Lewinsky

First Lady Hillary Rodham Clinton claimed that she and her husband were the victims of a "continuing political campaign . . . using the criminal justice system to try to achieve political ends in the country."[172] At the head of that campaign was Kenneth Starr, whom she characterized as a "politically motivated prosecutor who is allied with the right-wing opponents of [President Clinton]."[173] The First Lady infamously labeled the campaign against her and her husband as a "vast right-wing conspiracy," which consisted of people like Jerry Falwell, who had produced videos claiming that the Clintons had committed murder and engaged in drug trading, and the judge who appointed Starr as the independent counsel, who was himself appointed by two key conservative congressional Republicans.[174]

While Fall, Nixon, and their Republican Party supporters dismissed allegations of wrongdoing by claiming the accusations were nothing more than political rhetoric from the Democrats, the Clinton scandal was unique. While President Clinton dismissed any claims of wrongdoing, similar to Fall and Nixon, Clinton could not, however, claim the allegations were motivated by congressional Republicans. There were very few accusations coming from congressional Republicans, who believed "that when your opponent is shooting himself in the foot, you don't get in the way."[175] In other words, Republicans believed that Clinton's own malfeasance spoke for itself, and they feared that any finger-pointing would be perceived as making the apolitical political.[176]

Moreover, most Republicans were wary of directly attacking the president.[177] Their accusations might be seen as nothing more than the typical partisan rhetoric, capable of driving Democratic voters to the polls and jeopardizing the small majority Republicans held in Congress. In fact, Republican primaries had candidates attacking one another for their reluctance to speak out against Clinton. Also, if Republicans did oust Clinton, they would have to deal with the scandal-free Al Gore, who would then be running in 2000 with the advantage of being the heir apparent to the incumbent president during a time of political prosperity.[178] Keeping Clinton around allowed for the occasional nonlethal rhetorical blitz, which usually focused on "chastis[ing] the president on moral, more than legal, grounds."[179]

Additionally, some Republicans, who had relationships similar to Clinton and Lewinsky's, feared they would receive the same treatment that Clinton was getting if they spoke out. Republican Speaker of the House designate Rob Livingston admitted immediately prior to Clinton's impeachment that he had had an affair and then resigned. Livingston's actions came in response to Larry Flynt, publisher of the adult magazine *Hustler*, who offered $1 million to anyone who could prove that a member of Congress had an affair.[180]

Thus the majority of the accusations against Clinton did not come from partisan politicians but rather from the seemingly judicial and independent Kenneth Starr, who, despite the Republicans' view of him, was far from apolitical. Prior to his appointment as independent counsel in 1994, Starr was "considered the kind of centrist Republican that Democrats love, until he took over the Whitewater investigation and proceeded to squeeze witnesses and pursue leads with a zeal that troubled even people who lost no love for Bill Clinton."[181]

Others, however, claimed that Starr was always politically motivated. For example, as *Time* magazine claimed, "prosecutors are supposed to be above the political fray, but Starr has always had trouble fitting the model."[182] After his appointment as independent counsel, investigative reporters soon found that Starr had a "luggage cart's worth of political baggage."[183] That baggage included a potential run against the conservative Oliver North of Iran-Contra fame in Virginia's Republican Senate primary, nearly filing a brief in Paula Jones's sexual harassment lawsuit against Clinton, and, while serving as special prosecutor, representing private clients with a conservative political agenda. Moreover, in late 1997, Starr was about to resign as independent counsel to accept the offer to become a dean at Pepperdine University, which was heavily endowed by Richard Mellon Scaife, a severe critic of Clinton.[184] Starr, however, reversed his decision and continued as independent counsel; Pepperdine, nevertheless, held the position open for Starr.[185]

IMPLICATIONS

Early scandal discourse is framed as nonuseful, unimportant, and distracting by the accused. While there is some basis for the attacks due to the initial publicity of the accusations in the news, the attackers bear the burden of proof. Up until a smoking gun or other incriminating evidence is found, there is validity to the accused's *apologia*. Attacks, whether they are related to the public office or not, are seen as upending political deliberations of substantive matters that serve to benefit the people. Attacks are also seen as distractions from governmental functions that carry out those agendas that benefit the people. In other words, attacking another public person in politics or government shifts the focus away from doing the will of the people. Thus, political attacks are made to seem like an impediment to democracy. Democracy, as it is portrayed by the accused, is about much nobler issues than a person's private life, and not about making the most of a potential crisis for some political gain. In short, the stages of the scandal that follow the revelation of accusations portray the attacks and attempts to scandalize another as a disservice to democracy. However, we should be careful, for this stage of the scandal has several implications for free speech, public discourse, and democracy.

Free Speech

One of the prevailing theories of why we have free speech is based on John Stuart Mill's marketplace of ideas. The marketplace of ideas is the notion that we should protect all ideas, and through debate and discussion the best ideas will survive and weak ideas will not be able to bear the weight of criticism. The result is a sound and tested idea.

Even bad ideas have value in the marketplace. A weak and undeveloped idea may solicit criticism, which in turn may revise the bad idea and result in a new, better-developed idea. Furthermore, a flawed idea may cause another individual to think about an issue in a fundamentally different way and, by doing so, develop a more robust idea. To restrict an idea from entering the marketplace is to limit the potential output of the marketplace; consequently, we must protect all ideas. This includes partisan attacks.

One caveat should be noted. The marketplace does not necessarily produce the best idea but does often produce a popular idea. Frequently, criticism is abated not because an idea is inherently better than other ideas but because it is desirable, favorable, or well liked regardless of the merit of the idea.

Partisan discourse during scandals seems to offer little in the way of contribution to the marketplace. Scandal rhetoric is, as stated earlier, "low quality fare" with regard to the marketplace.[186] Alongside partisan rhetoric, Sunstein argues that political strategy and public impression are of more popular concern than the substantive issues of the day.[187] While political speech has long been recognized as the type of speech deriving the utmost protection, partisan rhetoric during scandals is not political speech in the strictest of senses to many. Political speech deals with the issues and policies of a state. There can be legitimate debate over what a government should and should not do. But partisan discourse during scandal does not focus primarily on that, at least from the point of view of the accused. Partisan discourse during a scandal, as the accused characterizes it, is about discrediting the accused. Scandal rhetoric is just one of the many means by which a political actor can attack and discredit a political opponent, who may or may not be of the opposing party or of a different branch of the government.

The distasteful nature of early scandal rhetoric may be low-quality fare, but, as time will show, often this low-quality fare results in substantial political matters. What were once ungrounded partisan attacks ultimately were the beginning of what ended as the first and only presidential resignation, a presidential impeachment, and the first presidential cabinet officer sentenced to jail. These are serious political matters and certainly worthy of the title of political speech. Consequently, scandal rhetoric has value to the metaphorical political marketplace; the problem is that no one really knows it, at least not until later in the scandal. However, not all scandal rhetoric results in such dire circumstances. If scandal rhetoric has potential legitimate value to the marketplace even in rare and extreme circumstances, then we must be careful about characterizing it as something less than pure political expression.

Public Discourse

Next we need to address the relationship between partisan discourse and public discourse. There are three related points on this issue. First, scandal rhetoric, the *kategoria-apologia* speech set, is a self-perpetuating form of rhetoric. An exigence, based on accusations of a transgression, creates the opportunity for attacks, which are exigences that call for a response. That response, in turn, becomes an exigence that begets further attacks. When and if new evidence of an alleged transgression appears, there is but another exigence, which calls for more attacks and then more responses. As such, scandal rhetoric builds upon itself and is self-perpetuating. In some scandals, the contextual and circumstantial factors can support weeks, months, or even years worth of public discourse about the transgression. In other scandals, the factors may support much less.

The same could be said of much of political life: a political policy is proposed, which calls for a response, which in turn calls for a response, and so forth. But scandal rhetoric is different. This public discourse is a guilty pleasure. Scandal rhetoric is seen as low value, and as such, many do not want to acknowledge that they enjoy such topics with such little value. Quite simply, scandal rhetoric is an indulgence that many enjoy, but few are willing to admit as much. The nuance and nature of specific foreign and domestic policies are not as alluring as accusing some political actor of a transgression. Talking about liars, cheaters, and no-good Charlies is a part of life and is also a part of political life. Talk of domestic and foreign policy simply does not have the same appeal as scandal rhetoric. Given the need to respond and then respond to that response on a topic that many secretly enjoy keeps scandal rhetoric going and never ending.

Second and relatedly, the very nature of the responses to the accusation call for more accusations. Bolstering, transcending, differentiating, and attacking the accuser do not directly deny the accusation, although they do address the attack. Rather, these genres of response attempt to diminish the attack by reframing it. Denial, on the other hand, does directly address and obviously deny the accusation. The denial, however, still calls for more attacks as the accused often has very little evidence to disprove the accusations. In other words, it is difficult if not impossible for the accused to disprove something that did not happen. While it is improper in the judicial sense to have to demonstrate that one is not guilty, the need to prove your innocence is different in the court of public opinion.

Nevertheless, the accused can deny the accusations, but it is very difficult to prove innocence, for there is no evidence except perhaps situational factors. For example, Reagan's national security advisor Bud McFarlane categorically denied *Al Shiraa*'s report that he visited Iran in October 1986, suggesting Reagan's administration had nothing to do with the Iran-Contra mess. McFarlane, however, was in Iran in May of that year. McFarlane himself said, "The gist of [the *Al Shiraa* report] rode close enough to the truth that . . . I knew without a shadow of a doubt that the spotlight was about to be turned full force on the White House and the president, and that the heat from it would be withering."[188] Thus, while there might be situational and contextual factors that allow for a denial, there is also the possibility that the denial is entirely false, is misleading, or is a partial denial of a specific aspect of the transgression. For example, Nixon said, "No one in the White House Staff, no one in this Administration, presently employed, was involved in this very bizarre incident."[189] The phrase "presently employed," naturally, raised some suspicions.[190] Consequently, in each of these contexts, there is room for the accuser to continue to push the attack, which allows for scandal rhetoric to perpetuate itself.

Third, early scandal rhetoric helps the accuser to achieve certain ends. Political actors, who for whatever reason cannot easily achieve certain ends due to opposition, may find it easier to achieve their goals by discrediting the sources of the opposition rather than confronting the oppositional arguments directly. This tactic is a means of shifting the merits of an idea or criticism away from the actual proposal or agenda and placing the onus on the person. By discrediting the political actor, the political actor's ideas are discredited. The connection between the person and his or her ideas is easily made in the public's mind.

Consequently, partisan and scandalous discourse is desirable from the point of view of those attempting to make policy. Scandal rhetoric attracts the attention of those with an interest in politics and especially those who are not interested in matters of politics. Those who are not interested in the finer points of domestic and foreign policy are often enticed by the allure of the powerful being accused of being up to no good—be it a political or personal transgression.

But, as stated earlier, we may not say we like it, but we do enjoy it and often it does serve a purpose: to engage the citizenry and to foster policy success. Scandal rhetoric and partisan discourse are an easy means to a difficult end in terms of policy, and the connection between policy and person is an easy connection in the public's mind. We may find it difficult to evaluate the finer points of a high-level policy, but we are quick and able to judge a person's actions. Because of our interest in such low-value political speech and its apparent ease at achieving some ends, it is nearly omnipresent.

Democracy

Bellah's conceptualization of democracy asks, "Does American civil religion need a satanic image in order to exist?" From the accuser and accused point of view, an evil is not necessary, but it is helpful. The accuser attempts to discredit the accused, but the accused also makes use of evil characterizations. The accused depicts the accuser as engaging in a red herring where the important, substantive matters of the day are pushed aside in favor of scandalmongering. To the accused, a democracy is where the people rule and are to be served. Clinton and Reagan made the most of this strategy.

In his denials, President Clinton depicted the allegations of misconduct as relatively unimportant by claiming there was more important work to be done. In response to questions about the early days of the scandal, Clinton told an interviewer, "But I want to focus on the work at hand," and "I've got to go on with the work of the country. I got hired to help the rest of the American people."[191] In a later speech he said, "And we've got a lot to do. I'm going to give [Congress] the first balanced budget in three years ahead of time, and a great child care initiative, and an important Medicare initiative."[192]

Later in Iran-Contra, the Reagan administration acted as if the scandal was not worth attention. As the televised congressional hearings gained a strong following, acting press secretary Marlin Fitzwater downplayed their impact on the president. Fitzwater stated, "We think it is more important to carry on the business of government than to be watching TV."[193]

Nixon indirectly appeared to be more focused on the business of the country. Nixon "hardly had any contact with the press," which he considered to be the enemy.[194] Nixon also refused to debate McGovern, which was a strategy adopted after losing to Kennedy in 1960. While Nixon's insecurities about the opposition were the private reasons for his insulation, his absence from debates and campaigns gave the illusion he was too busy running the country to engage in partisan and political affairs.

This is not to say that Nixon was in exile from the public. He typically spoke via television to an audience that could not ask questions. When he did speak publicly, it was to "handpicked audiences," who would ask the appropriate questions.[195] Furthermore, Nixon rarely held press conferences. He held only thirty-nine press conferences, which is far less than any other president, and "many of those amounted to ugly confrontations marked by name calling."[196]

Whether directly or indirectly stated, strategies that "convey a mood of calm, self-assurance, and normalcy" in response to the accusations depict the accuser as interrupting the business of running the country.[197] Clinton was specific. The accusations of sexual impropriety were keeping him from balancing the budget, taking care of children, and seeing to the health of our elders. These three initiatives seemed far more important than Clinton's sex life, at least as far as he was concerned.

Projecting a business-as-usual stance in the face of the accusations, the accused is placing himself on a higher moral and political ground. The well-being of the nation is the accused's top priority, not the petty and distracting attacks. The motivation for the accuser is to discredit; the motivation for the accused revolves around the high-value notions of change, progress, achievement, and success not only for the policies but for the people.

Interestingly, though, as in the major examples explored in this book, the high-value self-positioning of the accused is actually part of the cover-up. What once was seen as the noble statesman, who put the well-being of the country first and foremost is actually trying to diminish the wrongdoing. The accused, who is attacking the accuser for being petty, partisan, and distracting to the progress of the nation, is, as the case often plays out, the one whose transgression has done damage. Claiming to be better than those who are accusing you of what often eventually proves to be true makes the fall so much harder. Thus, what is an attempt at legitimate political discourse and action may very well be part of the cover-up, and what seems to be illegitimate political discourse is part of the uncovering. The difficult part for the viewers of scandals is the uncertainty.

The unsubstantiated attacks and responses result in a democratic ideology. Whether one positions him- or herself with the accuser or the accused, their voice is heard. Each has an evil to face—the accuser trying to block progress or the accused who is up to no good. The topic of debate is one that everyone can relate to—personal or power transgressions; consequently everyone can get involved.

CONCLUSION

This chapter addresses the political rhetoric that inevitably follows allegations of misconduct. This political rhetoric takes two forms: *kategoria* and *apologia*. *Kategoria* attempts to make a little thing into a big thing, whereas the accused attempts to thwart such attempts. This political rhetoric is partisan in nature and is seen as having little value to the more important pressing issues of the day.

The contestation between accusation and response has, up until a smoking gun is found later in the scandal, seemingly no end. The accusations are apparently motivated by the possibility, however unlikely it may be, of finding a weakness in another political actor (or even others affiliated with the accused) and exploiting it. To combat such characterizations, the accusers attempt to officialize their attacks to gain legitimacy. However, the accused engages in deofficialization to characterize the attacks as political gamesmanship.

While the public may perceive such scandal rhetoric as having little value despite finding it worth their attention, scandal rhetoric does have potential value. This potential value may not always manifest, but the potential value is enough to tolerate scandal rhetoric and see its value as political speech. Furthermore, we must recognize that a political landscape run amok with scandal rhetoric is due to several factors, including its self-perpetuating nature and the fact that it often serves as a political means to an end. However, we should be cautious because often the accused's attempts to seem above and better than those who engage in partisan rhetoric are, as the future will sometimes reveal, part of a cover-up, which will be revealed with a smoking gun.

Chapter Four

From Smoking Gun
to Impeachment

The discovery of a smoking gun marks the moment when we can say there was a before and an after, when a little thing does in fact become a big thing. That is, before the smoking gun, there is political contestation over the alleged misconduct, and the smoking gun provides "incontrovertible evidence" of the accused's guilt.[1] As such, the smoking gun, if it exists and if it is discovered, reveals that there has been some form of deception—an attempt to cover up some transgression—which firmly cements the status of the events as a scandal. In short, the smoking gun is often the key turning point in a scandal from predictable partisan attacks into a major constitutional crisis.

However, the smoking gun does more than demonstrate guilt. The smoking gun, as a term or as actual evidence, is a political strategy to discredit and possibly remove a person from office. The smoking gun, then, as Neuman states, is "a strategy that attempts to drive political opponents from office through an accusatory procedure, or threatens to do so in order to intimidate them, [but] partisan political impeachment and impeachment threats generally fail to produce results."[2]

This chapter challenges the notion of the smoking gun to suggest that it is not just a discrete event that reveals a cover-up and confirms guilt. In addition, the chapter argues, the smoking gun allows for the construction of *the* scandal problem.[3] In other words, *the* scandal problem points to the fact that the original transgression is usually not a problem or crime that Congress can readily address and is therefore moot, but the cover-up, which is obstruction of justice, is a serious crime and an impeachable offense, which is an act that only Congress can prosecute. Consequently, the cover-up is not worse than the crime; the cover-up *is* the crime from the point of view of Congress. Thus, the chapter concludes by arguing that American political scandals reflect the ancient Greek notion of scandal, σκανδάλον, which translates as "a trap laid for an enemy."[4]

In what follows, this chapter first explains how political actors attempt to construct reality (i.e., give meaning to the allegations or misconduct) in the wake of an allegation of some transgression or other exigence. Second, the chapter addresses how the smoking gun operates in the public discourse and is, in essence, a construction of *the* scandal problem. Third, the chapter reviews how the accused reluctantly participates in the attackers' definition of the scandal problem. The chapter then highlights the discovery and fight for the smoking gun in each major scandal. Finally, the chapter concludes with the implications for free speech, rhetoric, and democracy.

SMOKING GUN

The crisis of meaning covered in chapter 3 is abrogated when there is a discovery of a smoking gun. The smoking gun, according to William Safire, is "incontrovertible evidence" of guilt.[5] Safire, the popular political lexicographer, indicates that there is no question of the smoking gun's meaning. The smoking gun "is suggestive (sometimes too obvious) of guilt."[6] Furthermore, Billig and MacMillan state that the smoking gun is "the proof of criminality [that] is so obvious that it will not need persuasive rhetoric to convince onlookers of the perpetrator's guilt. Observers need only see the smoke to know who has just fired the gun."[7] Quite simply, the popular meaning of the smoking gun is that it is "irrefutable proof that will indubitably incriminate a powerful perpetrator."[8]

Safire's as well as Billig and MacMillan's delineations of a smoking gun resonate with the earlier criticisms of crisis communication reviewed in chapter 3. That is, the smoking gun is held to be an "objective thing out there" that determines guilt.[9] However, a social constructionist paradigm can bring a greater understanding of the smoking gun. As Bennet claims, "an event may 'happen,' but its meaning is constructed."[10] That is, the smoking gun may demonstrate that the alleged event happened, but the smoking gun can do much more than simply indicate guilt. The following section addresses the smoking gun as it is constructed in the context of *kategoria* and *apologia*. The section concludes by arguing that the smoking gun is the construction of *the* scandal problem.

SMOKING GUN RHETORIC

Kategoria

The term "smoking gun" has evolved since its introduction into American political discourse. The popularity of the term comes from Congressman Barber Conable, who is credited with first using it in the Watergate scandal.[11]

Conable recalled that when he heard the June 23, 1972, conversation between Richard Nixon and H. R. Haldeman, he knew that "the president had lied to us."[12] Importantly, Conable "only likened the Nixon tapes to a smoking gun after their discovery. He did not predict, in advance, that a smoking gun would be found."[13] The after-the-fact use of the term would change in later scandals.

In Watergate, the discovery of the actual smoking gun may mark a critical moment when we can say there was a before and after in the scandal. But it is also worthwhile to consider how this meaning of incontrovertible evidence used in Watergate affects subsequent uses of the term "smoking gun" in attempting to create meaning during other scandals.[14] Lakoff, Billig, and MacMillan believe that metaphors such as the "smoking gun" can "structure political discourse and, thus, political consciousness."[15] Undoubtedly, prior to the discovery of the actual smoking gun, accusers may very well use the term "smoking gun," as the term "belongs to a rhetoric of political accusation."[16] That is, prior to the discovery of incontrovertible evidence, an accuser can claim to be looking for an as yet undiscovered or unknown smoking gun, thereby "conveying that the confirmatory evidence is 'out there,' still to be discovered.'"[17]

The rhetorical strategy of looking for a smoking gun can be employed in two ways. First, accusers can be looking for *a* smoking gun, which implies that there might be evidence; second, accusers can be looking for *the* smoking gun, which implies that there is evidence out there that has not yet been discovered.[18] These strategies benefit the accuser, for they suggest that the accused is engaging in a cover-up since, at the least, there is a possibility of evidence. At the other end, the second strategy implies that the accused is actually covering up a crime, and it is only a matter of finding the evidence to prove the allegations.

Second, the use of looking for a/the smoking gun suggests that the accusers are seeking proof of their accusations, thereby attempting to raise their image and credibility as a legal (rather than political) entity. In Iran-Contra, for example, Sen. William Cohen, a member of the investigating committee, "suggested that a 'smoking gun' will never be found—that it disappeared into a 'smoking shredder.'"[19] Here, Sen. Cohen is stating that there might have been evidence out there to prove the guilt, but the accused has destroyed the evidence, which is in and of itself another accusation of wrongdoing. But Reagan seemingly also understood this rhetorical strategy of individuals seeking a phantom smoking gun as he boldly asserted, "There ain't no smoking gun!"[20]

Consequently, the smoking gun may be better understood as a form of *kategoria* in the political contestation over meaning rather than the incontrovertible evidence that many hold it to be. The accused, then, may need to respond to accusations of a/the smoking gun or the discovery of an actual smoking gun.

Apologia

If there are accusations of a/the smoking gun, then the critical evidence must be either found or obtained. The benefit of such a tactic is that the accused can then divert attention away from the accusations by focusing on the battle over the discovery or acquisition of whatever evidence there might be. Such a diversion strategy is akin to the rabbit who was caught by the hungry fox. The rabbit told the fox it was okay to eat him but pleaded for the fox not to throw him in the thorny briar patch—for that was a far worse fate. So the fox threw the rabbit in the briar patch. But unbeknownst to the hungry wolf, the briar patch actually allowed the rabbit to escape. Many believed Nixon used the White House tapes as his briar patch. That is, "once the Watergate committee learned of these tapes it had to make an issue of getting them," thereby distracting the public from the allegations, albeit in the example of Watergate, only temporarily.[21] More often than not, the battle for the evidence between executive and congressional investigators ends in the courts. If the court rules in favor of the executive, the smoking gun goes up in smoke. However, the court does not always rule in favor of the executive.

To understand how the discovery of an actual smoking gun creates meaning, we can look at two perspectives of social construction. Prior to the discovery of a smoking gun, there is a monist construction.[22] A monist construction is one in which "there are no objective features in the domain upon which to base a judgment of the adequacy of the social construction."[23]

In other words, a monist construction is when a speaker's discourse communicates some phenomenon into the public's consciousness, but there is no external support or evidence other than the speaker's own discourse to support the presence of the phenomenon. That is, the construction of an event and its meaning can only be assessed based on the symbolic (i.e., communicative) representations of the referent, which itself is unavailable or does not exist. For example, if politician A accuses politician B of lying but has no tangible evidence to prove the accusation, the lie is said to have a monist construction.

In terms of the scandal, there is no referent to judge accusers and apologists prior to the discovery of an actual smoking gun. After a smoking gun is discovered, however, one might say there is a dualist construction, which "distinguishes between actual states of affairs and perceptions, interpretations, or reactions to those affairs" employed by rhetors.[24] In other words, in a dualist construction, there is a referent to compare the competing discourses against. Returning to the previous example, if politician A accuses politician B of lying and has some evidence (banknotes, audiotapes, physical evidence, etc.), the accusations of lying are said to have a dualist construction. That is, there is tangible evidence to support the public discourse. Consequently, when the smoking gun is discovered and made public, there can be an evaluation of the competing discourses about the validity of the rhetoric.

If the accused's discourse is evaluated negatively, there is "a revelation that the deviant's identity has not been what he claimed it to be, but has been really deviant all along. Rather than saying the deviant is now unworthy of trust, the scandal shows how the deviant has in fact not been worthy of trust for some time."[25] This meaning of the smoking gun is attributed in part to the discourse of the accused. That is, the social construction of the cover-up is also the social construction of the apologist's own deviance. Nixon's statements, for example, that no one in the White House was involved in the Watergate burglary was an attempted construction to produce the meaning that no one in the White House participated in the burglary. With the revelation of the smoking gun conversation of June 23, 1972, however, it became clear that people from the White House were involved, and many, if not all, of Nixon's past statements became highly questionable.

The same turn of events happened in Teapot Dome. Albert Fall had initially said that his sudden affluence came from the *Washington Post* publisher Edward McLean, but the money really came from one of Fall's wealthy oil friends, Edward Doheny. Doheny, who had leased some of the oil lands, testified that he had loaned Fall the $100,000 a year before he had leased the naval oil reserves. The loan was "for friendship, not oil," and was delivered by Doheny's son in a small black bag.[26] Even if the exchange of funds between Doheny and Fall was a loan and not a bribe, the lie and perhaps even the nefariousness of a small black bag delivered by another only added to the intrigue and culpability of Fall. As a result, many of Fall's previous statements became questionable.

In essence, the purpose of the cover-up is to keep certain evidence hidden, for if publicized, it would be damning. A social constructionist approach, however, seems to suggest that the act of hiding evidence is the very element that makes it damning. This may be one of the reasons why the cover-up almost never works as a means of escape during a scandal. The cover-up creates the opportunity for the uncovering of a smoking gun, which exacerbates the original misconduct into something, as will be shown below, far more serious. Consequently, the accused has successfully aided his political opponents in their efforts. That is, the accused has attributed meaning (i.e., seriousness and responsibility) to an otherwise potentially unmeaningful event.

The accused's attribution of meaning to his own deviance suggests that the cover-up is often experienced via the accused's *apologia*, which is synonymous with the social construction of the accused's responsibility. This provides some insight into one of the reasons put forth as to why Clinton escaped an impeachment conviction in the Senate. Kramer and Olson claim that Clinton maintained "sufficient ambiguity and tentativeness" in his twenty public statements to "adapt to the unfolding controversy."[27] That is, Clinton's remarks "included the minimal amount of detail possible" so that he could adapt to future revelations and attacks. For example, a "'guilty' apologist may benefit from initial denial—as long as the denial is framed in such a way that allows one later to maintain that denial's 'technical' accuracy."[28] This ambiguity caused Clinton to lose some credibility, but it allowed future evidence against him to be addressed.

Silence

The accused also contributes meaning to the post–smoking gun discovery by his or her silence. In a legal context, silence, which is afforded by the Fifth Amendment, is a means of avoiding self-incrimination; importantly, in a legal context, the privilege against self-incrimination is in no way to be taken as a confession of guilt.[29] However, "in contrast to their legal counterparts, scholars in other disciplines have begun to recognize the significance of silence as a powerful means of communication."[30] Consequently, it is imperative to identify silences and to explain what they mean and how they are understood by the public.[31]

While silence in a legal context may be straightforward, in a sociopolitical context, Krieger states that "silence is ambiguous and therefore messy."[32] Silence can have a wide variety of meanings, including that the person is giving consent or withdrawing from the discourse in disagreement; silence may also mean that the person is carefully contemplating what to say next, or it could be a sign of disinterest.[33] Consequently, it is difficult to ascertain the meaning of silence; the smoking gun, however, offers a frame for determining the meaning of silence.

Prior to the discovery of the smoking gun, there can be innumerable attacks upon the accused. The accused cannot logistically respond to each individual attack simply because it would potentially be impossible to address each specific one. Moreover, the accused may very well draw (more) attention to the attacks by responding to them.[34] Yet, as the forms of *apologia* demonstrate, the attacks do allow the accused to refocus attention onto their accomplishments, albeit with a reactive posture.

After a smoking gun is discovered, the accused's silence can be damaging.[35] While the meaning of silence can be vague and messy, we can look to the "relationship between verbal utterances and the unspoken, which demonstrates the function of silence in a given situation."[36] In Teapot Dome, for example, Albert Fall spoke out against the charges but participated in congressional hearings. However, with the smoking gun testimony of Edward Doheny, Fall quickly became silent. In the hearings before and after Doheny's testimony, Fall had a pressing reason to speak; however, he was silent after the smoking gun discovery. Fall's turn to silence indicated that something had changed, which raised the suspicions of the press, the public, and Congress.

In other words, after a smoking gun is discovered and the accused quickly becomes taciturn after routinely speaking publicly, the silence violates expectations of a normally loquacious politician.[37] The expectation seems to follow "the utilitarian mantra held by all private citizens . . . speak up when you feel that it will help your cause [and] shut up when you feel it will help your cause."[38] Consequently, "when a public figure violates expectations by silence, the public's attention is riveted on the silence as it tries to attribute meanings to it."[39] Those meanings are often not favorable to those who turn to silence, as Schröter claims, "The ideals of democracy prohibit an appreciation of silence and secrecy."[40]

The meaning of Fall's silence could be interpreted as defensive posturing. In the pre–smoking gun political contestation over meaning, silence in the wake of a smoking gun clearly identifies the perpetrator, which tips the balance to the accuser's efforts at constructing meaning. The accuser is the "communicative 'controller,' [who] strives to diminish freedom of choice available to others involved in the rhetorical transaction by decreasing the perceived viability of alternatives other than the option [the accuser] advocates."[41] If the accused fails to provide meaning for his silence, the accused may become powerless in the public discourse; consequently, one must give silence meaning.[42] In Teapot Dome, Fall was able to limit the accuser's efforts by putting meaning to his silence by claiming that he would no longer participate in the congressional investigation but would save what he had to say for the more proper and officialized scene of a judicial court.

Claiming that an issue is in the courts further allows the accused not to comment on the matter publicly. Again, the accused must give meaning to that silence. Failure to do so results in allowing the accuser to create the meaning of the silence. While a matter is in the courts or is in preparation for legalities, the accused can refrain from commenting on allegations of wrongdoing, citing the constraint of an "ongoing criminal investigation."[43]

Citing the restraint of an ongoing criminal investigation is the attribution of the accused's silence to an external constraint rather than to an individual's choice to remain silent. Such a strategy "links their silence to a good greater than the maintenance of their own political capital. They effectively say to all those who want more information: 'Do not blame us! Blame the constraint!'"[44] Clinton, for example, stated that his refusal to comment was proper and responsible. Thus the accused's silence is given meaning based on respect for the law and not based on self-preservation or political contestation as the pre–smoking gun discourse has shown it to be. Albert Fall's silence was given meaning based on his earlier comments. Early in the scandal, Fall said he would speak in the courts but then backtracked on such promises by remaining silent; this reversal violated the sociopolitical expectation of speech from a public official (even if a former public official) accused of scandalous actions when confronted with near damning evidence.[45] This shift of the frame from political survival/success to the courts by the accused marks a critical move in scandal rhetoric.

THE JUDICIAL TURN

While the original allegations may very well be politically motivated and may therefore be dealt with in the political arena, the smoking gun introduces a new allegation of wrongdoing: the cover-up, which, as this section will argue, is dealt with under the auspices of a legal or pseudolegal context. This section will first address the nature of the cover-up and its relationship to the original misconduct, then the shift to a legal context, and conclude by arguing that this shift is the construction of *the* scandal problem.

Cover-Up and the Crime

A scandal can be broken into two constitutive elements: the substantive and the procedural.[46] The substantive element is the publicized wrongdoing; the procedural element involves the cover-up of misconduct.[47] In Watergate, for example, there was the break-in of the Democratic National Committee's office (i.e., the substantive component) and the cover-up (i.e., the procedural component). While, as many claim, Nixon was not involved in the break-in, his role in the cover-up is well documented, and it was his role in the cover-up, not the initial break-in, that sealed his fate. Thus, the cover-up can be a crime in and of itself—especially since a cover-up is obstruction of justice, which is an impeachable offense. Consequently, the procedural element can and often does subsume the substantive element, leading to the popular sentiment that "the cover-up is worse than the crime."

The Teapot Dome scandal allows one to better appreciate the relationship between these two elements of a scandal. In Teapot Dome, one could make the argument that the wealthy oilman Edward Doheny did not bribe Secretary of the Interior Albert Fall. That is, while Doheny did give Fall a large sum of money and was then awarded drilling rights to oil lands under Fall's control, there are some facts that seem worthy of noting. Doheny and Fall were longtime friends, so one might speculate that, as Doheny himself stated, the money was a matter between two friends, one in need and one with enormous resources to help his friend in need. But this fact alone could not overcome the high levels of the individuals involved and the important resources at stake. However, it is puzzling why Doheny, if he did "bribe" Fall, would be found not guilty of bribing Fall. That is, Fall was sentenced to prison for accepting a bribe that Doheny was found not guilty of giving. Perhaps, there was a legal technicality. Nevertheless, why did Doheny later foreclose, a common practice when one does not repay a loan, on Fall's estate when Fall did not pay back the bribe?

An answer to these questions might be found in the fact that the procedural element of the scandal exacerbated the appearance of guilt. Fall falsely testified that he had not received any money from Doheny for any reason whatsoever and that the money he received to improve his ranch came from Edward McLean, the owner of the *Washington Post*. The only problem was that McLean later testified that Fall returned his uncashed check as he received funds from another source, which turned out to be Doheny and Sinclair. Teapot Dome scholar David Stratton claimed, "This great lie cost Fall everything."[48] It was the cover-up, the procedural element, that did the damage. Similarly, Clinton's infidelity was not a crime, but his deception was. Thus, in Teapot Dome and Clinton/Lewinsky, as with Watergate, the substantive element of the scandal is overwhelmed by the procedural element in the eyes of Congress and other investigators who may be involved.

Recognizing the relationship between the substantive and procedural elements of the scandal is important. The cover-up is far from a point of political difference; a cover-up is often enacted via perjury or obstruction of justice, which are both criminal matters regardless of whether the accusation regarding the substantive element is a validated crime or not.[49] Obstruction of justice is broadly defined as when one attempts to subvert or interfere with the activities of the police, courts, or other investigatory agency of the government in their efforts to administer justice. There are a number of specific ways in which one can obstruct justice, such as lying to investigators or officers of the court, influencing the testimony of others, or destroying or tampering with evidence. Importantly, one can be found guilty of obstructing justice even if he or she is found not guilty of the focus of an investigation. This is because interfering with the administration of justice, whatever the outcome of the investigation is, is still a crime.

For the president, who is constitutionally charged with ensuring that the laws are faithfully executed, the seriousness of obstruction of justice is so profound that it "would so stain a president as to make his continuance in office dangerous to the public order."[50] Consequently, obstruction of justice is one of the few matters worthy of impeachment, for it seriously corrupts and subverts the governmental processes and democratic ideals.[51] Obstruction of justice is a serious matter that merits more than just simple attention in the political arena that the substantive element receives. Consequently, there is a shift in scene.

Shift in Scene

The public discourse in the wake of the smoking gun, which demonstrates a cover-up or potential cover-up, marks a shift in the scandal. The forgoing discussion of pre– and post–smoking gun discourse here and in chapter 3 has focused on the relationship between the rhetor's agency (i.e., *kategoria* and *apologia*) and his or her purpose in authoring meaning (establishing guilt or combating those attempts). However, when examining the rhetoric after an actual smoking gun is found, the relationship, or what Kenneth Burke calls the ratio, between agency and purpose is limiting; consequently, it is worthwhile to look to other relationships. Here it is valuable to recognize that an agent engages in some means (i.e., agency) for some purpose in a scene.[52] By adding the agent-scene ratio, we can gain a richer understanding of scandal rhetoric.

Specifically, examining the agent-scene relationship is beneficial in that it notes the status or "formal position of the actors."[53] For example, we can see that if the accused claims that it is improper to comment on an ongoing criminal investigation, they have propelled the matter into a scene of officialization, which they attempted to stop earlier in the scandal. That is, in the pre–smoking gun discourse, the accused attempted to deofficialize the attackers' efforts to officialize their accusations. But if the accused then cites the propriety of the courts, a legal principle, or a criminal investigation in the wake of the smoking gun, the accused has, in part, abandoned efforts at deofficialization and moved into the realm of officialization. That is, the accused has consented that those who are accusing or investigating have the valid role and authority to indict and that the process is unfolding in the "proper places."[54]

Those proper places can vary. In Teapot Dome, for example, the officialized places included the civil and criminal courtrooms. In Clinton/Lewinsky and nearly in Watergate, the proper place was Congress, which ultimately took on a role that differs from its normal legislative duties for impeachment. That is, while Congress is the legislative branch, one cannot disregard that the impeachment process (i.e., impeachment by the House of Representatives and conviction by the Senate) follows the auspices of a quasi-judicial proceeding.

The impeachment process is rhetorically significant, as Gronbeck suggests, for it marks a departure from the daily routine of politics and government. This is not to be understated. Impeachment itself is one of the most critical of all constitutional matters and is often dubbed a "constitutional crisis," thereby clearly marking it as a matter that affects the very footing of the American political system. The nonroutineness of impeachment (as well as formal, high-level congressional investigations into presidents and their administrations) marks a fully officialized scene in which the accused must participate, unlike the political contestation of the pre–smoking gun discourse.

The distinction between officialization as judicial and deofficialization as political can be clarified by using the distinction between executive actions and ministerial functions.[55] Executive actions are discretionary and are not legally enforceable and can be utilized as the executive sees fit, whereas ministerial functions are legally required to be completed regardless of the executive's desire. The accusers in the scandals are working toward a ministerial role in which the accused must be held legally accountable for the alleged misconduct—in the congressional hearings and, if necessary, through impeachment by the House of Representatives and potential conviction by the Senate. The accused, however, is responding in a discretionary manner; that is, they do not have to respond directly to the charges, for they are responding in a manner of deofficialization.

In the pre–smoking gun partisan discourse, each side is in the realm of contestation where each side is fighting for control and meaning of the debate as the last chapter addressed. If the accuser can successfully officialize, then they are in a stronger position to prosecute. If the accused, on the other hand, can deofficialize the debate, they can abrogate the accusations, putting themselves in a stronger position to vindicate themselves. Once a smoking gun is discovered, however, the silence of the accused due to the ongoing legal stage of the scandal firmly officializes the scandal.

The Scandal Problem

In a scandal, for example, the shift in scene recasts the original unsolvable conflict (i.e., political contestation/crisis of meaning) into a problem. As Bennet states, most political issues are too abstract and ill defined to be solved; consequently, "the essence of a political issue is that . . . it cannot be resolved."[56] Since a political conflict, by definition, cannot be solved, a redefinition of the issue must be made to create a problem.[57] That problem, in turn, offers the opportunity for a solution that was not available in the original, political (i.e., unsolvable) conflict. Consequently, if an act can be recast into a problem, then there is a potential solution, which "lends an air of finality, closure, and confidence to an otherwise unsatisfactory state of affairs."[58]

The smoking gun is a prime means for creating the problem. The smoking gun provides an opportunity for concrete action to resolve the contestation of meaning. That is, the smoking gun, in essence, redefines the issue of the scandal. The issue has gone from the substantive element, which is not necessarily a crime (i.e., a "little thing"), to the procedural element, which is always a serious crime (i.e., a "big thing") for those entrusted with faithfully executing the laws as charged by the Constitution. If Congress can investigate a substantive element, this provides an opportunity to uncover any potential obstruction of justice or perjury since the congressional investigation is an official inquiry.

As such, political scandals reflect the Ancient Greek notion of scandal, σκανδάλον. Literally translated, σκανδάλον is "the stick in a trap on which the bait is placed, and which springs up and shuts the trap at the touch of an animal."[59] In other words, the bait is the substantive allegations, which create an exigence to which the accused responds in public discourse or congressional investigations. But the trap is the procedural allegations, which are political but certainly do not have that appearance to the would-be victim. That is, allegations of wrongdoing create an exigence to which the accused responds via *apologia*; if the *apologia* is shown to be a cover-up with a smoking gun, then the allegations of the original, substantive misconduct are eclipsed by the more serious, procedural allegations that carry a far greater potential for punishment—impeachment and conviction for presidents (or members of their administration) that is carried out by Congress.

In the move from substantive to procedural, it is important to recognize that "we may lose sight of the fact that political 'solutions' generally involve rhetorical constructs which redefine the initial terms, demands, and issues of a political conflict."[60] For example, the impeachment process is a fundamental constitutional remedy (i.e., a form of checks and balances) and is not necessarily a purely judicial or political process.[61] Ideally, Congress assumes a role of looking into the facts and the law, "without partisan or narrow political bias, and proceeds to judgment."[62]

In practice, however, there are political overtones. For example, in the first presidential impeachment, Sen. Sumner stated that impeachment "is a political proceeding, before a political body, with political purposes; that it is founded on political offenses, proper for consideration of a political body and subject to a political judgment only."[63] Furthermore, Justice Wilson, who sat on the first Supreme Court in addition to signing the Declaration of Independence and participating in the constitutional convention, described impeachments as "proceedings of a political nature . . . confined to political characters, to political crimes and misdemeanors, and to political punishments."[64]

Impeachment is not about punishing a crime. Impeachment is about removal from office and disqualification from any future public position. Thus a criminal trial, if warranted, that might follow the impeachment process does not constitute double jeopardy.[65] Thus, the impeachment process is not a criminal trial.[66] But the impeachment process is portrayed under the auspices of a quasi-judicial process with judicial charges that often include obstruction of justice, which offers a greater warrant for the case of impeachment. Since obstruction of justice is an impeachable offense, the charge allows political actors such as Congress to resolve the scandal. That is, if the misconduct was criminal, that does not necessarily warrant any actionable process by the political accusers in Congress, which lacks the authority to try crimes. But again, if the original misconduct can be replaced or substantiated by impeachable offenses, then the political accusers (i.e., members of Congress) have the role and authority to take action. The ability of political actors to take action gives the appearance of officialization via an aura of judiciality as impeachment and "trial" in the Senate reflect a judicial process of indictment and trial in the court system. The aura of judiciality gives the impeachment process, a political process, an air of legal and judicial legitimacy over what began as a contestation over meaning of allegations of misconduct.

Consequently, impeachment, as Bennett explains, lends "an enormous sense of dignity to an otherwise undignified controversy."[67] However, we must not forget "the rhetorical strategies through which political outcomes are engineered within institutions of government" via political discourse.[68] That is, the accusers have successfully defined the post–smoking gun discourse in terms of the scene of justice by defining the cover-up, not the original allegations, as the problem. Thus, the phrase "*the* scandal problem" gets to the point that the original misconduct is not always a problem/crime and is therefore rather moot. Furthermore, if the original misconduct is a crime, the political actors are unable to rectify the issue—that is a matter for the judicial branch, and the impeachment process is a tool of the legislative branch. However, if the original misconduct is substantiated or replaced with an impeachable offense, then the political actors have successfully created a "preferred conception of an issue or event through the succession of scenarios" from the political to the quasi-judicial.[69] Consequently, the cover-up is not necessarily worse than the crime; the cover-up *is* the crime from the point of view of Congress.

In other words, in the relationship between the substantive and procedural elements, there is a grand opportunity for the accusers. That is, at best, Congress can only investigate substantive elements of alleged misconduct. However, if the substantive element of a scandal does not merit the seriousness of impeachment, members of Congress can focus on the procedural element, which might occur during the investigation. If this is done, then the investigation produced the opportunity for the actual crime, which is obstruction of justice. And since obstruction of justice is an impeachable offense regardless of the original transgression, Congress, which otherwise lacks agency to punish the substantive element, is now empowered to punish the procedural element.

RELUCTANT PARTICIPATION

In Teapot Dome, Watergate, and Clinton/Lewinsky, the smoking gun was found or forced to be handed over in a judicial or quasi-judicial context. The accused's denials and any other attempts at *apologia* would not be welcomed by investigators or accusers, for the smoking gun does exist. In such circumstances, the accused must work within the judicial scene to fight for control of the evidence. However, the accused is often not willing to fully participate. Presumably, as history has shown, the attempt to withhold or prevent release of key evidence is the last shot the accused has of maintaining innocence or delaying the acknowledgment of guilt. To allow for the release of or to hand over the smoking gun is to reveal the accused's guilt, which he knew all along but made public statements to the contrary.

There are two factors worth mentioning about the accused's reluctant participation. First, there is a public expectation that the accused, who has long denied such allegations through *apologia*, should not be willing to suppress any evidence whatsoever. For if the accused has done nothing wrong, then there should be no problem with any evidence because such evidence, if the person has committed no transgression, should be exculpatory. Any attempt to suppress evidence, be it the smoking gun or not, suggests that something is amiss, which contradicts earlier efforts of *apologia*. Furthermore the alleged transgression is seen as much worse, for not only has the transgression occurred, but the accused has lied about it.

Second, reluctant participation in a judicial or quasi-judicial scene is still participation and therefore confirms the shift from the political to judicial scene. In other words, by reluctantly participating in even a quasi-judicial scene, the accused gives up attempts at deofficialization, which occurs in a political scene. The accused has stopped attempting to politicize the attacks and has recognized that the situation calls for the work to be done in an officialized setting. Returning to the ancient Greek notion of scandal—a trap laid for an enemy—the accused has recognized the trap that they have been ensnared within but continues to fight. We can see this in three of the four scandals examined in this book.

WHERE THERE'S SMOKE . . .

Teapot Dome

Smoking Gun

As 1924 began, more evidence of the improvement in Fall's financial status appeared. The man who once considered resigning from the Senate before being appointed to secretary of the interior because he was in financial ruin and unable to pay his taxes from 1912 to 1922 and felt he could no longer afford the costs associated with being a senator became incredibly wealthy.[70] The congressional investigation, an attempt to officialize the criticism by holding the investigation in the proper place, discovered that Fall paid all his back taxes, made numerous improvements to his property, and purchased nearby land after leasing the lands to wealthy oil friends, Sinclair and Doheny. Fall also bought a great deal of quality livestock from Sinclair, who also included a former prizewinning racehorse as a gift to Fall's ranch manager.[71] From this, "newspapers were treated to a first-class front-page story."[72]

More news came from Archie Roosevelt, who was the son of the former president, assistant secretary of the navy, and a vice president in one of Sinclair's oil companies. Roosevelt had heard of the investigations and nervously quit working for Sinclair. Roosevelt testified that Sinclair gave $68,000 to Fall's ranch manager. But when Roosevelt's source for this information was questioned, the source claimed that Sinclair gave "six or eight cows," not $68,000.[73] The answer assuaged all concerns of the committee, but many still wondered and criticized Fall's sudden affluence.

In an attempt at deofficialization, Fall stated that in response to "evil minded person[s who] have seen fit to criticize [his newfound wealth] I want to say that I have never received one cent from Mr. Sinclair or from E. L. Doheny, or from any other corporation in which they are interested, in connection with the leases on Naval Reserve lands."[74] Less than a month later and in response to heavy criticism from Democratic senator Caraway from the great state of Arkansas, Fall reiterated that any direct claim or indirect innuendo that he received financial benefit from public office was "absolutely false" and "malicious."[75]

Soon the "national question" was, where did Fall get all the money?[76] A telegram to Sen. Walsh gave an initial answer. It stated that Edward McLean, the publisher and owner of the *Washington Post*, claimed he had loaned Fall $100,000 on a personal note and had never met any of the "oil crowd."[77] McLean's official testimony, however, stated that while he had given money to Fall, Fall had subsequently returned the uncashed check with a letter stating that he "had arranged to secure the funds elsewhere."[78] Fall testified that he agreed with McLean's account. This was the smoking gun of Teapot Dome. Fall had falsely stated that he received funds from the newspaper editor, which he did but returned, as he received funds elsewhere—from his wealthy oil friends who just happened to lease oil fields that Fall controlled.

"Sensational testimony" continued in January and February 1924.[79] Doheny, who had leased some of the oil lands, testified that he had loaned Fall the $100,000 a year before he had leased the naval oil reserves. The loan was "for friendship, not oil," and was delivered by Doheny's son in a small black bag.[80] Doheny claimed, "The order in which they [i.e., the loan, which predated the lease of the oil lands by a year] occurred disposes of any contention that they were influenced by my making a personal loan to a lifelong friend."[81] As for the sensational amount, Doheny, the millionaire, thought $100,000 "was no more than $25 or $50, perhaps, to the ordinary individual."[82]

"High political drama" soon swept over the nation.[83] With these revelations,

> four-column headlines leaped to the front page of the haughty *New York Times*. At once a horrified administration unloosed its thunder and began shouting wildly for criminal prosecution and suits to cancel the leases. Larger press tables were hastily dragged in. Senators, after introducing themselves to the chairman as members of the committee, took their seats at the table for the first time, wearing an air of stern resolve.[84]

The setting was improved for an investigation of such caliber. Such an effort required the proper place and people in the appropriate role. Officialization in Teapot Dome was in full swing. Congress had been looking into a questionable loan/lease deal, and in their investigation they were able to define the scandal problem. The former secretary of the interior had lied about what began as a questionable act of judgment by a cabinet officer.

Prior to Doheny's announcement, the crucial aspects of the investigation were the transferal of authority over the oil lands, the legality of the leases, the reversal of conservation, and the secrecy around the transfer of authority and the leasing of the oil fields. But these revelations had "awakened few echoes of interested response from the public until to them were added some further facts regarding Mr. Fall's personal affairs."[85] The idea of "the love of money as the root of all evil in the wrongdoing of Secretary Fall captured the public imagination. The deeper issues [of the leases] remained fuzzy and obscure."[86] Without the issue of Fall's personal finances, according to one senator, "there would hardly have been a scandal."[87] Thus Congress had defined the scandal problem as being about Fall's affluence, not the oil leases.

Fall, in a last-ditch effort at deofficialization, believed that Congress also did not care about the details of the leases. Fall told a reporter that if Congress did not approve of any detail of the leases, they could simply repeal them. In Fall's opinion, "instead of doing something so direct, it was the desire of certain senators to make a national sensation out of the leases for political advantage."[88] In effect, a quasi-judicial congressional committee defined the major issue of Teapot Dome.

Reluctant Participation

Fall and Sinclair spoke very little publicly during the Senate inquiry. When they did speak out, it was to decry the partisan rhetoric.[89] They also spoke of a desire for the nonpartisan sanctuary of the courts. Facing defeat from public opinion, Fall, Doheny, and Sinclair believed they would be vindicated in the courts where they could argue their positions fairly and impartially with, as

Fall stated, "the ultimate integrity of the courts" over the "ravings of some Senators."[90] Sinclair stated, "It is a great relief that the Teapot Dome controversy has at last been transferred to a court of justice," and he "welcomed the judicial determination."[91] Even more resolute in his innocence, Fall claimed, "I am convinced that the action contemplated will, if it gets into the courts, be upheld by them."[92] Moreover, Fall believed any comment would be made in, as he stated, a "dignified" and "official way."[93] Taking matters to court would separate fact from innuendo.

It soon became apparent that Fall, Sinclair, and Doheny took to the courts for political refuge and not to expose the truth themselves. Fall stated, "I am willing to tell all and when I say all, that is just what I mean . . . but due regard must be paid to legal procedure."[94] Fall claimed he would "tell all I know . . . at the proper place, and under the proper circumstances," which was a court of law.[95] After being recalled to the Senate's inquiry, Sinclair, like Fall, stated, "I shall reserve any evidence I may be able to give for those courts."[96] Doheny maintained his innocence throughout the ordeal and saved his testimony for the criminal trials. Not only did Doheny fail to testify in the two civil trials, but Fall and Sinclair also refused to speak at the trials. Furthermore, Sinclair and Fall refused to testify at their own criminal trials. Of the three, only Doheny testified at his own criminal trial.

Fall did, however, testify at Sinclair's retrial and claimed he enjoyed it very much. After he was cross-examined, he told the Associated Press, "I am happy now that I have told the truth about the leases. My story was not as complete as I would have liked it to be and did not cover some points that I thought the public should be told in fairness to me."[97] Nevertheless, Fall did not testify at any other time in the trials.

This reluctance was nothing new. Sinclair had escaped testifying before the Senate by "very quietly [sailing to Europe], without letting his name appear on the passenger list."[98] When he returned, he refused to answer any questions. Sinclair broke his silence only when the trials were over, claiming he was innocent. Sinclair himself was not tried for bribery, for he had put money into a Canadian bank, thereby forcing investigators to go through the Canadian legal system before he could be tried in the American courts. By the time the Canadian legal system ruled against Sinclair, the American judge refused to reopen the case. Sinclair was not the only one to evade the legal system. Other less prominent figures, including Fall's son-in-law, stealthily departed to various countries in Europe and one to Cuba to avoid testifying.

Throughout the trials, Fall suffered from perpetual illnesses, which absolved him from testifying. Early in the investigation, senators questioned Fall's constant sickness and asked for doctor's notes, and at times the investigators and courts appointed their own physicians to report on his health, which often confirmed but also sometimes disconfirmed Fall's doctors. After

Doheny's shocking testimony, Fall's appearance was definitely weak. Fall had lost more than forty pounds, and "his flesh hung in wrinkled folds about his face and neck."[99] Fall's illness forced the courts to reschedule trials and caused Senate investigators to come to him. His precarious health nearly ended his own criminal trial. Fall was incapable of standing when court was called and was carried in and out of the courtroom. When Fall did testify at Sinclair's retrial, it was from his sickbed in New Mexico.

Fall was given "whatever space [he] wished" from the press, but he refused the offers; "I have never fought a law case for a client nor myself through the columns of the press," he exclaimed.[100] Regarding the secrecy of the leasing, Fall stated, "My reticence in this matter may have justified some criticism."[101] The press applied this same sentiment to Fall's nearly wholesale reluctance to address Teapot Dome in nearly any place, even in court—where he earlier claimed he would. Despite this, Fall denied that he was "unwilling to cooperate."[102]

One editorialist claimed that Fall's reluctance had a "most unfortunate effect upon the public mind and [has] given his political enemies an opportunity to put the worst possible construction upon his official acts."[103] Another claimed that by his "unwillingness to testify Mr. Fall appears to admit wrongdoing."[104] Yet another suggested that Fall's actions were so heinous that he should continue to maintain "himself as inconspicuous as possible for the remainder of his life."[105]

Doheny and Sinclair's reluctance to testify labeled them "acquitted [in court] but not vindicated . . . in the public mind."[106] Fall found himself in a similar position. One writer claimed, "The defendant who employs technicalities to delay his trial, creates the presumption that he is guilty."[107] Others characterized Fall similarly: "A former member of the Cabinet, when charged with conspiracy and corruption [was] hiding behind every legal technicality."[108] Another commented, "If they are innocent, they should demonstrate that fact in open court" and "not to try to delay trial."[109] A few newspapers defended Fall, Sinclair, and Doheny by claiming that the accused were only exercising their legal rights by not testifying and delaying trial. Thus "the verdict of the jury [had to] be accepted as a legal record, but its acceptance by the public conscience [could not] be compelled by any charge from the bench," and the "public in general [was] convinced the whole transaction was crooked, no matter how many juries decide[d] otherwise."[110]

Watergate

Smoking Gun

In 1973, there was a shift in how the public became aware of the events. The media was no longer the "prime movers on Watergate."[111] While the investigative reporting of the *Washington Post* earned itself the Pulitzer Prize in 1973, the onus of the investigation now belonged to the televised Senate hearings, which were the "largest and most penetrating probe" of the scandal.[112] With the hearings broadcast, it was no longer just the attentive public who knew the details; television brought Watergate "into living rooms, where it could not be ignored."[113] All thirty-seven days of testimony were broadcast and "achieved extraordinarily high ratings" throughout the entire duration.[114] Thus the elevated proper places were easily accessible to all.

John Dean's "much anticipated" testimony was the first of "two astonishing moments" in the Senate hearings.[115] His testimony was delayed for one week due to Soviet communist leader Brezhnev's visit to the United States. Leaks to the press, however, foreshadowed his testimony.[116] Dean's official testimony began with a 245-page prepared statement, which took six hours to read. Dean then took questions throughout the rest of the week, and all three major networks carried the five days of testimony.[117] Dean's testimony described the Nixon administration's plans for dealing with identified political enemies prior to and after the break-in. But the biggest of Dean's claims was that President Nixon himself was involved with covering up the break-in. Dean claimed he had discussed a cover-up at least thirty-five times with Nixon. Furthermore, Dean stated that when G. Gordon Liddy and others were indicted, "the President then told me I had done a good job [in handling the White House's investigation of the break-in] and he appreciated how difficult a task it had been, and the President was pleased that the case had stopped with Liddy."[118]

The implication of Nixon's involvement, however, was not a clear breakthrough in the Senate's investigation. Dean was, in effect, calling Nixon a liar, but Dean had "little or no documentary evidence to support his charges against the President and most of his allegations [were] based on his own recollection of purported conversations with Mr. Nixon."[119] There was a need for a smoking gun, but at the time there was no clear evidence that one even existed.

Moreover, Dean, who had admitted his own guilt, was testifying in exchange for partial clemency against criminal charges. Many thought, as Dean later recounted, "that I was lying about the President to save my own skin."[120] It was a matter of political survival. Ultimately, the issue was Dean's credibility versus President Nixon's, and at the time more people believed the president, who had just won election by a landslide, than the "politically inexperienced" John Dean.[121]

But the deference for Nixon soon changed with the second major breakthrough in the Senate hearings. The existence of a smoking gun was discovered. Alexander Butterfield, a former White House aide to Nixon's chief of staff, inadvertently mentioned a taped conversation. The senators' ears perked up. The nation then became aware of the elaborate audio recording system that previously only seven people had known about. Nixon had recorded more than 3,500 hours of conversations with others who did not know they were being recorded. Nixon had installed the system "for historic purposes [and] to record the President's business."[122] Butterfield's revelation provided the means for confirming either Dean's accusations or Nixon's denials.

With this revelation, the Watergate drama would start a new chapter: the judicial showdown between the Senate investigators and the president. Before this, however, more was being heard. In response to the accusations of wrongdoing, the Nixon administration summarily responded by claiming the allegations were nothing more than political rhetoric. With the public's knowledge of the tapes, which did exist, Nixon's fight came to the courts.

Nixon Reluctantly Aids in the Inquiry

The Nixon administration's allegations of political rhetoric continued throughout the legal tug-of-war over whether Nixon should give up the tapes. Though this stage of the scandal occurred over eleven months, the events played out systematically.[123] Two major events did break up this chapter of the scandal: the two-week Yom Kippur War and the resignation of Vice President Spiro Agnew, who was replaced by Gerald Ford. Nonetheless, the public waited for the evidence that would condemn or exonerate Nixon.

The showdown began a week after the taping system became public knowledge in July 1973. Special Prosecutor Archibald Cox issued a subpoena for nine of the tapes. In response, Nixon delivered his second major speech on Watergate on August 15, 1973. He claimed the recordings were protected under executive privilege, a doctrine that legitimizes the executive branch's use of secrecy from legal inquiry similar to the relationship between lawyers and clients, priests and penitents, and wives and husbands. Nixon was not necessarily ignoring the subpoena to protect himself but gave reasons based on the separation of powers for refusing to turn the tapes over. Several days later he would reiterate this position in a news conference. Judge Sirica then ordered Nixon to give Cox the tapes so he could examine them privately. Nixon again refused. The decision was then appealed to the U.S. District Court of Appeals. Nixon's response now was to offer a typed summary of the tapes authenticated by Democratic senator John Stennis, who was considered a "respected elder statesman."[124] More and more, albeit reluctantly, Nixon attempted to show he was willing to participate in the investigation.

The Senate investigators, who also wanted the nine tapes, seemed to approve of the transcript idea, but Cox did not. Nixon's response was to ask Cox to resign. Cox refused. Nixon then ordered Attorney General Richardson to fire Cox. Richardson refused and resigned. Nixon then ordered Richardson's assistant to fire Cox. The assistant refused and resigned as well. Nixon then ordered Solicitor General Robert Bork to fire Cox, and Bork dutifully complied. These events of October 20, 1973, were labeled the Saturday Night Massacre. The press, including the *Washington Post*, the *Chicago Tribune*, the *Los Angeles Times*, the *New York Times*, and many, many more were highly critical of Nixon's actions. Nixon backtracked on his slow and reluctant participation, but it came at a cost.

The following Tuesday after the Saturday Night Massacre, Nixon's lawyer announced in Sirica's courtroom, "The President does not defy the law and he has authorized me to say he will comply in full with the orders of the Court."[125] Sirica was highly doubtful, but Nixon's lawyer maintained that Nixon would comply fully. Sirica "smiled broadly" and stated, "The court is very happy the President has reached this decision."[126] However, two of the nine tapes that were requested were found to have never existed (or perhaps to have disappeared), and one tape had an eighteen-and-a-half-minute gap for which Nixon's secretary took partial responsibility for accidentally erasing. Sirica ordered six technological experts to look at the tapes, and they concluded the erasing was no accident.[127] The gap had been recorded over anywhere from five to nine times.[128] Days prior to this discovery, Nixon famously announced, "I am not a crook."[129] Nevertheless, the Saturday Night Massacre and the eighteen-and-a-half-minute gap were "clear-cut wrong doing that the public could understand and relate to. . . . These were not complicated concepts."[130] The recording "had the sinister appearance of someone acting apparently out of desperation."[131] As a result, Nixon's credibility was falling.

The next major event came in April 1974 when the new special prosecutor, Leon Jaworski, who had been reviewing some of the already released tapes, then subpoenaed the White House for sixty-four more. Jaworski privately believed that one or more of the tapes would implicate Nixon. Nixon, in a television address, responded that he would turn over edited transcripts of some of the tapes. He wanted to demonstrate he was, to a certain degree, cooperating, but he also wanted to protect the presidency's executive privilege, the practice of withholding information from Congress and the judiciary that every president since Washington had exercised. In the address, Nixon noted a handful of instances where he had already waived his executive privilege during the investigation so that the House could come to an "informed judgment about the President's role in Watergate."[132] Nixon seemed to suggest that his offer of edited transcripts was a fair compromise given what he had already released and his level of cooperation. Jaworski was not satisfied with this offer and appealed to the Supreme Court in May 1974.

Two months after the subpoena, the Supreme Court heard the case. Nixon's argument, delivered by James St. Clair, was that the courts should not hear the case at all since this was a political matter between Congress and the president. That is, the judicial branch deals with judicial issues, not political matters. The justices were skeptical of this characterization of events because the case dealt with a criminal act (i.e., the break-in). St. Clair responded by arguing that the president's executive privilege was absolute in all areas—even in criminal matters. St. Clair even suggested that there was enough evidence available and that the release of any more tapes would be unnecessary. St. Clair's arguments were at odds with Nixon's earlier statements in April about waiving executive privilege in a few instances to get to the bottom of the situation.

Although Nixon attempted to portray himself as cooperating, the Supreme Court, minus the Nixon appointee who recused himself, unanimously gave the president no option other than to cooperate fully.[133] They quickly decided that the president's executive privilege was paramount in matters involving the military, diplomatic relations, or sensitive national matters. However, the break-in was a criminal act and did not deal with national security issues. Furthermore, the Court recognized that executive privilege was, in part, necessary to protect the confidentiality of communications among presidents and advisors; however, the importance of a specific criminal investigation was greater than a generalized need for confidentiality. Coupled with the fact that Nixon had already released some of the actual tapes (i.e., his reluctant participation), the Court ruled that Nixon had to turn over all the requested tapes. Their reasoning was that absolute executive privilege would "enable the president both to withhold potentially damaging evidence from an investigation and to produce evidence that would aid his case (or, at a minimum, confuse the issue) thereby distorting the investigative process."[134] In other words, absolute privilege could lead to an obstruction of justice. Simply put, the Supreme Court would not allow Nixon to participate to a limited degree; they wanted him to cooperate fully and hand over all the requested tapes.

Three days after the Court released their decision, the House Judiciary Committee began immediately investigating the possibility of impeaching Nixon.

Iran-Contra

Initiator and Participator

In late November 1986, after the initial accounts of the scandal were publicized in *Al Shiraa*, Reagan himself authorized Attorney General Edwin Meese to determine the facts, which he reported a few days later. Meese's findings did more than bring clarification. What Meese found exacerbated the already disastrous situation.

Meese reported his preliminary findings to the president, who then informed congressional leaders and the American public. Reagan, in "a shaken and grim-faced" manner, told reporters that he was not fully informed about the actions undertaken by his national security advisors.[135] Reagan also announced that Vice Adm. John Poindexter had resigned and his assistant, Lt. Col. Oliver North, had been fired. Meese finished the press conference and told the press the details of the diversion of funds, which the *Washington Post* called "the most shocking piece of news that Washington has heard since it first learned that Richard M. Nixon had taped the Oval Office."[136]

In the wake of this shocking disclosure, a number of official investigations began in December 1986 and January 1987. President Reagan appointed a bipartisan committee headed by John Tower. After Attorney General Meese's preliminary report on the diversion of funds, Lawrence Walsh was appointed as independent counsel.[137] While not a major inquiry, the Pentagon also looked into the dealings to determine if the Department of Defense was adequately compensated for the ammunition and parts sold to Iran.[138] The congressional investigations, however, sought out the spotlight. The Senate created its committee on January 6. The next day the House, which had apparently wished for the "celebratory status" that the Senate received during the Watergate investigation, formed their own committee.[139] But the necessity of two congressional investigations seemed questionable, and both were merged into one unified panel.[140] But before the congressional investigations even began, the Tower Commission had issued its report on February 26.

The Tower Commission report outlined three areas that led to the scandal. The report criticized Reagan's hands-off management style, the failure of his aides to keep him informed, and the fact that his administration largely ignored the proper processes in carrying out decisions. The report "portrayed President Reagan . . . as a confused and remote figure who failed to understand or control the secret arms deal with Iran."[141] The report also noted that some aides had kept information secret from the president to minimize his role. The report also stated that, though Reagan "did not intend to mislead the American public," he was not "totally candid at all times."[142] The findings from the Meese report and the Tower report, coupled with the fact that Reagan had initiated the investigations, not just participated or even reluctantly participated in them like Fall, Nixon, and Clinton had, arguably helped Reagan weather the storm.

Even though Reagan initiated his own investigations, he and his administration were completely willing to cooperate with other investigations. The White House would release documents to investigators—often without looking at them or making copies of them for fear of appearing to obstruct justice.[143] Investigators were shocked at their degree of access. The *Washington Post* reported, "'It baffles me to this day,' said one senior investigator of the White House attitude. 'It's like there is no other side,' said a senior attorney involved in one probe, adding that the lawyers investigating the Iran-Contra affair expected to be confronted by a high-powered White House legal team—the typical pattern in a major litigation."[144] The Reagan administration had learned the lesson Nixon failed to in terms of participation.

Smoking Gun?

After North and Poindexter's congressional testimony, people started to understand the basic plot of the scandal. However, there was much more detail to be revealed from the other investigations. As Sen. Nunn stated, "If you thought these hearings were just about a search for smoking guns, then they're probably over. But these hearings were always supposed to be more than that."[145] Such comments about the lack of importance regarding a smoking gun seem inevitable given that there were already two completed reports and the president himself had admitted the transgression.

The Tower Commission report had already been released three months before the congressional hearings began in May 1987. But while historians saw the Tower Commission as "having done a more thorough job in a shorter amount of time than the subsequent, televised Senate committee hearings," the congressional report went a bit further.[146] That is, the Tower report stopped "short of charging that Admiral Poindexter and Colonel North destroyed notes or invented cover stories to protect President Reagan. But it disclose[d] that in carrying out the Iran-Contra affair, members of the National Security Council repeatedly deceived Congress and other senior officials."[147]

Here is the beginning of Congress defining the scandal problem, which in this case was not about a smoking gun—the scandal problem was defined as the executive branch not respecting the congressional branch in foreign policy. Furthermore, the congressional report, released in November 1987, claimed that the National Security Council staff operated as if "it was the president's policy—not an isolated decision by North or Poindexter—to sell arms secretly to Iran."[148] With Congress's ability to investigate the executive branch, they defined the scandal problem as being Reagan's failure as president to communicate clearly and cultivate a respect for the Constitution and the law itself.

While the partisan rhetoric of Iran-Contra was much less severe compared to the other scandals initially, the congressional report ignited partisan rivalry.[149] Attorney General Edwin Meese dismissed the report by characterizing the majority report as "a great job of Monday morning quarterbacking" and stated that the report had come up with the same information as his own three-day probe a year earlier.[150] Additionally, eight Republicans, led by Rep. Dick Cheney, released a minority report that claimed the Reagan administration was guilty of "mistakes and nothing more."[151] The minority report also stated, "There was no constitutional crisis, no systematic disrespect for 'the rule of law,' no grand conspiracy, and no Administration-wide dishonesty or cover-up. In fact, the evidence will not support any of the more hysterical conclusions the committees' report tries to reach."[152] The minority report was released twenty-four hours before the much harsher majority report to dampen its impact. However, the reports did not gain much attention due to intervening events such as a Supreme Court nomination, a plunge in the stock market, and developments in the U.S.-Soviet relationship.[153]

The last chapter of Iran-Contra came with the trials and report of the independent counsel, Lawrence Walsh. Walsh indicted and tried a number of those involved in the scandal, including North and Poindexter. North was tried on twelve counts and was only convicted of obstructing Congress, destroying NSC documents, and accepting an illegal gratuity.[154] A year later, Poindexter was tried and convicted on all five counts against him.[155] Both appealed, and their convictions were overturned, as both North and Poindexter had testified under immunity, which meant that Walsh had the difficult task of proving that whatever evidence he had used against North and Poindexter did not come from their congressional testimony.[156] Thus Congress's desire for publicity and grandstanding in their investigations, which gave immunity to North and others, overtook the importance of finding a smoking gun and punishing wrongdoers.

North, who was running in the Republican Senate primary in Virginia, said the report had no "smoking guns [and] Walsh fired his last shot, and it was a blank."[157] North's description was accurate. The information in the report was well known, as it was used in the earlier trials. Also, the report came out a year into Bill Clinton's presidency, and virtually all those involved in the scandal had left public service. Moreover, Ayatollah Khomeini, who was at the center of the Iranian Revolution, had died, and the Sandinistas were no longer in power in Nicaragua.

In fact, Walsh's report only opened himself and his office to criticism, and he "may turn out to be the most widely scorned figure in the whole affair."[158] References to his report pointed to the outrageous expense of the investigation, $37.6 million, and the seven years it took to complete it, which provided few new details, resulted in few policy changes, and led to only a few major convictions, which were overturned on appeal.

Consequently, then president Bush attacked Walsh for focusing on "a political dispute between the executive and legislative branches over foreign policy, [and] we must be careful not to criminalize constitutional disputes of this kind."[159] That is, according to Bush, Walsh's accusations were based not on criminal actions but on political policy, which when prosecuted sets a dangerous precedent. Walsh had so angered Republicans that in 1992 when the independent counsel statute was to be reauthorized, Republicans blocked the reauthorization of the bill. However, in 1994, congressional Republicans did an about-face and reauthorized the statute for Kenneth Starr to begin his investigation into President Clinton's dealings in Whitewater, which would point to an affair with a young White House intern.[160]

Clinton/Lewinsky

Smoking Gun

The initial publicity of Lewinsky's relationship with the president in January 1998 would be the only major revelation until late July 1998. During that time, the media could only speculate on whether an affair had occurred and if President Clinton had lied and obstructed justice.

The next big break in the scandal came seven months after the initial allegations surfaced. On July 28, 1998, after numerous on again, off again deals, Monica Lewinsky accepted an offer from Starr for her full testimony in exchange for immunity.[161] Prior to Lewinsky's testimony, Starr had "little but circumstantial evidence, much of it messy, [and] none of it conclusive."[162] Now, however, Starr had his key witness, who also turned over the infamous blue dress, which supposedly had Clinton's genetic material on it, to the FBI for investigation. The dress, which Lewinsky had secretly withheld from Starr, "revive[d] perhaps the most sensational allegation in the case": the scandal was more than the "simple, he-said-she-said disagreement portrayed by Clinton advisers."[163] The following day, the president's lawyer announced that Clinton would voluntarily testify before the grand jury on August 17, 1998, via videotape.[164] Days later Clinton himself announced that he would testify "completely and truthfully."[165]

Later on September 21, after a "fierce partisan battle," congressional Republicans voted to release the president's grand jury testimony to the public, which they believed would be a near fatal blow to Clinton.[166] Yet Starr, who was once the "most dangerous man in America," was now on the defense, and Bill Clinton had once again become the comeback kid.[167] One of the reasons for the public's "violent mood swing" was that Clinton's videotaped testimony, which pundits thought might show the president "destroy[ing] himself by twitching, equivocating and storming out of the room," actually showed Clinton dodging the truth by infamously debating what "is" means but remaining cool under pressure while doing so.[168]

The president's response to the allegations of misconduct was unique compared to Watergate and Teapot Dome, in that Clinton used true candor.

On August 17, 1998, President Clinton testified for the grand jury via video from the White House. Later that day, Clinton addressed the country from the Map Room, not the Oval Office. The speech was "purposely depoliticized" to create a visual image of Clinton the man and not the president who was being attacked.[169] Clinton, as stated earlier, admitted in a brief four-and-a-half-minute speech that he had a relationship with Lewinsky and that he had misled the American public. Clinton stated that his answers to the grand jury were "legally accurate" but he "did not volunteer information."[170] Moreover, he called the relationship "wrong" and claimed that he committed "a critical lapse in judgment and a personal failure."[171]

Although Clinton addressed the nation and admitted to an affair after testifying on August 17, 1998, pundits still could only speculate on the details as they had done since the initial allegations of wrongdoing. Starr himself had remained somewhat tightlipped on the investigation prior to the release of his report on September 11, 1998, but did speak frequently to reporters who waited for him outside courthouses and beside his driveway. In the impromptu interviews, the judicial Starr presented himself as the finder of fact by continually repeating the word "facts" and at one point comparing himself to *Dragnet*'s Sgt. Joe Friday, who wanted "just the facts ma'am."[172] However, others disagreed with such judicial/officialized characterizations of Starr.

Despite his judicial role, it seemed as if Starr had a political grudge against Clinton before and after the allegations of an affair with Lewinsky. In September 1996, Jim Lehrer directly asked Clinton if Starr was out to "get you and Mrs. Clinton?" to which Clinton tersely responded, "Isn't it obvious?"[173] Lewinsky's lawyers cried "prosecutorial abuse."[174] Even critics of Clinton thought that Starr was "trying to bring down the President."[175] Moreover, following the initial allegations in 1998, people who may have been "disgusted by what the President might have done were [more] disturbed by what it might take to catch him."[176]

Due to the apparent political vendetta, media reports constantly insinuated the comparison between Kenneth Starr's investigation of the Lewinsky scandal and the Star Chamber, which was an arbitrary and oppressive tribunal that operated in England during the late Middle Ages. Consequently, due to the lack of overt political accusations and the use of covert judicial investigations, President Clinton and the First Lady both claimed there was a political conspiracy against them in addition to the denials of wrongdoing—and many in the press corroborated their framing.

Clinton Participates in the Inquiry

Like Albert Fall in Teapot Dome and Richard Nixon in Watergate, Clinton responded to the allegations by continually acknowledging that he would cooperate with the investigation (whereas Reagan called for investigations). In his initial responses to the accusation on January 22, 1998, Clinton repeatedly used the word "cooperate" over a dozen times. Specifically, Clinton claimed, "We are doing our best to cooperate here, but we don't know much. . . . I think it's important to cooperate. I will cooperate."[177] Clinton repeated this sentiment later that day on NPR's *Roll Call*, in which he claimed, "I intend to cooperate with this inquiry."[178] Reagan learned the lesson from Nixon in Watergate, and Clinton took it one step further by making it clear he was participating.

However, Clinton did something that Nixon and Fall had not done during their scandals. Despite Starr's accusations that the president was uncooperative, Clinton not only claimed he would participate in the investigation but actually did so. For example, Clinton became the first president to testify under a prosecutor's subpoena; he testified to a grand jury twice—which no other president had ever done—although, given the subpoena, he did not have much of an option. Moreover, when appearing before the grand jury, he did not take his Fifth Amendment right to not incriminate himself. Similarly, Clinton, who months earlier invoked executive privilege to keep his staff from testifying, soon retracted that right on June 1, 1998, rather than appealing the decision, which might have seemed as if he was delaying the investigation.[179]

Clinton specifically claimed that he would participate in the inquiry just as he had in all the previous investigations. Such comments implied that the attacks were nothing new, and he would likewise go on with business as usual. This allowed Clinton to marginalize but not ignore the accusations by depicting them as separate from his presidential work, which he presented as his real focus.[180] If anything, Clinton claimed the accusations were matters of his private life and for his family.

Not only did Clinton participate, but members of his administration also cooperated to near unprecedented levels that eclipsed the Reagan administration's willingness in Iran-Contra. Unlike the attorney generals in Watergate and Teapot Dome, who were involved in the wrongdoing and subsequent cover-ups, Clinton's attorney general, Janet Reno, quickly authorized the investigation of Whitewater to expand into the Lewinsky relationship when she had the legitimate legal authority to decline Starr's request.[181] Hillary Clinton explained Reno's decision on NBC's *Today Show*: "She doesn't want to appear as though she's interfering with an investigation."[182] As such, Clinton and his administration's participation in the scandal inquiry were very different from Fall's and Nixon's. Reno, who authorized another office to investigate the charges, also played a different role than Reagan's attorney general, Edwin Meese, who conducted an investigation of Iran-Contra through his own office. As such, Reno showed that the Clinton administration was willing to avoid any notion of impropriety. In effect, the smoking gun and participation stages of the Clinton/Lewinsky scandal are prime counter-examples to Teapot Dome and Watergate. Clinton fully participated, and the judicial/officialized investigator was not seen as such.

IMPLICATIONS

The shift in scene in the wake of a smoking gun has implications for free speech, rhetoric, and democracy. These implications explore how the post–smoking gun discourse perpetuates a democratic ideology. The democratic ideology presented in this stage of the scandal is that partisan actors, who were previously attempting to officialize their attacks, have achieved some degree of success. By defining the scandal problem as that which revolves around incriminating evidence, the political actors allow for the creation of democratically sanctioned investigation bodies and the development of already existing committees into properly officialized overseers. As such, the attacks are no longer partisan attempts; rather, they are officialized fact-finding bodies to determine, in part, to what extent their earlier accusations are valid. In other words, the smoking gun allows what was partisan discourse to become fodder for institutionalized and sanctioned investigations to hold the accused accountable to the people and the democratic system.

Free Speech

Political speech is highly prioritized in democratic contexts. The people, free from having their voices abridged, are able to inform their government, be informed of what their government is doing, and criticize their government when necessary. When political actors transgress some boundary, there is a natural tendency for people to want to call them out. The stage of the scandal addressed in this chapter highlights that there is one group checking the other: Congress, the representatives of the people, is checking the executive branch. This characterization has its roots in the notion of the people disagreeing with the king, which led to an empowered citizenry in the New World. The shift from political to judicial scenes in the scandal is an enactment of the popular memory of John Peter Zenger and even Woodward and Bernstein. With the power of the printing press, everyday people can call out the king and bring him down with truth on their side.

While Congress represents the people, it is important to remember that the members of Congress are much more. First, members of Congress are members of the government. Journalists, as chapter 2 argued, may be too closely aligned with government sources, and members of Congress are the government. They are overseeing the very organization they are a part of. Consequently, when it comes to examining the checking value of free speech in the smoking gun and impeachment stages of the scandal, it is critical to recognize that members of Congress also represent much more than the people. They also represent their party.

When one party becomes seemingly overzealous with so-called witch hunts and fishing expeditions to attack the executive, the executive's party will rally to defend their own early in the scandal. Congressional oversight of the executive branch becomes secondary to defending the party and its members. However, with the discovery of the smoking gun, the priorities change. The need to defend the accused, who earlier had proclaimed the attack as partisan rhetoric, becomes no longer necessary. Allegiances to the party and its members (i.e., political relationships) now become secondary to the differences between Congress and the executive branch (i.e., relationships based in the Constitution). For example, one of Nixon's "staunchest supporters," Republican senator Robert Griffin, and one of his "chief defenders," Republican representative Charles Wiggins, both defected from Nixon once the smoking-gun tape was released.[183]

Consequently, there is the checking of the government, which is a romantic and idealistic notion, but the people and the press are not the ones checking the government in the later stages of scandal. The government is investigating itself. That investigation is motivated not necessarily by means of enacting oversight but for reasons that deal with the self-interest of the members of Congress: their party and then their branch of government. Thus, there is the appearance of a democracy, but in fact the government is regulating itself. This self-regulation is not for the benefit of the people and a healthy democracy but for the benefit of party and power.

Public Discourse

The shift in scene also has implications for the political rhetoric of the scandal. The primary implication is who controls the public discourse. The discovery of the smoking gun or even the existence of it reveals the strong possibility that the accused, who had long engaged in *apologia*, was misleading everyone. This puts the accused on the defensive. The smoking gun also reveals that those who were once characterized as partisan muckrakers were actually on the mark, whether they knew it or not. They were unsubstantiated attackers but now are justified in their pursuits.

This polar shift of sorts builds momentum for the transition from the political to the judicial scene. Those who were discounted as partisan opportunists are now seen to have been correct all along. It is hard for the public to now see the accusers, who were once considered political and are now seen as judicial, and characterize them as anything but engaging in officially sanctioned congressional oversight with critical evidence in hand or within reach. As such, members of Congress who attacked the executive were forced to legitimize and justify their criticisms, but now, with the discovery of critical evidence, it is the accused who must justify his innocence. The examples used here demonstrate that the accused cannot do that, as they did in fact engage in some transgression. With no option other than silence or temporary sanctuary in the courts, the accusers are now the ones driving the public discourse of the scandal.

More specifically, prior to the smoking gun, partisan discourse about the allegations presented an issue with two major positions: either the accusations are, in part or whole, valid or not. Any number of factors but primarily one's preexisting view of the accused determines the potential validity of the accusations. However, once there is a smoking gun or the existence of a smoking gun is known about, the public discourse begins to focus on the consequences of whether the accusations are valid or not. If the accusations are accurate, then properly sanctioned committees and individuals must take action. Inversely, if the attacks are inaccurate, the problem is solved, but this is rarely the case. In the public's thinking, if there was no basis, there would be no investigation. If the attacks are inaccurate, then the investigations need not find guilt but what happened, if anything. Consequently, the attackers are able to justify their pursuits.

The one outlier is President Reagan, who initiated the investigations and therefore controlled the public discourse to a greater degree than others. When the congressional investigations occurred, they sought the spotlight, not a smoking gun, for the basic details of the scandal were already public information. Moreover, when the congressional investigations concluded years later, the resulting reports mentioned what had already been known. Reagan, who initially fumbled the handling of the scandal, was able to regain control of the public discourse and made the most of pointing out his administration's own errors years before Congress repeated what Reagan and his staff had already uncovered. By initiating the investigation, Reagan was better able to control and define what the scandal was actually about. However, it should be noted that we still do not know the full role, whatever it might be, of Reagan and then vice president Bush in the scandal.

Democracy

The ideals of democracy are present in the move from the political to the judicial scene of the scandal. The separation of powers ensures that one branch is no more powerful than others; consequently, Congress can investigate executive transgressions. The result, as the next chapter addresses, is often the expunging of the wrongdoer or his or her atonement. However, we must be careful of the motivations of the overseers.

One of the major potential motivations for defining the scandal problem in such a way that Congress can enact legitimate oversight is due to power. The very partisan nature of scandal rhetoric prior to the discovery or release of a smoking gun, which later confirms the accusations, suggests that one of the motivations is based on a need for power. The accusatory discourse against the executive comes early on not from the president's own party but from the political opposition, which is not oversight but political opportunism.

After the release or discovery of a smoking gun, the accused's party often abandons all efforts to support their own party member in order to fulfill their congressional role. To be associated with one who transgresses some standard and then attempts some form of concealment is to be as guilty as the accused in the public eye. Consequently, we can see individuals who once defended the accused quickly change positions based on new information from a smoking gun.

Defending the accused based on party and then, with the smoking gun, shifting the attack to focus on the branch of government allows the attacker to maintain positive relations with the public. In Watergate, Republicans supported Nixon and Democrats attacked until the smoking gun was revealed. Public support shifted, as did Nixon's initial supporters. The desire of members of Congress to follow public disapproval in the wake of the smoking gun outweighs their allegiance to those in their party. To maintain support for Nixon was to jeopardize themselves. In the Clinton/Lewinsky scandal, investigators like Kenneth Starr were seen as heavily partisan, which compromised the officialization of the inquiry. Consequently, many Democrats supported Clinton throughout the scandal. In other words, Watergate was initially a battle between Republicans and Democrats, and then, with the smoking gun, a war between Congress and the president. The Clinton/Lewinsky scandal pitted Democrats against Republicans from start to finish. In short, democracy requires, referring back to Bellah's conceptualization, an evil individual (or, as the case is here, a political party or branch of government), and other political actors make calculated decisions so as not to be grouped with the evil and to maintain favorable relationships with the majority of the people, thereby perpetuating the ideology of democratic representation despite the clearly partisan purpose.

CONCLUSION

Not all scandals reach the level of full scandal. Some little things remain little things, and some become big things. The argument presented here is that the scandal rhetoric during and after the discovery of a smoking gun is what makes a minor scandal into a large scandal. The accusers are able to define the scandal problem in such a way that they can address it. By defining the scandal problem this way, the accusers are empowered to take action, which would be difficult or impossible if the scandal problem were defined differently. Specifically, members of Congress can investigate some transgression, which may or may not be illegal, and in the course of the inquiry, Congress can determine if those they are investigating have obstructed the investigation, which is a problem they and they alone can address. This is the notion of σκανδάλον, a trap for the enemy.

Once the victim falls in the trap, deofficialization ceases to be a worthwhile and effective strategy. The only refuge is in the courts, which often leads to silence and reluctant participation. The by-product of such a move is to confirm the legitimacy of the entire ordeal and unwittingly officialize the entire investigation. But the investigation is not necessarily about truth and justice. The idea of the people, the citizenry, checking the government is true, but the checking is enacted not by the people but by the people's representatives, who also represent other interests: their political party and, after the discovery of damning evidence, their legal role of checking the executive branch. The primary motivation, at least in the context of pre–smoking gun discourse, is power. In other words, partisan discourse or interbranch investigations in judicial and pseudo-judicial contexts, which are made possible by a smoking gun, give the context of governmental oversight, but that oversight comes from within, thereby causing concern regarding the possibility of true oversight.

Thus, while it is imperative to recognize that the smoking gun allows for a shift in scene—from political/substantive to judicial/procedural—the shift in scene does more than tell us how some scandals gain mythic status in American political culture. The shift in scene tells us how one group has defined the scandal in such a way as to exercise power in their own interests and not necessarily in the interest of the people and democracy.

Chapter Five

Political Martyrdom

While the journalists, sources, accusers, and accused all are the primary agents in the scandal, the same cannot be said of the people. Certainly, the electorate exercises its democratic right by voting. But during the conclusion of the scandal in which the accused might be removed from office, the people have very limited sovereignty due to the democratic norms established by the Founding Fathers and reinforced by politicians in scandal after scandal. During the scandal, the people may maintain some agency in government through the identification with any one of the primary scandal agents, who in turn identify with those who had come before. In the end, the people, who have the power of the vote to put people into office, do not necessarily have the ability or opportunity to remove people from office. Quite simply, the electorate does not have the direct means to take away power from those who engage in scandalous malfeasance.

In other words, the democratic scandal allows for and legitimizes the self-regulation of government by the accused resigning, confirmation of guilt, scapegoating, or vindication by the very system of which the accused is a part. The scandalous politician transforms himself from wrongdoer to redeemer and allows for a symbolic rebirth of executive leadership. The scandal, then, ostensibly portrays democracy in action, but in actuality it misleads the people into believing that they are agents and have agency throughout the scandal.

To make this argument, this chapter examines the agents and their agency and then that of "the people." Next, the chapter discusses the nature of governmental self-regulation in the political scandal. The chapter concludes with a review of the self-regulation demonstrated in each major scandal.

POLITICIANS: AGENTS AND AGENCY

The accused politician's actions characterize the democratic scandal as a tragedy. As Burke claimed, "tragedy deals in crime."[1] Furthermore, "tragedy subjects the erring [figure] to trial, finds him or her to be criminal, and demands condemnation and penance."[2] In tragedy, the two methods of purification and redemption that help a society come to terms with a scandal include scapegoating and mortification since, as Burke stated, "guilt needs redemption (which is to say, a Victim!)."[3]

Burke's notions of scapegoating and mortification, which is self-scapegoating, illustrate how the accused politician is his own redeemer. The scapegoat mechanism provides redemption to the scandalized politician by restoring the prescandal political prosperity via a process in which the group places its iniquities upon a scapegoat in the hope of curing the evil that has manifested itself in the society.[4] To accomplish scapegoating, there must first be a merger of the iniquities between the culture and the actual scapegoat, which occurs in the election of the (soon-to-be-accused) politician. After the initial allegations and the development of the scandal, shocking testimony and/or evidence removes most of the doubt of the accused politician's innocence and thereby creates a "discord" between the accused and the electorate.[5] The result of the discord is the necessity of a scapegoat who, with his malfeasance, is the "essence of evil."[6]

Due to the accused politician's sacrifice or mortification at the end of the scandal, the accused is the "hero" or principal agent in the scandal.[7] While there are numerous agents involved in the scandal, the accused political agent is of primary concern when discussing the implications.[8] This is because the accused serves as the "prime mover" for most of the actions of the other agents in the scandal.[9] Simply put, without Fall, Nixon, Reagan, or Clinton, there would be no charges or countercharges of political rhetoric, no investigation, and no scapegoating or mortification, for the misconduct occurred through their own actions or within their administration.

Conceptualizing the scandal as a rhetorical event, the hero's commanding public performance comes in his own sacrifice or some variation. The hero separates himself or, in the case of Iran-Contra, others from nonheroic agents as he "risk[s] himself and dies [so] that others may be vicariously heroic" through their identification with the scapegoat, which Burke labels the "tragic hero."[10] Prior to the tragic hero's sacrifice or mortification, some may consider the accused politician to be a "villain" (i.e., an antihero).[11] For example, many judge Nixon to be the most egregious president due to Watergate. During the scandal, however, he was widely supported for his advances in foreign policy. Only at the point when incontrovertible evidence, the smoking gun, is uncovered does the accused hero rightfully become an antihero.

Only after much reluctance, the antihero then sacrifices himself, or an appointed scapegoat, to restore the prescandal political prosperity, thereby becoming the tragic hero. Thus the scandalized politician's journey starts by denying accusations, which later become publicly confirmed, resulting in the accused becoming an antihero (i.e., the dishonest public servant). The scandal ends with the selfless politician (or scapegoat) ending his exile of silence and sacrificing himself to restore the political system, thereby becoming a tragic hero. Consequently, the antihero may bring forth goodness and not only serve as a villain, much in the way that, as Burke stated, "a bitter fountain may give forth sweet waters."[12]

To this point in the book, the accused is the primary political agent, but he is not the only one involved. Burke distinguishes three types of nonheroic agents: co-agent, counteragent, and superagent.[13] For the purposes here, the superagent is the most critical, for it demonstrates the origin of the accused's agency. This is where Bellah's notion of civil religion, introduced in chapter 1, helps. The Founding Fathers ordained America's civil religion, which is based in part on a Protestant Christian theme of rebirth. We can see this biblical archetype manifested in presidential term limits. The tradition of a two-term president is credited to George Washington, and all but Franklin Roosevelt have followed it. The motivation for self-imposed term limits (until formally established by the Twenty-Second Amendment) is to allow the periodic rebirth of power so that no one individual will ever preside over the United States for any extended period. In a democratic system in which there has been only one exception to a frequent and periodic rebirth of power, the power of change cannot be overcome easily, if at all. Thus the necessity for a rebirth of power can also be seen in the political scandal. The accused is not simply following in Washington's footsteps; the accused's political fate is being driven by the culmination of over two hundred years of giving up power.

Accordingly, the accused politician similarly self-sacrifices (or presents himself as self-sacrificing rather than suffering the consequences of his own actions) or appoints a scapegoat to allow the government investigators and/or press to enact symbolic oversight. This is in accordance with Blasi's checking value of free speech. In the face of incontrovertible testimony supported by evidence, the accused politician can no longer dismiss the allegations as simple political partisan rhetoric. The accused must submit to the officialized investigation. Certainly the accused politician can acquiesce reluctantly by using all the available legal means to protect himself as a public official, who has the same legal means that are available to any private citizen. But the position as public official exposes the accused politician to a level of inquiry and scrutiny to which the normal citizen is not exposed. Consequently, the slightest attempt to protect himself legally in the face of incontrovertible evidence is an attempt to subvert government investigators' necessary act of oversight, thus further exacerbating the charges of a cover-up. Therefore, the accused politician must sacrifice himself under the implicit directive, which is inherent in the identification of those who had served before.

The accused politician becomes a "victim because the person cannot avoid suffering his or her fate. The tragic victim's discourse is fruitless because he or she appeals to . . . a force that is, in essence, beyond persuasion. The tragic framework requires a sacrificial scapegoat."[14] The accused must relieve himself of his personal ambitions for the good of the public. Richard Nixon made it clear in his resignation address, at least as he saw things publicly, that he was giving up his personal ambitions for the betterment of the democratic system:

> In all the decisions I have made in my public life, I have always tried to do what was best for the Nation. . . . I would have preferred to carry through to the finish whatever the personal agony it would have involved, and my family unanimously urged me to do so. But the interest of the Nation must always come before any personal considerations. . . . I have never been a quitter. To leave office before my term is completed is abhorrent to every instinct in my body. But as President, I must put the interest of America first. To continue to fight through the months ahead for my personal vindication would almost totally absorb the time and attention of both the President and the Congress.

Nixon believed that he had great personal motivation to help the nation. His own mind and body told him to fight until success was achieved. However, he had to give himself up for the sake of the country. He wanted to stay but left so that others might continue. However, Nixon's attempt at martyrdom stands in stark contrast to the reality that he had lost the support of even his loyal defenders after the release of the tapes.

Similarly, Fall and Clinton offered a variation on the theme of giving themselves up personally for the sake of the need for symbolic oversight. Clinton claimed that the discussion of his personal life was something that "no American politician ever" has been forced to perform, and that he was the victim of the "politics of personal destruction."[15] Fall believed that his personal affairs unfairly became public fodder and insisted that the money was not a bribe from oilmen but a loan from longtime personal friends. Nevertheless, Fall, Nixon, and Clinton all relinquished their personal ambitions and privacy to perform the role of the tragic hero who self-sacrifices to achieve redemption and purification from political pollution for the good of the nation.

Reagan flipped the relationship between the official and the personal. That is, Reagan did not relinquish his personal ambitions in order to self-sacrifice; he actually suggested that doing so would be detrimental. Reagan stated, "A few months ago I told the American people I did not trade arms for hostages. My heart and my best intentions still tell me that's true, but the facts and the evidence tell me it is not."[16] Here, rather than be guided by the officialized findings, Reagan continued to value his personal views rather than self-sacrifice in the face of evidence that directly contradicted what he believed. While Fall, Nixon, and Clinton demonstrated the necessity of giving up the personal for the sake of the nation, Reagan's March 4, 1987, speech characterized him as a president whose great assets included his personal qualities. That is, Reagan suggested, "if anything . . . [he] was guilty of caring too much for the hostages and their families."[17] Therefore, if Reagan followed the path taken by Fall, Nixon, and Clinton, who all relinquished the personal for the official, he would be giving up one of his great strengths, which would not be beneficial to the nation.

Nevertheless, as Fall, Nixon, and Clinton demonstrate, the tragic hero performs the redemptive task against personal temptation and thus recreates a new unified image of the group in opposition to the alienating of the scapegoat. By resigning, the scapegoat not only removes the responsible individual but also reconstitutes himself from transgressor of public standards to victim (i.e., the tragic hero), resulting in the appearance of obedience to the maintenance of the democratic political order. Obedience brings forth the "promise of reward (as payment for service)" whereas disobedience brings forth "punishment as enforced payment for disservice."[18] But obedience and disobedience come together in one figure, which Burke exemplified as "Christ as Servant" (in the physical world) evolving into "Christ as King" (in the spiritual world).[19] The resigned public official, however, moves in the opposite direction, from sovereign to subject, which demonstrates the symbolic rebirth of power.

While this pattern from sovereign to subject is present in U.S. politics, it is in no way unique to American democracy. As Burke claimed, "mortification is basic to the pattern of governance" and is essential to the social order "as an extreme form of self-control," which arises not from external sources but from within in an attempt to deny disorder and embrace order.[20] Nevertheless, the accused politician's internal regulation has its roots and operates from external sources. Politicians who have served and self-sacrificed before are the external sources with whom the accused vicariously identifies. The accused, in other words, subsequently internalizes his predecessors' motivations and acts on them, thereby begetting the reward for allowing the symbolic rebirth of power.

For example, while obviously guilty of attempting to cover up the Watergate break-in, Nixon averted any official declaration of his guilt and any subsequent punishment via mortification through resignation. In turn, Nixon received the payment for his selfless service through Ford's presidential pardon, effectively making him innocent, for he can never be proven guilty by the normal governmental institutions. Ford denied that Nixon's pardon was a quid pro quo for the presidency, but his denial, much like all the political rhetoric during a scandal, did very little to stop speculation at the time. Nevertheless, Nixon's resignation then allowed the government to free itself from Watergate and move on. Nixon continued to seek absolution in his later "writings [that] were designed to achieve historical redemption."[21]

Clinton also sacrificed himself by actually admitting his lack of candor, which in part earned him an acquittal and soaring approval ratings.

Fall never admitted that he was bribed, but he did admit that concealing the source of the money was wrong. Fall's claims that the transactions were personal have their merits, but his role as government official required him to sacrifice himself beyond what is expected of the private citizen.[22] Fall's punishment for his disobedience was a year in jail and a fine.

Interestingly enough, Fall and Clinton admitted to lying, but Nixon never admitted any wrongdoing. Nixon's stated reason for resigning was that he had lost support and could no longer govern effectively. One might conclude that, despite his achievements in foreign policy, Nixon's punishment for not admitting his wrongdoing has resulted in his popular characterization as the most scandalous president in the history of the United States.

Reagan, as stated earlier, did not self-sacrifice, but that is not to say there was no sacrifice at all. Oliver North was prepared to be "the fall guy."[23] North's role as scapegoat was to divert attention away from Reagan who was under fire. North accomplished this as he was seen as responsible for the diversion of funds from Iran to the Contras. The diversion of funds was a detail that, as North stated, was "so dramatic, so sexy, that it might actually divert public attention away from other, even more important aspects of the story, such as what else the president and his top advisors had known about and approved."[24] Thus, the diversion was the diversion—the diversion of funds was the diversion of attention away from Reagan and others. The focus was on North as personality and not on his role as scapegoat. For example, "news coverage of the testimony of Colonel Oliver North emphasized the military man as a personality, while the most damaging and serious of his actions remain secrets kept from the American public."[25]

As the scapegoat, North would not only take responsibility but also the prestige and popularity that came with it. North's popularity came from "his individuality, his lonely fight against state bureaucracy," and his patriotic defense that he was "only acting in the best interests of [his] country and at the behest of superiors."[26] As such, in response to the military man's testimony on Capitol Hill, *Newsweek* proclaimed that "Ollie Takes the Hill" and that the "Fall Guy" had become "a Folk Hero."[27] The low-ranking military officer, who was virtually unknown, was rewarded with mythical, folklore-like status in American political culture for his seemingly reluctant acceptance as the responsible party in Iran-Contra.

"THE PEOPLE": AGENT AND AGENCY

Although members of the electorate are agents in democracy, the people do not reach such a full stature in the scandal. While the politician is the primary agent and the press is an apparent agent, the people are not full agents in the scandal as they are during elections. The people, however, appear to have agency through identifying with the press and the politicians. McGee posited that "the people" is a "mass illusion" constituted into "objective reality" by a leader who "is transformed by their [i.e., the people's] faith in him and his ideas into a Leader, an image or mirror of collective forces."[28] Consequently, in the remainder of this chapter when the people are constituted into being through rhetoric, they are referred to in quotation marks (i.e., "the people").

McGee's conceptualization of "the people" is evident in the democratic scandal. That is, the removal of the official from public office does not come from the voice of the people (i.e., the electorate). Rather the removal from office comes from, in terms of resignation, the very person who performed the malfeasance or, in terms of confirmation of wrongdoing, the very system to which the accused belonged.

In a scandal, the politicians and the press invoke "the people" by claiming that the citizens are a "sovereign power."[29] Clinton, for example, constructed "the people" in his August 17, 1998, address, in which he announced that he had testified before the independent counsel and admitted to lying. Although Clinton claimed the investigation was focusing on his private life, the speech demonstrated that "the people" have the right to know the truth of the allegations against him, since he was a public official. Scholars have noted that the "rhetorical-mythic construction of 'the people' was made obvious" in Clinton's speech.[30]

Similarly, Nixon invoked "the people" in his first Watergate speech by claiming that he, as mandated by the electorate, was responsible for the actions of his administration; as Nixon stated, "the man at the top must bear the responsibility." Moreover, in his second Watergate speech, Nixon expanded on the need for responsibility, the need "to provide a perspective on the issue for the American people." Reagan echoed this theme in his March 4, 1987, address by stating, "The power of the Presidency is often thought to reside within this Oval Office. Yet it doesn't rest here; it rests in you, the American people, and in your trust. Your trust is what gives a President his powers of leadership and his personal strength," and "I'm still the one who must answer to the American people for this behavior." While Reagan and Nixon accepted responsibility in a general sense, they failed to take responsibility for any of the specifics. Such rhetorical responsibility is not necessarily a legitimate claim to having committed any transgression. Rather, claiming responsibility generally implies that they did not participate in the particular transgressions but are selflessly and grandiosely taking the blame nonetheless.

In the Teapot Dome scandal, the press invoked the "the people" as the sovereign who needed to be informed; the *Denver Post*, which first uncovered Fall's newfound wealth, printed a front-page editorial in large red letters entitled "So the Public Might Know."[31]

While "the people" are not the primary agents in the scandal narrative as they are in democracy, some have argued that the people are present but passive agents.[32] As Bottici related, "there are narrators, on the one hand, and receivers or potential re-narrators, on the other—without there being any possibility of tracing any sharp division between the two."[33] It might patently appear that there is a sharp distinction between the press and the people in the scandal, but this is not the case. Certainly the public experiences the press as a primary agent; however, as chapter 2 argued, a critical examination reveals that the press—including investigative journalists—narrates the scandal based on government sources and information. Moreover, one may claim that "the people" enact their sovereign agency via blogging and letters to the editor, which does create a robust public discussion. Nevertheless, "the people's" relationship to the media is equivalent to the press's relationship with government sources and investigators.

It would seem then that the press, like "the people," is not a primary agent, for their comments are similar to the press's, which are based on government-supplied information. The press's role, as described in chapter 2, identifies them as "blood brothers" with the official government investigators, for the reporters use the information provided by the government.[34] All the case studies have shown that the government investigators are fully capable of contending with the political pollution. Consequently, the press, which relies on official sources and information, has the ability, by identification with government investigators, to appear to contend with the scandal itself. Moreover, the very public act of publishing the allegations creates a scene in which the people experience the press as a primary agent. "The people," however, perform no similar public act during the scandal.

While the electorate has the ability to give power in elections, the people do not have the means to take away power as a form of punishment for scandalous malfeasance. Because self-regulation during the scandal limits the people's power as agents, the expunging of the scandalous official is a disservice to democracy but not to government. As Burke claimed, "redemption needs a redeemer," and that redeemer is the government to which the scandal belongs, not the people.[35] In other words, the scandal narrative "encourages passivity on the part of the general public and unwise concentrations of power in ostensible redeemers. It betrays the ideals of democratic responsibility and denies the reliance on human intelligence that is basic to the democratic hope"; the democratic scandal narrative "instructs both the public and the superheroes [i.e., the politicians and press] how to respond to evil, and their actions are thought to become effective when properly ritualized."[36]

While "the people" are not primary agents, they nevertheless have agency in that the politicians constitute them into being, as does the press, which is aided by the government that provides information to report. "The people," like the press, have symbolic agency through their identification with the government.[37] The power of persuasion through identification has the power not only to unite us when we know we share interests but also to align our interests even when they are dissimilar but we see similarity. Burke continues:

> The concept of identification begins in a problem of this sort: Aristotle's rhetoric centers in the speaker's explicit designs with regard to the confronting of an audience. But there are also ways in which we spontaneously, intuitively, even unconsciously persuade ourselves.[38]

Here Burke builds upon identification in the face of dissimilarity by differentiating the old and new understandings of rhetoric. Aristotle's rhetoric dealt with the relationship between the self and other; Burke, however, understands rhetoric to be self-persuasion. But this self-encounter is not entirely solipsistic. We are persuaded to believe what we believe even in the face of dissimilarity by an ambiguous other with whom we identify. Briefly, Malinowski and Csapo claim that it is myth and, more important for the purposes here, its archetypes that frame and guide our self-persuasion. As a specific example, Frentz claimed in his analysis of Phaedrus that not only do Phaedrus and Socrates learn about themselves from one another, but the reader is guided "towards a heightened self-knowledge" by identifying with Phaedrus and Socrates.[39] This is true in the democratic scandal as well. We can learn a great deal about ourselves, the people, in the political scandal.

As politicians and members of the press identify with their cultural exemplary models from America's civil religion (i.e., Washington, Zenger, etc.), the people identify with those directly involved in the scandal itself (i.e., Fall, Paul Y. Anderson, Nixon, Woodward and Bernstein, Clinton, etc.), who ritually perform their obligation to demonstrate democracy in action. During Watergate, for instance, the Republican electorate was a co-agent with Nixon and counteragent to Woodward and Bernstein. During the Lewinsky affair, the Democrat public was a co-agent with Clinton and counteragent to Starr and the relentless media. The Teapot Dome electorate was a counteragent to most of the government, as both Republicans and Democrats were covered in oil.

Nevertheless, there are three heroes during the scandal with whom the people can identify. First, there is the politician as villain (i.e., the wrongdoer) turned tragic hero (i.e., the scapegoat or one who mortifies). Second, there is the press, and third, there is the accuser. The press and the accuser evolve from villain (i.e., disrupter of prosperity) to hero (i.e., overseer of government). When the press breaks a scandal and disrupts the political prosperity, there are two possible outcomes: government investigators, who often give the press the information, may confirm or disconfirm the allegations. If the allegations reported by the press are confirmed, the press has demonstrated its heroic role of symbolically providing oversight of the government, which began with the press's cultural archetype that originated with Zenger—even if the press only represented government information. If, on the other hand, the reports are disconfirmed or if a news outlet has given false information, the news agency, like the scandalized government, demonstrates its heroic ability to regulate itself. Likewise, the accused politician is heroic if he (e.g., Nixon) removes himself from public life; if he (e.g., Clinton) confronts and overcomes the allegations, thereby defending the office of presidency; if he (e.g., Fall) accepts his personal responsibility; or if he (e.g., Reagan) expunges the wrongdoer (e.g., North), who valiantly falls on his sword for his commander in chief and consequently becomes a national sensation for doing so.

Consequently, while the democratic scandal allows for the coexistence of numerous heroes, there is no separate universal villain. Some may claim that the politician sees the press as the enemy and vice versa; however, when the scandal is viewed through the eyes of the people, both politician and press have the ability to be heroes, albeit at different times in the scandal. Therefore, the politician, the press, and the people, through vicarious identification, all have the opportunity to be the hero at the end of a scandal. But again, the people's only power as actor in the scandal derives from their secondhand identifications with either the press or the public official.

Retuning to this project's framing of democracy as civil religion, we can offer an answer to one of the major questions of civil religion: "Does American civil religion need a satanic image in order to exist?"[40] The satanic archetype represents the tester of the righteous. In every scandal, there is a test of what is right, which comes from the politician, who transgresses a public standard only to right the wrong himself. The politician is both evildoer and purifier.[41] The evolution from violator to redeemer reaffirms the integrity of the democratic system, which, nevertheless, continues to produce innumerable scandals. Thus, while scandalous politicians come and go, the system remains the same due to the legitimizing authority of the scandal as it plays out from beginning to end.

The scandal narrative is powerful, and those who view it under a hermeneutic of suspicion may nevertheless find that it is an ineluctable force. As Burke claimed,

> Once you grasp the trend of the form, it invites participation regardless of the subject matter. Formally, you will find yourself swinging along with the succession of antithesis, even though you may not agree with the proposition that is being presented in this form. Or it may even be an opponent's proposition which you resent—yet for the duration of the statement itself you might "help him out" to the extent of yielding to the formal development, surrendering to its symmetry as such.[42]

The scandal is a tragedy built on ritual that demonstrates how "political processes are structured in ways that limit the scope of possible outcomes while organizing support for the government and reinforcing particular images of polity and society."[43] As such, democracy becomes an ideology operating in the scandal. From the 1920s and 1970s to the 1980s and 1990s and even into the present day, the scandal narrative ideally represented by Teapot Dome and Watergate manifests itself in America's unconsciousness through smaller scandals such as, most recently, Jack Abramoff, Randy Cunningham, Tom Delay, Conrad Burns, Bill Frist, "Scooter" Libby, and many, many more. It seems then that scandals will always occur, but there are alternative options that allow the people to become agents and rule with their own agency rather than acquiring it through identification.

SELF-REGULATION IN THE SCANDAL

In each scandal, there are two main transgressions. First, there is the actual wrongdoing—bribery, political espionage, or what have you. Second, and universal to nearly every political scandal, is the cover-up, which is often cast as the most serious offense.[44] Fall, Nixon, Reagan, and Clinton all appear to have known this. Fall claimed that his lies made a "bad matter very, very much worse."[45] Nixon was well aware that the lie is worse than the crime as he remarked about an alleged communist spy, "If you cover up, you're going to get caught."[46] Reagan was advised by his chief of staff, "The cover is blown here. We have got to go public with it, we have got to tell Congress, we have got to tell the American public exactly what went on so they are aware of it"; Reagan, however, out of concern for the hostages, agreed with his national security advisor, who stated, "We got to keep the lid on this, we got to deny it, we're endangering their lives."[47] Clinton's chief "scandal spinner" claimed, "Tell the truth. Tell it early. Tell it all. Tell it yourself. And if it's bad, tell it sooner."[48] Clinton seemed to take the advice only after he attempted to cover up his actions by simply lying and not involving anyone else except Lewinsky.

There is, nevertheless, a third latent transgression that the scandal exposes, one which at first may appear to be a virtue of government rather than a vice. The democratic scandal demonstrates the government's ability to self-regulate, which occurs by the accused resigning or being confirmed guilty by the very government of which he or she is a part. Since the government regulates itself, the people are not agents and consequently are denied their power to act as primary actors; however, the people identify with and are constituted by the scandal's primary agents and thereby appear to have only limited power. The scandal denies the power of the people to participate in any form in the punishment of the malfeasant public official. By bringing the question of ethics (i.e., "What should one do in the political realm?") to the political scandal, one might inquire into the possible scenarios for allowing members of the public to become agents in their own right.

There are two current possible means for giving the people rhetorical space to constitute themselves as primary agents in the scandal. First, assuming that presidential scandals continue in their present patterns, the people can take power away by voting for another in an election, but such an event would be extremely rare if it did ever happen. The reason for this rare occurrence is that the political party or government would ostensibly not allow the accused politician on the ballot and face unquestioned defeat at the polls, thereby giving the opposing party an easy victory. The threat of an accused politician losing an election is even more real in that those associated with the accused often receive retribution from the voters. The vice presidents of Nixon and Clinton were tarnished in their campaign efforts following the scandals.

Vice President Calvin Coolidge and Secretary of Commerce Herbert Hoover, who both served alongside Albert Fall in Harding's cabinet, managed to alleviate any voter vengeance by taking a hard stance against their former colleague.

The second means for creating a rhetorical space for the people is the use of polling, which journalists and politicians employ. Polling gives citizens a voice, albeit one shaped by the questions asked. The voice is also dependent on the few selected to represent the many. Moreover, the press expresses the voice that comes from the poll. Polling as an alternative to a self-regulating government has its roots in the Clinton/Lewinsky scandal. The Lewinsky scandal and the Clinton presidency in general were one of the most extensively polled political events and administrations to date.[49] It may even be argued that public opinion (as expressed in polling results) demonstrated that the people had agency in the Clinton/Lewinsky scandal. That is, polling results generally favored Clinton's job performance, showed that the public wanted a punishment but impeachment was too harsh, and that by December 1998 the public was "sick" of the scandal.[50] Regardless, the polls had little effect, thereby denying the people their status as full-fledged actors. As the *Washington Post* reported,

> Neither public opinion polls nor the strong Democratic showing in last month's midterm elections has prompted more than a trickle of House GOP members to come out against impeachment. For a White House that has lived on polls, the idea that the House would defy opinion so brazenly is both baffling and frightening.[51]

Ultimately, the Senate's final vote to acquit Clinton was based primarily on party lines, and public opinion appeared to have little impact on the vote.

The two options provide alternative means to abdication and self-regulation, but, as shown, they have their weaknesses. In terms of voting, the cure may be worse than the disease, and the expression of public opinion via polls is ineffective. It may seem, then, that the only option is to maintain the method of self-regulation, which produces results, but at a cost.

Thompson explained this cost by writing,

> The most perplexing kind of immorality in public office displays a more noble countenance. It is that committed, not in the interest of personal goals, but in the service of the public good. The problem of dirty hands concerns the political leader who for the sake of public purposes violates moral principles.[52]

In essence, the political leader who believes him- or herself to be doing what is right may simultaneously be doing what is wrong. This is as reassuring as it is frightening. The conscious acts of malfeasance (i.e., bribery, espionage, etc.) are recognized as being wrong, but the denial of the people's ability to enact their own agency (rather than acquiring it through identification) is the greatest threat to democracy while being a great virtue for the government.

The people can retain their sovereignty through direct participation in the scandal by appointing nonpolitical investigators from the electorate, but this option, like the others, may fall short of the ideal of democracy, as can be seen in each of the critical case studies.

MARTYRS

Teapot Dome

The last stage of Teapot Dome came with a number of court trials. Public interest was briefly piqued when the trials against Fall and Doheny commenced, but the public soon lost interest as there were eight cases to be heard, and with "so many different suits . . . confusion concerning them has sprung up in the popular mind."[53] Moreover, there was little novelty in the cases. In each trial the evidence presented was no different than that from the widely publicized Senate hearings.

The cases record a highly complex and bitterly contested litigation with both sides represented by some of the most brilliant advocates of their generation. For laymen, these cases represent democracy's boast that no man, rich or poor, of high or low estate, is above the law.[54] All the public wanted to know was, is Fall guilty? whereas the government was more specific and wanted to know if Fall conspired to defraud the government.[55]

The Senate investigation resulted in two civil cases and six criminal cases. In the civil cases, Doheny and Sinclair were tried separately for conspiring with Fall, who was indicted alongside them in both civil cases. Doheny and Fall's trial started in October 1924; the verdict was appealed all the way to the Supreme Court, which, in February 1927, agreed with the previous decisions that the two conspired to defraud the United States. Sinclair and Fall's trial started in March 1925; using much the same evidence as the previous case, Sinclair and Fall were found not guilty. The government appealed, and the decision was overturned, which the Supreme Court agreed with in October 1927. After nearly six years since Fall leased the oil lands to Doheny and Sinclair, the United States once again had control of their property.

Fall, Sinclair, and Doheny were all expected to be found guilty in the criminal cases as they were in the civil cases.[56] The criminal cases, however, took a different turn. The first case was against Doheny and Fall. The trial started in late November 1926; the jury found them not guilty of defrauding the United States in mid-December 1926. The "public discouragedly predicted that the other indictments would be dismissed."[57] The second trial was against Sinclair and Fall for the same charge; the trial was soon declared a mistrial because Sinclair had hired detectives to spy on the jurors. Paul Y. Anderson equated this "sensational halt" to a curtain falling on an unfinished play.[58] The show, nevertheless, continued.

The third trial was against Sinclair for contempt of court and for refusing to answer the Senate investigation's questions; Sinclair was later found guilty and sentenced to nine months, and the Supreme Court eventually agreed with the lower courts. The fourth was a retrial of Sinclair for bribery; the trial began on April 10 and ended on April 28, 1928. The jury found him not guilty in less than two hours. Some newspapers "satirically commented that the jurors were the only people thus far in the long-drawn-out scandals who had been locked up."[59]

The fifth trial was against Fall for accepting a bribe. The trial started on October 7, 1929, and ended on October 25, 1929. Due to the conclusions of the previous trials, it was thought "Fall might escape trial."[60] But strangely Fall was found guilty of accepting a bribe that Doheny was acquitted of giving in the sixth trial in which the jury only deliberated for fifteen minutes. The courtroom was shocked at the guilty verdict. Fall's family broke into tears, and one of Fall's attorneys fainted and fell to the floor. Fall was sentenced to one year in jail and a fine of $100,000, which he could not afford. Moreover, years later in 1935, Doheny would evict Fall from his home since he had not repaid the "loan," which was adjudicated as a "bribe."[61] Fall appealed to the Supreme Court, which refused to hear his case. Fall even applied for a presidential pardon from Herbert Hoover, whom he served alongside in Harding's cabinet.

Fall was found guilty but "broke the silence that [had] been his policy since the Senate investigations that led up to the criminal and civil cases. . . . His statement was a declaration of innocence . . . [that] the verdict of the jury was an 'astonishment' to him."[62] On July 21, 1931, Fall entered prison and spent most of his time in the institution's hospital due to his ill health until he was released on May 9, 1932, which brought a close to the story of the Teapot Dome scandal. The system had worked. The scandalous public official was punished.

Watergate

While Teapot Dome had a long series of events to bring the scandal to an end, Watergate ended very quickly following the release of the smoking gun. On August 5, 1974, eleven days after the Supreme Court ordered Nixon to turn over the actual audiotapes, Nixon released the smoking gun conversations, which proved he knew of the break-in and participated in the cover-up. With this, Nixon had lost the support of the Republican Party. The eleven Republicans on the House Judiciary Committee who voted earlier against impeachment rescinded their votes, and it was clear Nixon would be impeached.

Three days after releasing the smoking gun, President Nixon declared, "I shall resign the Presidency, effective at noon tomorrow," August 9, and that Vice President Ford would become president. With his resignation, Nixon moved from public official to private citizen. However, less than a month after taking office, Gerald Ford pardoned the former president, thereby ensuring that Nixon would never be brought back into the official inquiry. While speculation and uncertainty about what happened and who was involved continues, the Watergate scandal was effectively over.

By resigning, Nixon had avoided all external oversight. Cemented with the pardon, all the investigations and trails were over. In the end, the man who ascended from House minority leader to vice president to president pardoned Nixon, which Democrats soon would call scandalous.[63] After becoming president, Gerald Ford delivered his inaugural address without the traditional rhetorical ruffles and flourishes. In his brief speech, he stated, "My fellow Americans, our long national nightmare is over." No other phrase better highlights the dystopian nature of events infamously known as Watergate.

The resignation distinguished Watergate from all other presidential scandals before and since. As Leonard Downie, an editor for the *Washington Post* who worked with Woodward and Bernstein, claimed, "We didn't really believe the president was going to resign. Most of us were dysfunctional the night that he resigned because the role which we had played."[64] Moreover, Nixon's secretary of defense, James Schlesinger, ordered top military generals not to act on any White House order without his approval in the days prior to Nixon's resignation due to the political instability at the time. Schlesinger feared Nixon might incite a war as a means to redirect attention away from the scandal. Also, the president's chief of staff directed Nixon's physician not to give him any sleeping pills or tranquilizers for fear of possible suicide. From this, Michael Schudson writes, "if the president's closest aides wondered about his stability, it is no surprise that people elsewhere grew fearful."[65] Evans and Myers summarize the conclusion of Watergate: "No one in the Nixon gang would have foreseen the eventual results of the Watergate break-in but it required no great insight to realize that all the elements of a juicy scandal were present—particularly in an election year."[66] However, Nixon's gang acted outside the norms and laws, and Nixon avoided punishment in much the same manner.

Iran-Contra

In response to Attorney General Meese's initial investigation, Reagan announced that Vice Adm. John Poindexter had resigned and his assistant, Lt. Col. Oliver North, had been fired. The accused, who, as it seemed, was Oliver North, boldly stood up and accepted responsibility for the scandal. North proudly and unapologetically claimed that yes he did lie to Congress, because, quite simply, that was the nature of business at the National Security Council (NSC).

A relatively low-ranking military officer, Oliver North was seen as the fall guy. As opposed to John Dean, who refused to be Nixon's scapegoat in Watergate, North was "defined by the media as the individual most responsible for the entire Iran-Contra scandal" even before his congressional testimony.[67] North's role was to divert attention away from the involvement of high-ranking members of the administration.[68] Thus, in Iran-Contra, the cover-up was not enacted via denials and dismissal of allegations; it was North himself who was the cover-up. North and the independent counsel's report would later suggest that the diversion of funds was the diversion; in other words, the focus of the investigations on what actually happened in the scandal kept the focus off of who was actually involved in the scandal.[69] Consequently, North himself was the diversion.

While the basic plot of Iran-Contra became known relatively quickly compared to the other scandals, major details still remain uncertain.[70] One of the details includes who was responsible for the scandal. In Iran-Contra, responsibility "was passed around like a live coal from hand to hand, now resting with one player, [then] with another."[71] Responsibility evaded high-level officials, such as President Ronald Reagan, Vice President George Bush, and the secretaries of state and defense. What accusations Reagan faced he responded to by claiming he was uncertain about what had happened or that he simply did not remember. Reagan repeatedly stated that he could not recall having approved or even having seen the entire Iran-Contra plan. For example, Reagan stated,

> I'm having some trouble remembering that . . . but then I want to tell you that there were so many things going on, so many reports, and some of this was during the time that I was laid up in the hospital, and so forth. I don't recall ever anything being suggested in the line of ransom. I do know that we were constantly receiving ideas and exploring ways in which we could try to get our hostages back. . . . But it is possible that what we were talking about was the use of money to pay people . . . who could effect a rescue of our people and I have never thought of that as ransom. . . . There was an awful lot going on and it's awful easy to be a little short of memory.[72]

Such statements, however, became problematic after testimony in the congressional investigations pointed to the idea that Reagan did in fact know about the Iran-Contra plan. Reagan did an about-face when he later claimed, "I've known what's going on there, as a matter of fact, for quite a long time now, a matter of years"; Reagan further claimed that funding the Contras "was my idea to begin with."[73]

Reagan's apparent forgetfulness was contextualized by the opportunistic memory lapses of his aides. In the congressional hearings, Sen. Mitchell lamented that NSC director Bud McFarlane's "apparent frankness was marred by bouts of amnesia."[74] Moreover, Adm. Poindexter, who took ultimate responsibility by claiming that he insulated Reagan with plausible deniability, was often forgetful himself. Poindexter repeatedly claimed, "I don't know" or "I don't recall," 184 times in five days of testimony.[75] Poindexter's constant forgetfulness did not convince and angered many congressional investigators, who pointed to Poindexter's naval medical reports that indicated he had a "photographic memory" and was constantly lauded for his "retentive memory."[76] Although some speculate that Reagan's postpresidential health might explain his forgetfulness, at the time numerous polls found that Reagan and his aides' memory lapses were seen as deception. Nevertheless, Reagan, who did not regain his prescandal approval ratings, finished his term with the highest approval rating of any president in forty years.[77]

The scandal affected Bush, but he too was able to dodge any serious damage. As vice president, Bush claimed he was "out of the loop."[78] However, on November 5, Vice President Bush wrote in his diary, "I'm one of the few people that fully know the details, and there is a lot of flack and misinformation out there. It is not a subject we can talk about."[79] After succeeding Reagan, President Bush then avoided further damage when indictments were handed down on October 30, 1992, just days before the presidential election. Furthermore, the potential disclosures from the upcoming trial of Secretary of Defense Caspar Weinberger worried Bush. With concerns that his complicity might be revealed and having lost the 1992 election, Bush granted pardons to Weinberger as well as the others convicted in relation to Iran-Contra on Christmas afternoon when few would be paying attention to the news. Walsh responded, "The pardons in themselves perfect[ed] the cover up."[80] The *New York Times* stated that the editorials seem to suggest that Bush "pardoned himself."[81]

The tremendous amount of attention on North as he battled the investigators meant that there was less attention spent on the culpability of Reagan or others. Thus, the Iran-Contra scandal, as it was publicly experienced, was not about high-level malfeasance and disrespect for the letter and spirit of the law. Rather the scandal was the story about how a low-level solider was willing to take a metaphoric bullet for his commander in chief and became a national hero for doing so. As such, the congressional investigation, which began after North's dismissal, was not necessarily a fact-finding body but a showdown between the large, unwieldy Washington bureaucracy and a simple, boots-on-the-ground marine.

Clinton/Lewinsky

On September 9, 1998, Kenneth Starr submitted his official report to Congress, which then released the report to the public and to the White House two days later.[82] The Starr report outlined eleven possible grounds for impeachment, and many newspapers reprinted selections of or the entire independent counsel's 453-page report the following day. Although the grounds for impeachment were expected, few anticipated one element: the graphic nature of the report. As the *Washington Post* claimed, the report was perhaps the biggest such undertaking since the 1974 release of Richard M. Nixon's Oval Office tapes, whose salty language was often replaced by the phrase "expletive deleted." That bit of self-restraint seemed almost quaint compared to the lurid passages concerning oral sex and phone sex between Clinton and Monica S. Lewinsky, which ordinarily would be deemed unfit to print.[83]

When news outlets printed or reported sections of the report, they had to offer disclaimers mentioning the inappropriateness of the government's report for children and some adults.[84] Bob Woodward called it "the most detailed pornographic government report in history."[85] One editorialist called it the "dirtiest paperback ever to top the best-seller list."[86]

The report was shocking for its graphic detail, not for its damning evidence. Clinton had already spoken publicly about his testimony on August 17. He admitted in a brief four-and-a-half-minute speech that he had a relationship with Lewinsky and that he had misled the American public. Clinton called the relationship "wrong" and claimed that he committed "a critical lapse in judgment and a personal failure."[87] Clinton then shifted gears. He issued the directive to "stop the pursuit of personal destruction . . . and get on with our national life" and attacked the investigation.[88] The inevitable avalanche of polls that followed became the focus for endless media commentary. The basic outcome of the polls showed that the public thought Clinton could have been more apologetic and less critical of Starr.[89]

After the release of the Starr report, Clinton once again addressed the situation. But this time he presumably kept in mind the results of the opinions poll from his August speech. Speaking at the White House Prayer Breakfast, he stated, "I agree with those who have said in my first statement after I testified I was not contrite enough. I don't think there is a fancy way to say that I have sinned."[90] Clinton claimed that the sorrow he felt was "genuine" and that he had asked for forgiveness from his friends, family, staff, cabinet, Lewinsky as well as her family, and the American people. He expressed "genuine repentance" with "determination to change and to repair breaches of my own making." Clinton continued that it was time to move on to healing for both him and the country. In these two speeches, Clinton had done something that Fall, Nixon, and Reagan had not done. Clinton admitted he did wrong. In addition, Clinton said, "I'm sorry," days earlier for his actions.[91]

The investigation of the scandal resulted in Clinton's impeachment. The partisan atmosphere was in full effect. The inquiry into impeachment was held in the House Judiciary Committee, which was the most partisan committee in the House of Representatives. Despite the bickering, the House impeached the president on December 19, 1998. Nearly a month later, the Senate trial began. The defense agreed with the prosecutors that Clinton had done wrong, but they also argued that the president had not violated any public trust.

The four articles of impeachment mirrored the stages of the scandal narrative. Clinton was accused of failing to publicize his misconduct and of reluctantly participating, which delayed the investigation. Thus, there were two indictments for providing false information and one for attempting to delay justice. While Clinton arguably committed these actions, they were not as egregious as the presidents' actions in Teapot Dome or Watergate. Clinton did lie, but he eventually told the truth. Clinton did use strategies available to him to delay the inquiry, but he eventually conceded. Consequently, these indictments, as well as the fourth (for bringing disrepute to the office of the presidency), were voted down, and Clinton, although impeached, was acquitted of all charges.

While the impeachment "trial" followed the auspices of a judicial court, the proceedings were considered to be in the "political realm," as they occurred in the Senate.[92] This was confirmed by the votes. No Democrat voted guilty on the charge of perjury or on obstruction of justice. The public, as throughout the scandal and despite the constant media attention, had little interest in the trial, which marked a stark difference between Clinton's and Nixon's scandals. Whereas the public anxiously tuned in to the day-by-day coverage of the Watergate hearings in the summer of 1973, the Clinton impeachment proceedings in the winter of 1998 were cold. Most of the cable networks (e.g., CNN, MSNBC, and C-SPAN) all planned to devote time to Clinton's impeachment, but ABC, NBC, and CBS broadcast the impeachment votes, the occasional breaking news from Baghdad, and what the viewers mostly preferred: soap operas.[93] Moreover, there were two million viewers of CNN's coverage of the acquittal. Twice as many tuned in to professional wrestling a few channels away.[94] Most of the public stopped paying attention to the issue after Clinton's full confession.

Those who did watch did not seem to care. Days after being impeached, Clinton's approval rating hit an all-time high of 73 percent. Clinton's lowest approval ratings hovered around 50 percent and came only during the initial publicity of misconduct in January 1998.[95] A majority of Americans believed that Clinton did not deserve to be impeached for his actions. Many deplored his personal actions but were happy with his public leadership. If the public was unhappy with anyone, it was Kenneth Starr.

IMPLICATIONS

The concluding stages of a scandal have several implications for understanding how the scandal in American politics perpetuates a democratic ideology.

Specifically, the conclusion of the scandal perpetuates a democratic ideology in that democracy is saved by the apparent selflessness of the accused giving up his or her personal ambitions and goals for the greater good of democracy. This is the political-cultural depiction of the dying and rising savior archetype. The accused dies a political death so that he may save democracy. This political martyrdom is created through the accused's own actions; the voice of the people takes a subordinate position to the self-regulating government. We the people only need to sit back and relax as the very system that creates the problem solves the problem.

Ascending to the presidency is a feat that only a very few individuals have accomplished; consequently it is a very prestigious, powerful, and coveted position. To give it up is a great sacrifice. The magnitude of the sacrifice matches the magnitude of that for which the sacrifice is made: democracy is, in abstract and practical terms, highly valued. The end of a scandal does not always point to punishment; it points to the demonstration of a self-regulating government and the health of a democracy, or so it seems.

Free Speech

The First Amendment serves many purposes, but the focus on free speech in this book has been on the checking value. There are other important aspects of free speech too, though. The voice of the electorate is a clear example. One of the great hallmarks of a democracy is that the voice of the people, actual voting citizens, can empower a fellow citizen to govern. One of the other great hallmarks is the ability of the electorate to influence and, if necessary, criticize those who have been empowered. The resignation of the accused effectively silences criticism, for the source of the transgression has been removed and is no longer a threat to the institution he or she is a part of and to the larger democratic system. The evil has been expunged.

Yet there is an imbalance. The voice of the people can elevate fellow citizens to powerful positions, but the voice of the people cannot rescind that elevation—at least in the cases presented here. States have recall elections in which, after a sufficient number of voter signatures have been collected through a petition process, a state politician or official can be made to run again in a special election before the expiration of his or her term; however, the U.S. Constitution does not provide for a federal recall process. Nevertheless, a recall election does not necessarily provide for the checking of the official. Let us not forget that Reagan and Nixon won their prescandal elections with significant landslides. A politician's popularity could potentially be enough to weather a scandal. Clinton, for example, ended his time in office with high approval ratings.

However, the heir apparent of each accused president suffered on account of his predecessors. Gerald Ford, who became president and never faced the voters outside of Michigan until he was roundly defeated by Jimmy Carter; George H. W. Bush, who was out of the loop publicly but was well aware of the situation privately; and Al Gore, who lost a bitterly contested election in 2000—all suffered to some degree by the votes of the people. However, the reasons for their lack of success were not primarily due to the scandal of their predecessor. One might argue that Gerald Ford lost the 1976 election not due to Watergate but because of his pardon of Nixon, which was scandalous in its own right, at least at the time. Many initially believed the pardon was a quid pro quo for the presidency; however, as time has passed, so have the scandalous perceptions of the pardon. Many, including Bob Woodward, now agree that the pardon was the right and courageous thing to do.[96]

This implication is not to suggest that a scandal-tainted politician must or should stay in office only to be potentially expunged at the next election to ensure that the voice of the people is heard. There are two primary concerns with such a suggestion. First, in the examples discussed here, all of the presidents were on their second and final term as president—they would never have been in another election. Albert Fall had already left public office and never faced the voters in becoming the secretary of the interior, as President Harding appointed him. Second, and most important, is that the value of people checking their government officials is not greater than the value of removing the offending person in a timely manner. The greater harm with the potential for causing further damage is the offender staying in office, not in lacking the ability to express one's views to remove the person from office.

Moreover, the people can still voice their opinions through various platforms such as public meetings, letters to the editor, online postings, and even public opinion polls. But these methods are restrained as explained earlier in the chapter. Thus, the point remains the same: the voice of the people cannot directly remove a person from office due to federal-level scandals.

Public Discourse

The conclusion of the scandal, be it resignation, removal from office, or vindication, also has implications for the public discourse. The public discourse up until the conclusion of the scandal has focused on the public's right to know. The initial allegations via the journalists have focused on informing the public about an alleged transgression, the partisan discourse has focused on trying to substantiate or to disavow the allegations, and the smoking gun is the ultimate aspect of the scandal that informs the public about what actually happened in the scandal. The final chapter of the scandal, however, is a departure from the right-to-know narrative. The conclusion of the scandal is how the accused deals with the informed public. The event itself is over.

The public discourse focuses on the guilt of the individual. Fall was found guilty, Nixon resigned, Oliver North was fired, and Clinton was impeached but not convicted. This is what is talked about at the end of the scandal. It seems natural to focus on this aspect of the conclusion, for the punishment, self-inflicted or not, or vindication is the most recent event in the scandal. Such a focus comes at a price. What is not the focus of public discourse is what actually happened and the consequences of the transgression. In Teapot Dome, the remaining unanswered question was what happened to the ill-gotten money made by Sinclair and Doheny, who drilled on the oil lands for many years before the contracts were invalidated. In Watergate, the question remains as to Nixon's involvement in the actual break-in and the eighteen-and-a-half-minute erasure from the tape. If Nixon gave up the tapes that were his own undoing, then it is even more troubling what he presumably did not want others to know; this assumes that the technical experts were correct in determining that the eighteen-and-a-half-minute erasure was no accident.[97] In Iran-Contra, we do not know the full involvement of Reagan and Bush in breaking U.S. law. The exception is the Clinton/Lewinsky scandal, where we know exactly, in graphic detail, what happened; the issue here is that many did not want to know that level of detail or thought it was inappropriate for such a national-level conversation.

Another important implication for public discourse at the end of the scandal is the context of democracy. In all the scandals, public discourse by the accused is contextualized by democratic values. The accused is always able to maintain a commitment to democracy even in defeat. In the beginning the accused is committed to democracy in terms of doing the work of "the people." The discourse of the accused is to not focus on the allegations of wrongdoing but to get back to the business of the nation. Democratic values even contextualize the accused's silence when the scandal hits the courts. That is, those involved will remain silent publicly in order to preserve a fair trial. Democratic values contextualize the conclusion of the scandal as well. In the end, the accused is committed to leaving or accepting punishment so that democracy prevails, which will be discussed further in the next section. As such, democracy is always the rhetorical mover of discourse even as the accused is punished. This perpetuates a democratic ideology throughout the scandal.

By framing discourse in this manner, the scandal ends with the will of "the people" being done. In essence, the muckraking press, who publicized unbelievable accusations, upheld democracy; the partisan fighting, which seemed to distract from the business of government, upheld democracy; and the accused, who was found guilty either in court or via congressional investigation, upheld democracy by being convicted or resigning. If the accused is not guilty, there is a surge of support for the vindication. The will of "the people" is always spoken.

Framing public discourse around the punishment dramatically insulates the accused from any further criticism. The building momentum against the accused is all about the transgression and the cover-up. But by resigning or resolving the issue in the courts, the discourse no longer focuses on the wrongdoings, as the conviction, resignation, or abdication marks the end of the scandal. Consequently, there is no further opportunity for attacks or criticism. The scandal is over. There has been punishment, and to continue attacking is to return to the partisan nature of earlier scandal rhetoric, which has been concluded by the martyrdom of the accused. Consequently, with the evil removed, the topic of the evil in the public discourse fades relative to the earlier stages of the scandal. The concern here is that with the fading of the discourse and the perceived "beating a dead horse" partisan mentality, the remaining unresolved questions are difficult to answer or even address.

Democracy

By resigning or being expunged from the governance system, the accused has made a sacrifice for the sake of democratic ideals. That sacrifice can be very personal. In his resignation speech, Nixon's remarks were very personal. It was about him, his family, and his plans, but he, as he saw it, selflessly gave it all up so that the system could proceed. This act made him not guilty of any crime or of any cover-up. He had become an impediment to the system. By removing himself, he allowed the system to carry on. His actions were for the greater good. But serving the greater good is not always a selfless act. By removing himself rather than being removed, Nixon was in control of the situation, which he had lost when the tapes became public. Throughout the scandal, Nixon was in charge. The allegations came about at a time when he had won a landslide reelection; then it was up to political opponents, who had to fight the incumbent president, and it was he who had the tapes. Nixon had power until he lost it when he was forced to release the smoking gun. Yet, even in defeat, he took the sword and fell on it, robbing the democratic system of the opportunity to exercise punishment. Yet the system allows for resignation, and Nixon took the remaining time in power to control his own fate and sacrifice himself. But we must not forget that Gerald Ford had some control of Nixon's fate after his self-sacrifice.

Richard Nixon resigned, as he stated, for the good of the country, and his actions seemed to do just that. The partisan criticism that plagued Nixon's administration stopped nearly immediately with Ford's ascension to the presidency. The approval of the president (from Nixon to Ford) jumped fifty points in just a few days.

Clinton, Reagan, and Fall all sacrificed as well. Their sacrifices were not necessarily as personal as Nixon saw his own, regardless of his near complete lack of support and inevitable removal from office. Rather, their sacrifice was oriented toward the ends of democracy—toward letting the system work, regardless of whether the scandalous actions were contradictory to the ends of democracy. Despite their immoral, illegal, and questionable actions, each of the accused participated in the democratic system. This system not only allowed for the scandal to happen but also allowed for the scandal to be rectified. Each of the accused individuals participated fully in both sides of the system. This is not to say they participated fully or participated in good faith. Clinton's testimony was technically and legally accurate, but it was also evasive and questionable. Fall's public statements and courtroom antics seemed legitimate and questionable too. Publicly claiming he would speak in court and then refusing to do so, while feigning illness and then being legitimately ill, all speak to his participation, even if not full participation; he cooperated with the system and accepted the results. Reagan took control of the situation and was able to manage his scandal with far greater ability than Clinton, Nixon, and Fall by firing Oliver North and accepting the resignations of others. As a result, however, there are aspects of Iran-Contra that are still unknown. This is the case with Watergate (i.e., the eighteen-and-a-half-minute gap) and Teapot Dome (i.e., where all the profits went from Doheny and Sinclair's drilling of the government's oil).

The scandal serves as an "embodiment of enduring images of polity and society" by perpetuating an ideology of a democracy where the scandalous individual is his or her own redeemer, which subsequently denies "the people" an opportunity to be redeemed or serve redemption.[98] This is particularly evident in the Watergate example. With the impending investigation, President Nixon resigned and was pardoned by his vice president, Gerald Ford, who succeeded to the presidency. Thus the investigations and their findings were moot. Moreover, Ford became the only person in history to be vice president and president without ever being elected to those positions. Ford moved from House minority leader to vice president after Nixon's first vice president resigned, not surprisingly, over allegations of tax evasion and money laundering. Thus, scandals are certainly widespread, but the scandal gives the appearance that democracy is fully functioning, which undermines the dark, hidden reality of the elimination of the protagonist of the scandal.

CONCLUSION

There are numerous implications of the closing of the democratic scandal. Perhaps most significant, a democratic scandal allows for the self-regulation of government: when the accused is confirmed as guilty, resigns, or is removed, the democratic ideals of government are upheld. There was an evil, which has been identified and punished and/or removed from the system. The democratic ideal of the people participating, however, is absent.

When the agents in the scandal vicariously identify with the ideals of the Founding Fathers and all those who have followed in their footsteps, those ideals serve as an indirect, outer control over the actions of the accused politician, journalist, and, by extension, "the people." Thus, "the people" unconsciously persuade themselves to believe in their role as sovereign agents in democracy, as do the accused politicians, who are persuaded by their own vicarious identification to enact the symbolic rebirth of power. Subsequently, neither "the people" nor the politicians consciously aim to undermine core democratic principles. The people, politicians, and the press's actions are all unconsciously driven. However well-intended the actions, they nevertheless are detrimental.

Teapot Dome taught us to examine all politicians as government officials, not as people (who may be financially destitute and require money from friends); Watergate taught us that the nation is a country of laws, not of men; Iran-Contra demonstrated that we had learned a lesson about the severity of impeachment from Watergate; and the Clinton/Lewinsky scandal taught us that we should investigate crimes, not people. But, from another perspective, what we the people have become aware of is that the scandal serves not as a means to ensure the success of democracy but as a legitimizing narrative that we all ritually, albeit vicariously, perform to believe in the power of democracy—when in reality we reinforce the power of the government.

Chapter Six

Contemporary Issues and Scandals

People love talking about scandals. Whenever I mention my research on scandal, people inevitably raise a few smaller-scale and contemporary scandals in the news. Sometimes the conversation turns to "scandals" that would not be considered as such given this book's definition. These could be nonscandals or pseudoscandals. Nonscandals, as addressed in chapter 1, are events that could be popularly called scandals but fail to meet the scholarly definition. For example, there may be no substantive attempt at a cover-up that is different from the alleged wrongdoing. Pseudoscandals, which may also be commonly called scandals, are often driven by cynicism and derision and lack any real transgression or cover-up.[1] In the case of pseudoscandals, I always reply that not all mistakes and poor policy decisions are scandals. However, these conversations about nonscandals, pseudoscandals, and smaller and contemporary scandals have been fruitful.

Rather than simply dismissing points that can be made from congressional scandals, nonscandals (or pseudoscandals), and scandals from outside of politics, I include them here in the hopes that they can provide more insight into the patterns of American political scandal, the focus of this book. While the four critical cases are the yardstick by which all other scandals are measured, finer points of scandal can and should be addressed.

Accordingly, this chapter will examine the case of former U.S. representative Anthony Weiner, who was involved in a sexting scandal in which he sent lewd pictures of himself to a number of young women. Although it is not a presidential scandal, the case demonstrates the applicability of theory presented in earlier chapters to a wide range of political scandals.

The chapter then explores a number of other scandals and controversies to highlight variations on the themes presented in this book. They include the tabloid press in scandals, nuances of officialization, how cover-ups have gone digital, alternative means by which a scandal can conclude, and how self-regulation operates in nonpolitical scandals.

THE SEXTING SCANDAL

The political scandal begins in relative prosperity. The same could be said of Anthony Weiner's scandal in which he sent sexually explicit photos of himself to women and then attempted to conceal his transgression. In mid- to late July 2010, Rep. Anthony Weiner's private and professional life started getting serious, in a good way. He was married in a ceremony officiated over by none other than former president Bill Clinton. He gave an angry and impassioned one-and-a-half-minute speech on the importance of medical relief for the rescuers and victims of the September 11 attacks. The video of the speech quickly went viral. Due to his feisty firebrand style, which symbolized Democrats' frustrations with congressional Republicans, he soon earned a seat at several popular political news and talk shows. The representative had become nationally known. While Teapot Dome, Watergate, Iran-Contra, and Clinton/Lewinsky all began in a period of relative public prosperity, Weiner's sexting scandal began in a period of personal prosperity.

Unlike other scandals, the nature of the initial transgression was embarrassingly public. During a brief moment on Friday, May 27, 2011, a lewd photo of a man's lower half clad in boxer briefs appeared on Rep. Weiner's Twitter page. The image was sent to a twenty-one-year-old college student in Seattle. As quickly as the photo appeared, it was deleted.

The Press in Weiner's Scandal

The first reports of the sexting scandal appeared on a conservative news website run by Andrew Breitbart, who straddled the line between activist and journalist.[2] An anonymous Twitter user alerted Breitbart of the tweet. Less than an hour and a half later, the story was prominently displayed online. Breitbart had no government or inside sources. However, he did serve as a shaman in that he relayed one person's unshared vision to the rest of the world.

Breitbart knew that the accusations could be easily dismissed as a partisan attack on the now popular representative. Breitbart clearly leaned right politically, contrary to the New York City Democrat. However, Breitbart had a greater concern than partisan dismissals as he was no stranger to chicanery himself. He was involved in two large media controversies, both of which involved extensive editing of videos.

These controversies are worth noting for two reasons. First, the controversies are a further example of how the partisan nature of news is becoming a more prominent player in contemporary scandals. As the Clinton/Lewinsky scandal demonstrated, there is often a press scandal in the political scandal. Second, the nature of digital media has allowed for the corruption of the smoking gun and other incriminating evidence. The alteration of the Watergate tapes is clear in the eighteen and a half minutes of silence. The altering of the tapes by Breitbart is not so obvious. The unscrupulous editing was not discovered until after the evidence had significant and irreversible impact.

One controversy dealt with the nonprofit community organization ACORN, which was nonpartisan but supported social issues that generally aligned with the Democratic Party. Two conservative operatives secretly taped meetings with ACORN representatives. These recordings were then highly edited so as to falsely portray the organization as assisting the secret operatives with evading taxes, child prostitution, and human trafficking. The videos alarmed everyone, including Congress, which cut their funding. Even though the heavy use of editing was later discovered, the videos effectively brought down the forty-year-old organization.

The other controversy involved a U.S. Agriculture Department employee who was recorded speaking to the National Association for the Advancement of Colored People. The speech was heavily edited so as to depict the African American speaker as being prejudiced against whites. The employee, Shirley Sherrod, was condemned by President Obama and fired by the secretary of agriculture. After discovering that the tapes were heavily edited, Sherrod was offered another government job and numerous apologies but turned them down. She then sued Breitbart for defamation.

In an apparent attempt at redemption for these controversies, Breitbart released information about Weiner in a strategic manner. He released just a bit of information and withheld more damning evidence to show later that he had not hacked Weiner's Twitter page. By withholding additional non-Twitter-based evidence, Breitbart was later able to confirm that there were multiple instances of Weiner's impropriety across a variety of online platforms. Breitbart also gave some evidence to the more trusted ABC News, who then released that information.

Responding

Much like the other scandals discussed in this book, Weiner attempted to overcome the situation through implicit denials and transcendence. After deleting the photo, Weiner subsequently announced that he had been hacked and stated, "The wiener gags never get old, I guess."[3] In doing so, Rep. Weiner indirectly denied sending the photo and further dismissed the issue by putting the situation into the larger context of the innumerable jabs people have taken at him throughout his life based on his last name.

Weiner continued by saying that the photo and the growing number of questions was a distraction getting in the way of his taking care of his constituents. The distraction *apologia* is a classic response seen in many other scandals. Not surprisingly, the public and press did not readily accept such responses. In response to the disbelief, Weiner further substantiated the indirect denials and routine nature of the incident: "Look, this is a prank and not a terribly creative one. . . . I was hacked. It happens to people. You move on."[4] The pundits did not move on.

Officialization

At this point in the scandal, after the newsbreaks and after the initial rounds of *apologia*, there is typically partisan discourse where the attackers attempt to officialize their accusations. This did not happen in Weiner's scandal. But this is not to say there was no officialization whatsoever. Instead, it was the accused who engaged in officialization.

Weiner sought to officialize his own indirect denials and transcendent characterization of the actions as a prank by hiring a law firm to investigate the incident. By hiring lawyers to investigate, Weiner equated the incident with something serious enough to merit a lawyer who could look into the matter and then take whatever legal actions were necessary in the official context of the courts. However, this attempt at officialization was met with skepticism. Why would something that was described as just another jab at his name merit serious legal scrutiny? Furthermore, why was law enforcement not involved if the situation possibly involved criminal actions? Weiner's answer was that he did not want to waste federal resources on an investigation.

This technique is telling based on the earlier examinations of Watergate, Iran-Contra, and Clinton/Lewinsky. Nixon sought to minimize the disclosure of his involvement in the cover-up by assigning John Dean to write up a report. Reagan also got his own administration in on his investigation. Clinton's attorney general outsourced the investigation to an independent individual. Weiner obviously hired the law firm, if only symbolically, to control the results of any investigation, for the lawyer answers to his client, whereas the police would most likely uncover what really happened, thereby sealing Weiner's fate.

Partisan Discourse?

There was relatively little partisan discourse in Weiner's scandal, and there are a few reasons for this. First, the scandal was rather short. It was only ten days from the initial tweet to Weiner's admission of wrongdoing. Such brevity did not allow for much public discourse. Second, much of the discourse was from Weiner himself, and he did not appear in public during half of the short scandal. Pundits, however, speculated nonstop. Third, the impropriety of the event spoke for itself. No substantive commentary was needed. Fourth, the initial photo served as one of the smoking guns. Weiner could not deny that the picture was of him. The pundits were clearly skeptical at anything that resembled a denial.

The atmosphere of skepticism against Weiner only grew when he claimed that he did not know whether the photos were of him or not. In an interview, Weiner stated, "You know, I can't say with certitude. My system was hacked. Pictures can be manipulated. Pictures can be dropped in and inserted."[5] Perhaps this statement was motivated by the fact that Breitbart, who was no stranger to digital and video manipulation, released the pictures. It was worth a try; yet Weiner's uncertainty was not viable. It is difficult to believe a person does not recognize their very own body. After the interview, Weiner did not appear in public for a few days.

As the scandal progressed, Republicans were relatively silent. A few called for Weiner's resignation. However, given the clear impropriety of his actions, the scandal did not need their help. If anything, it was best to let the ordeal play out as long as possible to shame Weiner and his party.

Early on, some Democrats said that his future was up to him and his constituents. They later changed their tune after his admission of guilt. However, one representative supported Weiner. Charles Rangel believed that Weiner would be fine if the press would leave him alone. Rangel said that Weiner was not messing around with "little boys" and was not "going into men's rooms with broad stances."[6]

Each of Rangel's examples had a decidedly partisan point. Both came from a Republican sex scandal: Rep. Mark Foley's sexually suggestive communications with male teenage pages in 2006 and Sen. Larry Craig's attempted solicitation of sex in a men's restroom at an airport in 2007. Craig claimed he was not signaling a person, who turned out to be a police officer, with his foot; he just had a wide stance in the stall.

Admission, Apology, and Alternative Resolution

Weiner reappeared on Monday, June 6, 2011, after Breitbart released more photos from another woman. The man in these photos was clearly Weiner, who called a press conference later that day. He finally acknowledged that he had sent the photos and that he had inappropriate conversations with women before and during his marriage. He apologized and said that he would not resign, and Democratic leaders begin to express disappointment and embarrassment.

Perhaps he believed that acknowledging his wrongdoing was the blood the newshounds wanted.

On the same day, the Democratic Speaker of the House, Nancy Pelosi, called for an investigation to see if he used any government resources. Typically, officialization is when one party or group attempts to legitimize their accusations. However, Pelosi's request was not officialization for two reasons. First, Democrats were in a tough position. They wanted to support their own yet not endorse Weiner's actions. Calling for an investigation to determine if someone used government resources is limited in scope compared to the other potential areas for scrutiny in the unfolding scandal. Second and relatedly, Pelosi was not attacking Weiner. Her actions seemed motivated to protect the legitimacy of her position as Speaker.

After his admission, Weiner again stepped out of the public spotlight until his wife, who was confirmed to be pregnant during the week the scandal broke, returned from her trip in which she was an aide to Hillary Clinton. Weiner then sought to end the scandal by seeking a leave from Congress to receive treatment. This strategy is unique compared to other scandals discussed in this book. Weiner sought to remove the wrongdoer, himself, temporarily, which offered the opportunity to come back once he had redeemed himself. However, more photos were released the following day. In the wake of the new disclosure, President Obama and Speaker of the House Pelosi suggested resignation. Finally, Weiner resigned from Congress on June 16, 2011. That brought the scandal to a close, or so it seemed.

Attempted Redemption and Resurrection

Weiner was out of office for almost two years when he announced his candidacy for New York City mayor on May 23, 2013. He evidently believed that he had paid the price for his indiscretions and it was time for political resurrection. At the very least, he thought it was time the voters had the chance to give him a second shot. His campaign ads depicted him as a responsible family man who had gone through some tough times and learned some tough lessons.

In an attempt to be completely clean, Weiner acknowledged during a radio interview that there might be more photos and online chats that might emerge.[7] Nearly a month after he announced his campaign, new disclosures rocked his campaign. Weiner now said, "I said that other texts and photos were likely to come out and today they have."[8] Though he was forthright about the possibility of more disclosures, this offered no credibility compared to his actions.

This book argues that at the end of the scandal, the accused's punishment can serve as a means to save democracy. This was not the case for Weiner, who attempted political resurrection without having been fully or even partly redeemed. Weiner would lose the Democratic mayoral primary with only 5 percent of the vote. But this is not to say that political redemption is unachievable. For example, South Carolina governor Mark Sanford disappeared for nearly a week in the summer of 2009. His staff said he was hiking the Appalachian Trial, but he was having an extramarital affair in Argentina. He resigned as chair of the Republican Governor's Association but insisted that he would not resign. The state legislature began impeachment proceedings, but timing served as a constraint. Sanford would be out of office due to term limits in less time than it would take to impeach him; consequently, Sanford was censured after he left office in January 2011. Many had long speculated that Sanford was going to run for president in 2012, but the scandal stopped such plans. However, Sanford announced that he would run in the special election for the House of Representatives in late 2012, and he won the election in 2013. Weiner's and Sanford's scandals are not exactly comparable, but together they both demonstrate conditions that impede and allow for political resurrection and redemption.

The Critical Issues

The press was not reliant on government investigations for information in the Weiner scandal. Breitbart did rely on a nongovernmental source, but this does not assuage concerns of the press's role in scandals. Breitbart, as described above, was not above mixing activism in his journalistic reporting. To claim that he was simply reporting information is not enough to prove that he was fulfilling the checking role assigned to the press. The decision to publish the information was made quickly, deliberately, and strategically for a seemingly partisan purpose: to besmirch the rising Democratic star. Not every deleted tweet is newsworthy, but Breitbart apparently found Weiner's tweet to be worthy of publication. In Breitbart's defense, Weiner's tweet was not the typical deleted tweet, and the congressman's own actions did not hurt the journalist/activist's chance of success.

The public discourse during Weiner's scandal exhibited the notion of governmental self-regulation, thereby perpetuating a democratic ideology. That ideology is that "the people," who are rhetorically constructed into being, are in power. However, it is the accused who controls his own fate, and he did his best to do so given the unrolling evidence. First there was denial, then admission of wrongdoing, then a leave of absence, and ultimately resignation. Certainly, many tried to influence Weiner to resign, but they left that decision to him and his constituents. Moreover, those who did speak out did so in a very calculated way, which resulted in allowing Weiner to self-regulate himself to save democracy. That is, there was pressure, but no one was forcing him from office with any serious investigation. Those who urged resignation suggested what Weiner himself should do, not what should be done to him. In effect, they wanted him to self-sacrifice so as to protect them from having to wield the sword themselves.

Weiner-gate allows for an interesting insight into the nature of democracy amid a scandal. The Weiner scandal demonstrates, in essence, what can happen in the rare event when a politician, who was accused of some transgression, faces the voters again. As stated earlier in chapter 5, a political party may attempt to stop a tarnished politician from running again and thereby risking a potential loss to an opposing party. However, Weiner's election was a primary election, and he was running against fellow Democrats. After his initial entry, Weiner polled very high, but it was subsequent disclosures of indecent and lewd interactions that finally cost him the primary election. The voters seemed to understand that people make mistakes, but apparently they are able to forgive just a few. While there are a tremendous number of variables at play in an election, the idea of second chances gives some insight into why Weiner failed while Sanford succeeded. Weiner continually erred, whereas Sanford erred once.

VARIATIONS ON A THEME

There have been other smaller scandals and other controversies throughout the years. This section draws upon some more recent examples, which will help reinforce and point to subtle nuances in the scandal narrative presented in previous chapters.

Evolution of the Journalist and News Outlet

In chapter 2, the role of the journalist in scandal was covered, beginning with Teapot Dome. But the nature of the journalist has changed as a result of the tremendous evolution of journalism and media since that time. Some may even claim that there have been multiple major evolutions since then. The public of the 1920s received its news through the press. In the 1920s, television had not yet been invented, and radio was in its infancy; "newspapers and word-of-mouth were the major means of national communication."[9] It was "the press" composed of "chain-smoking, wise cracking reporters in rumpled raincoats" who delivered the news.[10] Some of these reporters engaged in the precursor of modern investigative journalism: muckraking.[11]

The idea of muckraking had disappeared by the time of Watergate, but the reporter was still seen as pounding the pavement in search of the truth.

One reason for this characterization is that there was intermittent television reporting early in Watergate. Television coverage virtually disappeared from October to January 1973, when one of the first trials began. Then, after covering the first of the trials, televised news coverage once again fell silent for months. Not only did the television reporting ebb and flow; it lacked "'original' or 'investigative' reporting."[12] Even an NBC executive claimed Watergate was better suited for newspapers because "it's not visual and it's also very complicated."[13]

However, television news played a more significant role in Iran-Contra and Clinton/Lewinsky. During these scandals, the term "the media" conjured up images of "bright young men and women with blow-dried hair and perfect teeth" engaging in investigative reporting.[14] Not only were the television reporters attractive, but they were also available. The twenty-four-hour news media guaranteed that the latest information was known immediately. However, the immediacy of television did not compare to the new media that emerged in the 1990s and has grown exponentially ever since.

It is no longer the newspaper reporter or television correspondent but the Internet reporter who has taken over as the breaker of scandal. The evolution has continued to this day. Access to the technology and knowledge required to spread the word of some politician's conduct is easily available. A simple video camera, which many carry in their pockets all day every day, is all that is required. Unlike Drudge, no webpage is needed. Simply upload a video to YouTube and send the link out, and a scandal can be born. Those who break the scandal are no longer the dogged professional journalist engaged in shoe-leather reporting. This classic journalistic archetype has evolved and opened up to include the everyday citizen and less reputable sources. But we must be careful not to let our opinions of the source override the value of the news. Let us not forget that *Newsweek* was set to break the Clinton/Lewinsky scandal but delayed because of the personal nature of the story. The far less reputable *Drudge Report* has only benefited from quickly doing what *Newsweek* was reluctant to do. Breitbart, who had crossed the line of journalistic integrity, was careful not to do the same with Weiner.

One journalistic outlet with a negative reputation is the supermarket tabloid *National Enquirer*. The *Enquirer* has published stories that range from the domestic squabbles of celebrities and royalty to NASA astronauts making contact with space aliens. With such stories and the *Enquirer*'s policy of paying for information, which often leads to the publication of fabricated news, the *National Enquirer* is not very credible.

There have been times, however, when the supermarket tabloid was on the mark with political scandals. During the 1988 election, it was speculated that Democratic presidential candidate and frontrunner, Gary Hart, was having an affair. Hart challenged the media: "Follow me around. I don't care. I'm serious. If anybody wants to put a tail on me, go ahead. They'll be very bored."[15] Some journalists took him up on this dare and printed their findings of him with a much younger woman. Hart and his wife simply said there was no improper relationship with the woman. The *National Enquirer*, however, soon published a photo of the young woman sitting suggestively on his lap while holding his hand. Hart subsequently dropped out of the race.

During the 1996 election, the *National Enquirer* broke the story about Republican presidential candidate Bob Dole, who was running on a family values platform, having an affair in the late 1960s while married.[16] The Dole campaign replied in a carefully worded statement that attacked the *Enquirer* rather than responding to the truth of the statement.[17] A few other publications reported the allegations, but the story never went anywhere. Two years later, the winner of the 1996 election was caught in a sex scandal.

The *National Enquirer* also broke a scandal in the 2008 election. Democratic presidential candidate John Edwards had already admitted to having an affair with Rielle Hunter but denied being the father of her child. Initially, the mainstream media did not readily believe the *Enquirer*'s reports, which said that Edwards was the father. But eventually the *Enquirer* was vindicated as Edwards admitted to being the father. For their efforts, the *National Enquirer* was nominated for a Pulitzer Prize.

Many were shocked that a supermarket tabloid with a reputation for being wrong (despite the earlier examples stated here) and paying for information could merit such recognition. After all, the Pulitzer Prize is the most prestigious award there is for journalism. The *Enquirer* did not win the award, but the nomination was a victory in itself. The history of the *National Enquirer* and its record with sex scandals in U.S. politics shows us that scandals can be revealed by many questionable sources.

The evolution of the journalist and the news outlet tells us we should be careful consumers of the content of scandalous news reports in addition to being mindful of the source and the publication. One can very easily dismiss a news report based on the source whether that be the reporter or the publication. We no longer live in the age of a few large national newspapers and television stations. Lyndon Johnson had three televisions in the oval office so he could watch all the major networks. He would need many more today, and that does not even address the online news. There are a myriad of sources and outlets, and all have their strengths and weaknesses. In Watergate, the much heroized Woodward and Bernstein were not always right. The same is true today. Questionable reporters and sources are easy to dismiss, but they may sometimes be right. The tabloids have a bad reputation, but, as shown, they can be, and have been, right about scandals.

Contemporary Issues with Officialization

Partisan Officialization

As covered in chapter 3, political attacks are officialized when they come from an individual with the proper role and authority, which validates the accusations. However, there are instances where the proper credentials do not fully validate and legitimize partisan discourse. There are two potential outcomes to this.[18] First, scandal rhetoric can devalue the officialized office and title. Second, scandal rhetoric can become institutionalized. Both of these outcomes can be seen in the recent examples of Reps. Darrell Issa, Henry A. Waxman, and Dan Burton, who all served as the chairman of the Oversight and Government Reform Committee.

The Oversight Committee, which is the primary investigative committee in Congress, has two primary goals: first, to ensure that the people's money is well spent, and second, to ensure an effective and efficient government. Yet there seems to be a third unofficial role of the committee: to cause trouble for the White House when the committee is being led by a member of the opposite party than the president.

Rep. Issa was a member of the 111th Congress, which saw the first presidential term of Barack Obama. During this time, the House of Representatives was described as having a "poisonous atmosphere" where "each party appears to be in a near-constant state of outrage over the behavior of the other."[19] This characterization holds true of members of the House Oversight Committee. One such member was Rep. Issa, who was promoted to chair of the committee in 2011. Prior to becoming chair, it was clear how Issa would conduct himself and how bad it would be. Issa was described as the "White House's worst nightmare" and would become the "annoyer in chief" as chair of the Oversight Committee.[20] Regardless of these characterizations, Issa himself said, "Oversight is not and should not be used as a political weapon against the occupant of the Oval Office. It should not be an instrument of fear or the exclusive domain of the party that controls Congress."[21] Eight days after this comment, Issa called President Obama "one of the most corrupt presidents in modern times."[22] Many found it difficult to reconcile these two statements.

Rep. Henry Waxman was to President Bush as Issa was to Obama. As Republicans lost control of the House in the 2006 elections, many expected that organizations closely aligned with Bush and his administration would "be in for a rough few years" when Waxman become chair of the Oversight Committee. He was called the "the Democrats' Eliot Ness."[23] Regardless of being characterized as a partisan by Republicans, Waxman was still praised by his critics for his tenacity.[24] Such praise came from none other than Rep. Dan Burton, who was chair of the Oversight Committee during the last years of the Clinton administration.

Rep. Dan Burton fulfilled the same role that Waxman and Issa did for Obama and Bush during the last half of President Clinton's tenure in the White House. Burton was well known for some of his extreme positions. He advocated using nuclear attacks on Iraq in the Persian Gulf War and claimed that White House aide Vince Foster, who had committed suicide, was in fact murdered and even went so far as to reenact the murder.[25] He called President Clinton a "scumbag."[26] Nevertheless, once appointed to the chair of the Oversight Committee, he promised to be "thorough and uncompromising" in his investigations and not to engage in any witch hunts.[27] Burton's fierce partisan nature was apparent, however, to Democrats, who routinely characterized his investigations as scandal politics, political witch hunts, and the determination to go on a "mad pursuit of a partisan agenda to break the president."[28]

A more thorough review of who has chaired the Oversight Committee demonstrates that when the president's party is the same as that which controls the House, and which therefore appoints the chair of the Oversight Committee, there is less rigor in the investigations of the executive branch.[29] When the president and the chair of the Oversight Committee are of different parties, the rigor of investigations increases dramatically. The difference in the level of scrutiny strongly suggests that congressional investigations of the executive branch are not motivated by ensuring an effective government but to cause problems and be a constant thorn in the side of the president. Consequently, even though it would appear that the duly appointed chair of a standing congressional committee that is charged with investigating the executive branch has the proper officialization to engage in oversight, the partisan reputation, actions, and even public statements of those very chairs can very well undermine their own credibility as officialized investigators. As the four major scandals covered in this book demonstrate, what was once partisan rancor could very well eventually turn out to be a major constitutional crisis. Nevertheless, as one journalist noted in the case of Rep. Issa, "sometimes, certainly, the whiff of smoke exposes fire. Sometimes, too, it's worth chasing smoke simply to ensure that no fire is smoldering unseen. But Issa, if it comes to that, must keep in mind: The fireman needs to be careful how he wields the ax."[30]

Symbolic Officialization

Chapter 3 addressed how little things become big things through officialization via high-level investigations, which may, as suggested in chapter 4, be carried out in a political process under the guise of judiciality. Contemporary examples demonstrate that officialization may be enacted through direct appeals to the judicial process. That is, the threat and filing of a lawsuit is one way in which contemporary partisan attacks attempt to officialize criticism of the chief executive.

On July 30, 2014, the House of Representatives voted along party lines (i.e., five Republicans and all the Democrats voted against the lawsuit; all other Republicans voted for the lawsuit) to sue President Obama for failure to follow the Constitution. Specifically, the concern addressed the president's failure to implement some parts of the law and not others. Obama has not yet enforced the Affordable Care Act's (aka "Obamacare") mandate that employers must provide insurance or face a penalty. Obama has repeatedly delayed the implementation of the mandate to give employers more time to comply with the law. Interestingly, Republicans, who criticized Obama for failing to implement certain aspects of the law, have voted to repeal those same aspects numerous times.[31]

Also, Obama campaigned on repealing the Defense of Marriage Act (DOMA) in court in 2008; in 2011, Obama and his attorney general formally announced they would no longer defend the law in court, citing their belief that the law is unconstitutional. Thus, while Obama has not enforced every detail of every law, he has stated reasons for his (in)action, which are not driven by a disrespect for the Constitution's instruction that the chief executive faithfully execute the laws, which is exactly what Republicans accuse him of doing.

This is not the first time members of Congress have sued Obama or any other president in regard to their official duties. Some of these lawsuits have resulted in legal precedents being established. In *Nixon v. Fitzgerald*, the Court noted that not protecting the president from lawsuits seeking civil damage would "inevitably subject presidential actions to undue judicial scrutiny as well as subject the president to harassment."[32] The court claimed that there are several existing methods to prevent presidential misconduct, including "strict scrutiny by the press," "vigilant oversight by Congress," and the "credible threat of impeachment."[33] Twenty-five years later, the Supreme Court again discussed the issue of executive immunity with regard to a lawsuit in which Paula Jones claimed then governor Bill Clinton had sexually harassed her.[34] The decision clarified that a president is not immune from civil lawsuits for actions prior to and unrelated to the office.

Despite Supreme Court rulings, the threat and filing of lawsuits continues to occur. The reason seems apparent: it is a partisan political weapon cloaked in the guise of the judiciary. As discussed in chapters 3 and 4, to justify and officialize accusations requires the use of the proper people and the proper places. The accusers, to properly officialize the accusations, must have the proper position, title, and authority to indict the accused. If the accusations come from a partisan opponent, the attacks are less severe. Furthermore, the accusations must also be in the proper place. The setting must be different and separate from the everyday routine of public discourse. Such examples can be special congressional committees.

The Obama lawsuit reveals that the use of the courts is a more serious symbolic attempt at officialization. That is, there is the attempted use of the courts as attempted officialization, which may not always be successful or legal given the legal precedents addressed above. Nevertheless, there is the use of the courts as the site of officialization rather than congressional committees, as the site of the court is separate and distinct and therefore more officialized than the partisan politics in Congress.

The chances are extremely unlikely that lawsuits against the president brought forth by members of Congress will ever be heard in a courtroom for a few reasons. First, the judicial branch has long been reluctant to hear congressional lawsuits against the president because there are other options for overseeing the chief executive, as mentioned earlier. Second, the legal justification for dismissing most of the lawsuits is that Congress cannot demonstrate standing. Standing requires that the person(s) bringing the lawsuit are being or have been harmed. No member of Congress has yet been able to demonstrate that they have been harmed by Obama's nondefense of Obamacare or DOMA.

Whether the lawsuits will ever be heard is most likely ancillary to the real motivation behind them. The apparent purpose of the lawsuits is not to demonstrate that there has been some injury, but to attempt to symbolically officialize congressional criticisms of the president. Congressional criticism is fair game in politics, but moving the criticism from Congress to the judiciary allows for attempted officialization regardless of the fact that the courts will most likely dismiss the case.

The dismissal actually helps the accusers in a certain way. While having a court hear and render a verdict in the courts is officialization, attempting to engage in a lawsuit is an attempt at officialization, not officialization per se. Nevertheless, attempted officialization serves a similar role as officialization but not to the same extent. Consequently, there are degrees of officialization. Officialization is not an either-or situation. There is an in-between. Not all attempts at officialization are successful, but they are attempts nonetheless.

In response to courts dismissing attempted officialization lawsuits, members of Congress have been given a prime talking point. That point is that the case was dismissed because of a legal technicality (i.e., standing), not because the accused is innocent of the substance of the lawsuit or because there is a lack of convincing and incriminating evidence. While standing is a critical legal concept, it holds secondary status in the mind of the public compared to the lofty charges of failing to faithfully execute the laws as required by the Constitution, especially to those who side with those bringing forth the case.

However, President Obama is no novice to partisan warfare and has engaged in deofficialization. He has called the lawsuit a "political stunt" that is not a pressing issue for the nation.[35] This responsive rhetoric is similar to *apologia* in the scandals discussed in previous chapters.

The press and pundits are also skeptical of congressional Republicans' attempts at officialization via lawsuits. For example, some have described the legal effort as a "campaign-season lawsuit, [which has] underscored the harshly partisan tone that has dominated the current Congress."[36] Pundits have noted that the lawsuit is political theater and a foolish move.

While delaying or refusing to implement all or part of a law is not a scandal per se, it is worthwhile to note that what constitutes scandal rhetoric is similar to other partisan political rhetoric. Fall, Nixon, Reagan, and Clinton all replied similarly to Obama against their criticisms. Yet the difference lies in the fact that officialization via the judiciary in Teapot Dome, Watergate, Iran-Contra, and Clinton/Lewinsky addressed a significant legal issue such as obstruction of justice.

Even if the lawsuits were to proceed, the wheels of justice turn slowly. Any lawsuit against the president would have no remedy. By the time the cases are heard, decided, and potentially appealed, Obama will have left office after his two terms. Thus, it is not the lawsuit itself but the threat of a lawsuit, including the filing of charges—which, as history and precedent have shown, will most likely be dismissed—that is an attempt at officializing criticism of the president.

The officialization via threat of lawsuit comes at a cost. First, the ploy of officializing criticism via a lawsuit is transparent. The news media of Teapot Dome, Watergate, Iran-Contra, and Clinton/Lewinsky did not readily address such political tactics during the officialization process. This is not the case today. The new media of the twenty-first century is quick to spot and report such tactics. Second, when one party attempts officialization, there is an inherent difficulty in being successful. Rather than being congressional criticism of Obama, it is clear when the House votes along party lines that the attacks are based on party and not on Congress as an institution. When Congress votes on party lines, Congress is no longer seen as a branch of government but as a means that Republicans and Democrats use to attack one another, thereby devaluing the legitimacy of Congress as an institution.

The Cover-Up and Digital Edit

The four major scandals discussed throughout this book had four major cover-ups. But there are smaller cover-ups happening too. The small cover-ups attempt to suppress previous actions or statements that might put some politician in a compromising position. Due to the rise of online resources such as Wikipedia, the popular online encyclopedia, the cover-up has a new brother: the edit. In 2006, Wikipedia was the nineteenth busiest site on the Internet. Given the increasing popularity of the site for information, politicians running for reelection favorably edited their own pages, presumably with the help of their staffers. U.S. representative Marty Meehan, whose first campaign for Congress in 1992 involved a strong position on term limits, found himself in an awkward position as he was running for his eighth reelection in 2006.[37] Perhaps thinking that his constituents had forgotten about his platform of long ago, his staff thought it best to delete any reference to his previous views on term limits from his Wikipedia entry.

Other representatives were able to edit their pages without criticism. Wikipedia tracks every edit and the IP addresses of computers that anonymously edit the entries. Computers in the House of Representatives share an IP address; consequently, we know that people on House computers were editing. We just do not know whom. Senators, however, all have a unique IP address.[38]

Five senators were criticized for deleting past transgressions while some bolstered the positives. Sen. Joe Biden's staff deleted references to plagiarizing speeches and work in law school. Sen. Dianne Feinstein removed information regarding a fine she had paid for not disclosing financial information. Sen. Conrad Burns's entry referenced a comment where he called Arabs "ragheads," which was deleted. Sen. Tom Harkin's office deleted references to his gross mischaracterization of his service in Vietnam.

Many members of Congress claimed they were simply fixing erroneous information. Some, like Rep. Lee Terry, were erasing false accusations from their entries. An apparently unhappy constituent wrote that Rep. Terry "likes to beat his wife and children."[39] Sen. Coburn deleted the "fact" that he was "the most annoying senator."[40]

In each of the earlier incidents, a member of Congress had committed some transgression and then attempted to conceal it, if only by deleting it from Wikipedia. However, the Congress-Wikipedia scandal of 2006 never really had staying power for a few reasons. First, Wikipedia is open for virtually anyone to edit, including government officials and their staff. It should therefore be no surprise that members of Congress did so. Second, it is almost expected that bolstering one's image is fair game during election season. Third, the nation was already in the midst of two significant scandals. The Jack Abramoff bribery scandal was in full swing, and those not interested in politics were shocked by a nonpolitical scandal at the time. James Frey was facing the music from Oprah for his memoir, *A Million Little Pieces*, which turned out to be fabricated.

In 2014, Wikipedia has become the sixth-busiest website, and the need for politicians to edit their own and others' entries continues. A computer associated with Republican congressman Tim Huelskamp, who has been a critic of the Republican congressional leadership and has slowly been losing the support of his constituency, was used to include a "profile boosting section labeled 'National Conservative Leader'" on his Wikipedia page.[41] His profile was updated as it was becoming clear that he would face a tough reelection.

Some of the edits are strategic, others are grammatical and stylistic in nature, and others are just plain silly. A silly but accurate edit came from a computer associated with the U.S. Senate. The edit added a brief note on the entry for "Horse head mask." The edit was the inclusion of a photo of a man wearing a horse head mask shaking hands with President Obama in Denver, Colorado.[42] However, some edits are silly and disruptive. A computer with an IP address associated with the House of Representatives changed Donald Rumsfeld's biography to describe him as an "alien lizard who eats Mexican babies."[43] In response to such disruptive editing, Wikipedia soon began restricting edits from congressional offices. While there are many computers that share the same IP address, some House staffers are upset at the restriction because of the actions of a few pranksters.

In editing Wikipedia, the opportunities to bolster one's biography and to engage in silly pranks come at a cost, but there is also the potential for more. Congressional edits can subtly alter the neutral point of view that Wikipedia insists upon. One of the "five pillars" of Wikipedia is that all entries are written in an "impartial tone . . . and we characterize information and issues rather than debate them."[44] Subtle edits to current events and the issues of the day allow for editors associated with Congress to support their own policy goals and criticize others. For example, a Senate computer subtly changed the entry for Edward Snowden, who disclosed classified information that revealed the existence and extent of global surveillance, from "dissident" to "traitor."[45] The change occurred one day after Russia granted Snowden political asylum. The entry now reads, "Snowden has been variously called a hero, a whistleblower, a dissident, a traitor, and a patriot," with numerous citations for each characterization.

To combat disruptive edits as well as to provide unmatched transparency, computer programmers such as Ed Summers have developed automated bots that post to Twitter any and all changes to Wikipedia in real time from computers associated with Congress. The bot has been praised as a new watchdog of government.[46] The problem of politicians editing Wikipedia to bolster their own image is not a problem just in the United States, and many countries including Sweden, Ireland, and Germany have their own Twitter bots that tweet edits from their own government. There is also a website that keeps an archive of deleted tweets since June 22, 2012, from state and federal politicians and candidates.[47] A user can easily search for politicians by position, party, or state. Undoubtedly these tools will soon reveal a scandal.

(In)credible Threats of Impeachment

Chapter 4 argued that the smoking gun turns the scandal into a problem that Congress can address with impeachment. Impeachment is a constitutional remedy to be taken in response to a very serious democratic problem: the president, vice president, or a federal officer has engaged in bribery, treason, or some other high crime or misdemeanor. Given the heinous circumstances that call for its implementation and the significant potential results, impeachment is and should be used in only the most extreme cases. However, impeachment is perhaps the highest and most publicized form of officialization; consequently, threats of impeachment are becoming more and more frequent as a means for substantiating accusations. However, the frequent deployment of impeachment devalues it, which is a serious problem. The politician who constantly calls for impeachment is the political boy who cries wolf.

In terms of impeachment, there are various forms. There are threats of impeachment, which some presidents have faced. There is the actual drafting and discussion of articles of impeachment, which has happened to a few presidents, either by committees or the full House. Some of these proposals may actually be voted on by Congress and pass, which has happened only twice. Then, after impeachment, there is a trial in the Senate. If convicted, the guilty party is removed from office, which has never happened.

Of the two presidents who have been impeached, Andrew Johnson and Bill Clinton, both are widely considered to have been politically motivated. After becoming president, Johnson removed Lincoln's secretary of war, which many in Congress felt violated a federal law. That law would later be repealed by Congress and ruled unconstitutional by the Supreme Court. Nevertheless, it became clear early that the president has jurisdiction over his administration. Clinton, who has been addressed throughout this book, was hounded by a well-known investigator who was out for political blood.

There have also been some close calls. Nixon, had he not resigned, would certainly have faced impeachment after the tapes became public. If we take the success of impeachment efforts as any indicator of their legitimacy, then we can dismiss most, if not all, impeachment proceedings as nothing more than political officialization.

Moreover, the threat of impeachment is becoming more and more common. Every president since Ronald Reagan has faced the threat of impeachment. While many earlier presidents have faced impeachment threats, demands for impeachment have now focused on five consecutive presidents, which is unprecedented. What was once sporadic is now becoming more of a continual practice. As a consequence, the legitimacy of impeachment becomes questionable. Impeachment no longer appears to be the last step but is the go-to for political disparagement. As such, threats of impeachment do not carry much officializing power. Political attackers have seemingly recognized this and stopped using the I-word.

Impeachment should be done in the most extreme circumstances, and it seems the word "impeachment" should be used in the most extreme circumstances. Those who engage in impeachment-like accusations but do not label them as such are said to be engaging in "impeachment light" (or "lite"). The term appeared as early as 1998 during the Clinton/Lewinsky scandal. Rep. Henry Hyde, who served as the chief prosecutor against President Clinton in the Senate, argued against censure, which he described as "impeachment lite," where there are "no real consequences except as history chooses to impose them."[48] Impeachment light, then, is nothing more than accusing the president of high crimes and misdemeanors and not taking any more action.

"Impeachment light" was also used to describe a hearing in 2008 to examine President Bush's actions. Those actions included the pretenses for the Iraq war, the use of torture, and outing a CIA agent, who was married to a critic of the Bush administration. Democrats said the inquiry was into "executive power and its constitutional limitations."[49] Republicans called it "impeachment lite," and one paper called it an un-impeachment hearing where Bush could be accused of impeachment-level offenses but not be actually impeached.[50]

The next time the term was used in the same context was in July 31, 2014, against President Obama. Speaker of the House John Boehner's lawsuit against the president for failing to enforce certain aspects of certain laws was described by the *New York Times* as "impeachment-light—a way to send a signal that Republicans would fight the president's efforts to revise laws Congress had passed while not going as far as many on the right would like."[51] As such, impeachment light is also about building and maintaining political support.

Republicans are calling Obama's failing to enforce certain aspects of the Affordable Care Act unconstitutional. It would seem that the failure of the chief executive to follow the Constitution would be an impeachable offense. However, Republicans are cautious to use the politically loaded I-word as the *Washington Post* has stated: "It's a political loser to champion impeachment. So Republicans used other words Wednesday, such as treason, monarchy and usurpation" in their debates about bringing forth the lawsuit.[52] Democrats, on the other hands, are using "impeachment" in abundance in describing the lawsuit. The net result is that there are more financial contributions coming in to the Democratic Party.

Threats of impeachment with no follow-through or impeachment-like actions create an interstitial rhetorical moment. As Rep. Dan Lungren said in regard to the Obama lawsuit, "We're sort of in that Never-Neverland of accusing the president of impeachable offenses but not taking actions to im-peach him, which I guess impugns him but does not impeach him, but maybe it has the same effect in the court of public opinion."[53] Thus, if we hold im-peachment as a political process that operates under a judicial guise, so too does the threat of impeachment, where the charges are public accusations and the jury is the public. The result of such characterizations is that partisan rhetoric, which once led to officialization, now becomes de facto officializa-tion. In other words, partisan rhetoric is not the means to get to officialization; partisan rhetoric now is officialization. Consequently, Boehner's lawsuit is largely symbolic, but we should not dismiss it, for the lawsuit symbolizes the very act of officialization. Even though in practical terms the lawsuit has very little chance of success, the threat of a lawsuit suggests official actions are being undertaken.

Exclusion and Expulsion

There are a number of ways the scandal can end other than the impeachment process, scapegoating or mortification, or being found guilty or not guilty in the courts. These alternative ends offer an opportunity to address some of the concerns raised in the implications of chapter 5. While most of the examples in this chapter are more contemporary, here it is worthwhile to go a bit further back in time.

Adam Clayton Powell Jr. was a powerful and outspoken U.S. representa-tive from 1945 to 1971.[54] He represented the Harlem, New York, congres-sional district. He gained prominence as chair of the Committee on Education and Labor. However, he was soon criticized for how he used the committee's funds. A congressional investigation found that he had used the funds for extravagant travel expenses and that he had made questionable salary pay-ments to his wife.

When the Ninetieth Congress was sworn in, Rep. Powell was asked to step aside. House members decided to form a special committee to determine if Powell, due to his previous actions, deserved his seat in Congress. Powell testified before the committee only about matters relating to his eligibility for office under Article 1, Section 2, of the Constitution (i.e., age, citizenship, and residency). The special committee finally concluded that Powell should be sworn in, censured, fined $40,000, and deprived of his seniority. The full House debated the matter and bypassed the committee's recommendation and passed a motion to exclude Powell from Congress. Powell then filed suit against the Speaker of the House; the sergeant at arms, who refused to pay Powell; and the doorkeeper, who refused Powell entry as he was a duly elected member of Congress. While the case progressed through the courts, a special election was held. Powell won with 86 percent of the vote, but he was not seated. In 1968, Powell was reelected by 80 percent, and he was sworn in with all other members.

Although some issues were now moot as Powell was seated in Congress, there were still pressing questions to answer. The most relevant question for the purposes here is whether Congress can exclude a duly elected representative due to scandalous actions. Eventually the Supreme Court ruled that since Powell was excluded before taking the oath of office, the exclusion was unconstitutional. Congress can only expel members, not prohibit them from becoming members. The only restrictions on becoming a representative are listed in the Constitution—age, citizenship, and residency—not whether you have been involved in scandalous actions.

The court refused to address the issue of Powell being sworn in and then expelled because of his actions. The court only addressed the facts of the case as they were. However, the court noted that the special committee's recommendations (i.e., fine, censure, and loss of seniority) were partly based on history and practice. No member has ever been expelled from office for actions they committed in a prior Congress. In other words, the Ninetieth Congress could not punish a reelected representative for actions during the Eighty-Ninth Congress, the reasoning being that whatever actions were done in a previous Congress were germane only to that specific Congress.

The example of Powell offers some insight into the alternatives in which the people retain their voice, but first we should determine whether Powell's actions were a scandal. There is no clear indication that Powell attempted to conceal his actions. A biographer noted, "If anything, he seemed to revel in it, almost taunting his critics—in and out of Congress—and daring them to make an issue of the way he acted."[55] Powell did not believe his actions were any different than what others had done. This is not to say his actions transgressed some norm. Powell believed that he was being criticized for what all other congressional chairmen have done, but he was receiving undue attention because of his critical disposition and his race. Although his actions did not reach the level of full scandal, there was public, media, and congressional criticism about his activities.

His activities, whatever they may have been, were not grave enough for his own constituents to remove him from office. Perhaps, as Powell repeatedly claimed, his behavior was no different than other committee chairs—they were the ones covering it up, not him. Perhaps he was a victim of the racial politics of the time. Whatever the reason, Powell's constituents responded favorably to his counteraccusations of hypocrisy and racism. Regardless of the potential harm his presence brought about, his actions were not so bad in the eyes and ballots of those he represented. After being prohibited from

Congress, he was reelected twice, once in a special election to fill his very own seat.

However, given a more egregious transgression, Powell's constituency may have preferred him not to be in office. By expelling a fellow member of Congress for some controversial behavior and then forcing them to run again in a special election, the people are allowed more of a voice, but there are still consequences. Forcing a representative to campaign in a special election would burden the already busy campaign season members face every two years, thereby limiting the representation of the people in the House. Moreover, given the exponential costs of running a campaign, this tactic could result in abuse. One party, if they had the votes, could expel a member and make them deplete their campaign monies in a special election.

Eventually in the 1970 congressional campaign, Powell lost the primary election by a scant 150 votes. His loss was not due to scandalous accusations. His congressional district had recently been redrawn, and he was bombarded with constant criticism from his primary campaign opponents about his frequent absenteeism. Charles Rangel defeated Powell in the primary, and Rangel would go on to become the next representative for the district. Rangel would later be censured in 2010 for his own scandalous behavior, which is discussed in the next section.

Although it is rare, some members of Congress have been expelled after taking the oath of office. The reason for all but one of the fifteen senatorial expulsions was supporting the Confederacy during the Civil War; the other senator was removed in 1796 for treason. Only five representatives have been expelled: three for supporting the Confederacy, and two for bribery and related offenses. Many others have been faced with expulsion, but those accused were vindicated, they resigned, their term expired, or they died during the controversy. Regardless, expulsion carries the same concerns as impeachment and conviction, as discussed in chapter 5.

Facing the Music

One critical aspect of such punishment is its public nature. Nixon delivered his resignation speech to sixty million television viewers, but he only faced two people. He had ordered everyone out of the Oval Office except two members of the CBS news crew, who were filming the event. However, some scandalous individuals have to face much more, and others face much less. Take the example of Charles Rangel, who followed in the footsteps of Powell in more than one way. Rangel became the long-standing representative of Harlem, just like Powell. Rangel became a chairman of a powerful congressional committee, just like Powell. And Rangel became the target of his peers for ethics violations, just like Powell.

Using official congressional stationery, Rangel reached out to corporations that had business before his powerful Ways and Means Committee
and asked for funds to build a postcongressional library for his papers.[56]
Many called out the apparent conflict of interest in addition to the fact that
Rangel requested funds from Congress to build the center that would carry
his own name. Critics believed he was working hard for himself when the
funds could have better supported his community. Rangel also failed to
report income associated with a rental house in the Dominican Republic on
his tax forms and congressional disclosure forms. The failure to report and
pay taxes for several years was particularly embarrassing as Rangel was
the chair of the committee that writes the tax code. In effect, he failed to
follow the very rules his committee is in charge of writing and overseeing.
There were other incidents including benefiting from extremely favorable
leases on four apartments and being reimbursed for travel to the Caribbean
by companies with matters before his committee. Rangel claimed, "No one
would ever be able to say that it's a scandal or that I was corrupt," and
blamed most of the incidents on sloppy record keeping.[57] Just like Powell,
Rangel's constituency overwhelmingly reelected him in the face of such
scandalous accusations. While the voters were forgiving, the House was
not and censured Rangel.

There was much anticipation for the "once-in-decades happening."[58] After
the case for and against censure was made, an amendment was proposed to
reprimand Rangel. The reprimand, which was supported by then representative Weiner, would be less severe in that Rangel need not stand in front of his
colleagues. Yet the votes were cast, and Rangel would be required to stand
in front of everyone. Speaker of the House Nancy Pelosi called him front
and center to the well of the floor. Rangel pushed himself out of his chair,
adjusted his suit jacket, took a few steps forward, and stood with his feet apart
and hands clasped in front of himself with "the vigor washed out of him."[59]
Pelosi "solemnly read the one-paragraph admonition properly known as
House Resolution 1737. No florid rhetoric was flaunted for this pressing bit
of protocol, but the stiff, cut-and-dried language of censure"[60] while everyone
was hushed for the event. When it was over, Rangel spoke remorsefully but
defiantly about the ordeal.

The difference between censure and reprimand is not necessarily in the
alleged transgression but in the publicity of the disciplinary procedure. In
essence, the more public the punishment, the worse it is. This is true for the
apology too. Politicians, who have to apologize as punishment for transgress-
ing some boundary, may strategically pick a more private or public place for
their atonement. For example, Clinton apologized for his personal actions in
the Map Room, which is a more personal, social space in the White House.
This strategy depicted Clinton as a person, not as president.

In addition to locations, politicians now have a number of mediums to use in their apologies. Politicians can strategically use certain locations and mediums to assuage the often awkward and difficult nature of a public apology. Former representative Todd Akin once stated that women could not get pregnant if they are victims of "legitimate rape."[61] The Missouri representative's statement implied that those who got pregnant from rape were not really raped. Unsurprisingly, he was quickly and heavily criticized for his statement.

While not necessarily a scandal, the example demonstrates a key feature of the mediated apology, which is common in scandals. Akin eventually apologized, and he did so in a very convenient place. The Republican representative went on the conservative-friendly Fox News show, *Huckabee*, which is hosted by Mike Huckabee. Huckabee is a former Republican presidential candidate; a former governor of Arkansas, which shares a border with Missouri; and the founder and leader of a political action committee that supported Akin.

Apologizing to those you have offended is difficult, and there is a very uncomfortable vulnerability to it; however, apologizing while surrounded by forgiving friends is far easier. Akin's close associations with Huckabee certainly made the apology a more bearable experience for him.

Anthony Weiner's apology was more vulnerable. Weiner apologized in a public press conference. As the conference began, Weiner approached the lectern, immediately grabbed a drink of water and sipped at it nervously, and sheepishly looked up at the crowd of reporters. The normally brazen congressman admitted the truth while his voice cracked in a tearful admission. Weiner's approach differed substantially from that of Akin's. It is not clear whether Weiner's apology was strategic or not. Since not all political apologies are easily accepted, one could speculate that putting oneself completely in front of the press, which Weiner had attacked for fanning the flames just a week earlier, allowed the press to treat him like he treated them. Moreover, the vulnerable public apology could further support the sincerity of the apology. Those who apologize, as if looking those they have wronged directly in the eye, have a more noble countenance, albeit flawed from the transgression, than those who do not.

There are those who apologize face-to-face, those who apologize in front of a camera, and those who apologize online. The advantage the people have in seeing the accused, whether electronically or in person, is that we can see the sincerity or lack thereof in the delivery. Take the example of Minnesota state representative Ryan Winkler, who compared the lone African American Supreme Court justice Clarence Thomas to "Uncle Tom" via Twitter in response to Thomas being part of the majority who voted down part of the Voting Rights Act.[62] The phrase is popularly understood to mean a black person who unquestionably and subserviently follows white people. After deleting the tweet, Winkler, a state representative who holds a history degree from Harvard University, tweeted that he did not know the term was derogatory and apologized. While the online apology affords less vulnerability, there are costs. The primary cost is the ability for the audience to determine the sincerity. The words on a page can be sculpted, edited, and reworked to frame the apology, but the delivery is often very telling. The online apology does not allow such an opportunity.

This is not to say all in-person apologies are sincere. Speaking about business practices, Oklahoma state representative Dennis Johnson said that a customer might try to "Jew me down on a price."[63] The video of the proceedings shows fellow representatives snap to attention, not believing what they had just heard. Johnson then stopped speaking as he was handed a note. After reading the note, he turned to someone off camera and whispered, "Did I?" Returning to full volume after several seconds of quiet, he boldly and succinctly offered an obviously unscripted, in the moment apology—"I apologize to the Jews"—which received awkward laughter. He attempted to segue back into his speech with "They're good small businessmen as well," smilingly. The apology comes off clearly as mechanical and patronizing. He later would offer a more sincere apology, but the point remains that not all face-to-face apologies are sincere.

Self-Regulation in Nonpolitical Scandals

One of the overriding aspects of political scandals addressed in this book is that the political scandal allows for governmental self-regulation. But nongovernmental organizations do not operate in the same self-regulating manner. The press, for example, has its own scandals involving the fabrication of news stories. Stephen Glass fabricated dozens of stories for the *New Republic*; Jayson Blair did the same for the *New York Times*, and Jack Kelley for *USA Today*; and then there was the botched coverage of the 2004 election by Fox News and CBS regarding President Bush's military career.

Ostensibly, media scandals are resolved similarly to their political counterparts. Each scandal was investigated in-house and involved the removal of the (ir)responsible party, thereby demonstrating the self-regulatory function of the press to be much like their blood brother, the government in dealing with the scandalous politician. Moreover, echoing the conclusions of some political scandals, the *New Republic* news fabricator Stephen Glass and Jayson Blair of the *New York Times* resigned, as did *USA Today*'s Jack Kelley, who claimed he had done nothing wrong. Thus some antiheroes resigned, thereby becoming redeemers for the benefit of the organization. In these respects, political and nonpolitical scandals are similar.

However, such an interpretation is to misunderstand the agent and agency of the authority giver in a press scandal as compared to its political counterpart. In a democracy, the electorate is the sovereign agent, but in a private organization, the ruler is the employer. That is, citizens elect someone to serve as their representative and speak on their behalf, which is not the case for a hiring manager at an organization. In a democracy, the representative is the agency of the electorate in government, which operates for the benefit of the sovereign agents (i.e., the voters). The worker, however, is the agency of a capitalist corporation (i.e., the agent) that operates for, in most cases, the benefit of the organization and not for the people who patronize the business. Consequently, the scandal is a rare type of political rhetoric separate from other forms of discourse. Scandal rhetoric is unique, for it vicariously invokes "the people" who are normally the sovereign agents in democracy.

Bitzer claims that scholars make no clear distinction between political rhetoric and other forms of rhetoric.[64] Some issues may be seen as private, and others may see the same issues as public. In terms of purely political rhetoric, the public-private nature was muddled beginning with Gary Hart in 1988 and then with Bill Clinton's infidelity.[65] Those who defended Clinton claimed that sex was a private matter; those who accused him claimed that lying to governmental investigators was a very public matter.

But looking beyond the political scandal, the relationship between public and private is very different. For most nonpolitical scandals in private organizations, the investigators of the scandal are governmental or government related. For example, baseball commissioner Bob Selig initiated the baseball steroid investigation by appointing former U.S. senator George Mitchell to head the inquiry. Prior to the appointment of Mitchell, Selig continually remarked that he had done all he could to stop steroid use, but a 2005 congressional hearing found that Selig's comments were, in actuality, covering up a widespread problem in baseball.

Another example that demonstrates outside regulation by government investigation is the energy corporation Enron. The scandalous accounting practices by Enron resulted in massive corporate gains that ultimately deflated, causing the company to be investigated by the government's Securities and Exchange Commission. These two examples demonstrate that nonpolitical organizations that affect the public's business (i.e., the national pastime and the economy) are not internally regulated and investigated but are scrutinized by the government.

One may claim that the press is a private organization and that its scandals are not investigated by the government but instead are self-regulated much like the government. This is certainly true. However, the press is a far different organization than baseball and energy corporations, which are not ingrained in the national spotlight as overseers of the government. The history of free speech in the colonies and then the United States makes clear that only in very limited and truly extraordinary instances can the government regulate the press.

Moreover, the press's relationship with the government, as described in chapter 2, supports the view that the press is entrenched as a fundamental element of the government, unlike many other businesses. Thus, one could reasonably believe that the press would self-regulate in a manner similar to their blood brother. However, this is not the case. The government investigates private organizations that affect the public's business and thereby provides a separate entity to impartially investigate another. Though the government provides oversight to the other, it does not act similarly when investigating public officials. Rather, the government investigates itself and manages to redeem itself by expunging the evil.

CONCLUSION

Scandals come, scandals go, and some—like Teapot Dome, Watergate, and the others discussed in the preceding chapters—stand as significant beyond their historical moment. But there are smaller scandals, nonscandals, and others that help us understand the extent to which the scandal remains the same, albeit with variation, in more contemporary cases. Anthony Weiner's sexting scandal, for example, follows the scandal narrative. Weiner's scandal started with allegations of wrongdoing by a press source that was characterized as being questionable; then there was *apologia*, which consisted of denials and transcendence, then very minimal but present partisan discourse, officialization, silence, and finally mortification. However, there were variations. Weiner, for example, engaged in officialization, and there was very little partisan rhetoric. These variations demonstrate that current and future scandals may provide further nuance and subtleties to the scandal narrative.

The chapter also reviewed some recent and a few not-so-recent smaller scandals and controversies to note some variations on a theme. It is worth noting that the scandal narrative developed in chapters 2, 3, 4, and 5 provides the overarching scandal narrative. The four major critical cases used are the scandals that stand above all others. Thus minor scandals, even with their variations, still follow the thematic scandal narrative. That is, Weiner's sexting scandal involved officialization, although the accusers did not use it. Future scandals and controversies will undoubtedly provide more nuances, and a future major scandal may even alter the overriding scandal narrative.

Chapter Seven

Yesterday, Today, and Tomorrow

Addressing scandals from the point of view of history reveals all the hidden aspects that were not known while the events were playing out. But we experience scandals as they happen, not in the rearview mirror of history. We experience scandals as they unfold in real time in the newspaper headlines, television news, and online news reports, not through classified reports that were later released; complex legal arguments, decisions, and appeals; or tell-all books published long after the fact.

In essence, this book does more than explain what happened in the past during Teapot Dome, Watergate, Iran-Contra, and Clinton/Lewinsky. The ideas in this book can help us understand what might happen in the future or what is going on around us currently. Consequently, this final chapter addresses three issues. First, how those who were at the center of each of the four major scandals made sense of the then uncertain events unfolding around them. Second, that the very thematic narrative of the scandal itself is a model that provides understanding to those participating in and those observing a series of events in the news that may turn into scandal. Lastly, this chapter concludes with an ongoing scandal that, as of the writing of this book, has not reached a conclusion.

RECOGNIZING SCANDAL

Teapot Dome

Although Teapot Dome has been pushed to the back pages of "political folklore," it is a substantial scandal in contemporary American political history and was told to the people in a familiar dramatic pattern.[1] The reporting on the

Teapot Dome scandal "missed no detail of a movie plot" and included numerous summaries of the "drama" complete with a "cast of characters" to keep the public up to date.[2] Moreover, the reporters and editorialists recognized Teapot Dome's importance with Doheny's testimony. But before this explosion of publicity and while Teapot Dome was common gossip in 1922 Washington, insiders knew it would "be a national scandal before all" was done."[3]

Fall himself realized early on how the story of Teapot Dome would unravel. In December 1923, he had been out of office for ten months, and the Senate's inquiry was just starting. Fall knew of the impending political rhetoric and the strategies needed to evade the accusations. He claimed, "I knew perfectly well, at that time that the Democratic leaders were preparing to wage war on the Republican Administration by making charges of general dishonesty."[4] "I knew the power of the public press," he continued, "and how it could be used under such circumstances . . . that my reputation would be defamed, and that I would be unable to adequately meet in the public press the charges against me."[5] Later, in 1928, he realized that his attempt to cover up his actions had made a "bad matter very, very much worse."[6] Nevertheless, he maintained he was innocent of receiving bribes. At his sentencing, Fall repeated that he had lied about the source of the money to "prevent a volcano of political abuse pouring upon the [Harding] Administration."[7]

The press also recognized the familiar political rhetoric of the scandal myth during Teapot Dome. Early in October 1923, before the Senate investigation began, the *Washington Post* reported that "the first political rumblings" from Democrats were expected to be heard.[8] The *Post* continued, "It is not clear how the political insinuations can be brought into the hearings, but it is understood that a pronounced effort may be made."[9] In other words, the press knew that politics in some way would enter the picture, but they did not know exactly how; so too thought the "opponents of the administration."[10]

Democrats were attacked and blamed for exhibiting partisanship. As one editorialist wrote, "that the politicians would respond to what has happened only by a particular display of partisanship was also inevitable."[11] Another claimed, "If the situation was reversed . . . the Republicans would take good care to use the political advantage placed in their hands."[12] In short, "the political charges [were] what might be expected."[13]

Watergate

Countless accounts and investigations have since been written on Watergate, and all benefit from hindsight information that the public, the press, and the government did not have as the scandal unfolded in the early 1970s. But by some intuitive sense they all knew what was happening. Just two weeks after the break-in, *Newsweek* reported, "Washington had one of the juiciest political scandals in memory."[14] A veteran reporter for ABC recalled being questioned by superiors for his immediate covering of the break-in; he justified his coverage with a "journalist's hunch."[15] It was not, however, entirely intuitive. The reporter claimed, "There was a sense of inevitably" for political connections to be made because the burglars "could not have been seeking money or valuables" in the DNC office.[16] Bob Woodward, who along with Carl Bernstein is famously remembered for his reporting of the scandal for the *Washington Post*, later recalled, "The outline of the Watergate cover-up was so clear in retrospect."[17]

Even Richard Nixon himself seemed to have a sense of how the story would play out. In 1948, Nixon investigated Alger Hiss in a spy scandal. In a recorded conversation, Nixon once told Dean,

> That son-of-a-bitch Hiss would be free today if he hadn't lied about his espionage. . . . He could have said, "I—look, I knew Chambers. And, yes, as a young man I was involved with some Communist activities but I broke it off many years ago." But the son-of-a-bitch lied and he goes to jail for the lie rather than the crime.[18]

Nixon also told his domestic policy advisor, alluding to Hiss, "If you cover-up, you're going to get caught."[19] The president obviously ignored his own advice.

Iran-Contra

Iran-Contra has become a "part of the primary text of American history."[20] Iran-Contra came some fifteen years after the most notable scandal in U.S. political history, and the wounds were fresh in the eyes of many, some of whom were actively involved in the Iran-Contra scandal. Moreover, the Clinton/Lewinsky scandal, in terms of the potential political punishment, would eclipse the, at best, slap on the wrist Reagan received. However, Iran-Contra, like the Watergate and Clinton/Lewinsky scandals, "produced a similar fare of drama, emotion and unexpected twists."[21] As Iran-Contra played out, many attempted to detour the public discourse of the scandal, perhaps in the hopes that the ordeal would not rise to the severity of Watergate. Others, however, could not deny Iran-Contra's significance.

During the Iran-Contra scandal, Watergate was still fresh in the minds of many, who were weary of the lessons learned some fifteen years earlier. Some sought to differentiate it from Watergate. For example, the popularity and likability of Reagan was far greater than that of Nixon. For this and similar reasons, using the suffix "-gate" was questioned for Iran-Contra. The

New Republic offered a free subscription to anyone who could come up with the best moniker for the scandal. The contest generated several options, such as "Contra-diction," "Contra-deception," "Contra-versy," "Saudi Night Fever and the Old Iranaround," "Irantics," and the winner, "Iranamok." These suggestions playfully capture the essence of the scandal as serious but not a severe constitutional crisis that the ominous "-gate" suffix would seem to suggest. Such a contest points to the idea that Iran-Contra was seen potentially as the next in line of major political scandals and that some, such as the *New Republic*, tried to resist the casting of Iran-Contra into the mythic proportions of Watergate.

Such efforts, however, can be hard to resist. With the "-gate" suffix excluded, one submission reverted back to the major scandal before Watergate. Combining Teapot Dome with Reagan's ability to escape political grease and grime, the idea was "Teflon Dome."[22] This idea mirrored another well-known individual, the mob boss John Gotti, who was labeled the Teflon Don, as many juries did not find him guilty of any crimes throughout the 1980s. It is difficult to determine which is worse, being compared to Watergate or to an infamous mobster. Regardless, the debate over the name is telling.

Many believed that the scandal reflected the narratives of soap operas and movies. Those involved in the scandal such as Albert Hakim, who worked with the Reagan administration to use the profits from the Iranian arms sales to arm the Contras, called the ordeal a "soap opera."[23] Others saw parallels, as one scholar noted, "North's testimony replaced soap operas on the networks and commentators assumed that the same needs drove people to watch both."[24] Others suggested that North himself exceeded the soap opera as he "hit the bedrock of fundamentally masculine mythologies quite removed from the soap opera."[25] Such perspectives seemingly caused *Newsweek* to wonder if the televised hearings would "outdraw the soaps," and to claim, "If it all works out, the [Iran-Contra] show will be a hit spinoff" from the earlier Watergate hearings. In response to comparisons between the scandal and the soaps, on the first day of the hearings, news anchors such as Dan Rather lectured his audience, "This is not a television show. . . . This is the real thing."[26] While the scandal was very real, the scandal narrative was the fodder for film. Purportedly, when Reagan fired North the president remarked, "One day this will make a great movie."[27]

While some saw North as the fall guy, others saw him as destined for Hollywood. As early as December 1986, Hollywood producers were looking at the idea of a biographical film, with Mel Gibson or Treat Williams as North.[28] The producer Jaw Weston said, "It's almost impossible to sell anything with politics . . . but North touches a deep wellspring in the American spirit."[29] Moreover, a New York magazine film critic described North as "a type of composite mythological figure, ready to step into a set constructed from 200 years of American archetype and 50 years of the cinema."[30] North was characterized as an amalgamation of Batman, Superman, and Rambo.[31] North's larger-than-life persona was evident as the iconic "Hollywood" sign was vandalized during his testimony. The letter "H" was removed, and the sign simply read, "Ollywood." North, however, was not the only one who seemed to be playing a role; one longtime supporter of the president criticized his handling of the scandal by saying, "I'm beginning to think I misjudged Ronald Reagan all along. . . . I think he was just a politician, just mouthing the lines."[32]

While the Iran-Contra "cover-up demonstrated that little had been learned from past scandals," there were other elements of Iran-Contra that demonstrated something had been learned from scandals such as Watergate.[33] Learning from the Woodward and Bernstein–inspired archetypal journalist, "editors and reporters [were] clearly more sensitive than in the past—such as during the Watergate scandal—to the potential for a backlash against the media."[34] Thus "the Watergate parallel served to restrain the press, to beckon the ever-lurking gremlin of self-censorship to the forefront of the press consciousness."[35] That is, popular culture suggested that it was Woodward and Bernstein who brought down Nixon, and the Iran-Contra press corps did not want to appear to be out for Reagan's blood. Reagan himself fed this imagery in early December 1986 as he described the press as "sharks circling" with "blood in the water."[36] The press had learned from Watergate, but they could not stand idly by once the story was out. Consequently, the press ran critical coverage "side by side" with news coverage "pleading with the president simply to admit mistakes had been made, fire those deemed responsible, apologize and move on."[37]

It was not just journalists who had learned from past scandals, either, but politicians too had learned to operate differently from previous major scandals. Both Reagan and Nixon had won landslide victories in the years before their respective scandals; however, the voters saw the two quite differently. While Watergate was the precedent for Iran-Contra, there were notable differences in how politicians reacted. First, Reagan was no Nixon. Reagan was "outgoing, usually open and good-humored, whereas there was a dark and brooding side to Nixon that sometimes troubled the electorate."[38] Second, while the reasons behind the Iran-Contra scandal were illegal and did not have the support of Congress, the scandal was not based on pitting one party against the other. Thus impeachment talk "was kept to a minimum and never seriously considered."[39] One *Washington Post* editorialist also commented, "The idea of impeaching Ronald Reagan seems preposterous, even to his sharpest critics. It has the flavor of regicide, or patricide, or shooting a lovable old dog."[40] The lesson from Iran-Contra, then, is that the seriousness of the charges is often weighed disproportionally against the likability of the wrongdoer. Bill Clinton would benefit from such a lesson, and he would also update it to address the motives of his accuser.

Clinton/Lewinsky

The Clinton/Lewinsky scandal has entered into American political folklore not for the actual misconduct but for how the scandal ended. Certainly the nation was somewhat shocked at the initial allegations, but when viewed in context, it seemed unreasonable to punish Clinton for what most already knew about him when he first ran for office and for what other presidents such as Thomas Jefferson, Franklin Roosevelt, John Kennedy, and Lyndon Johnson had all done. Regardless, "Lewinsky [was] hardly the only woman ever alleged to have had an affair with an American president, [but] she became the first to testify about it in a criminal investigation of the commander-in-chief."[41]

A hundred years after Johnson's impeachment and subsequent acquittal, Richard Nixon faced impeachment but absconded before the proceedings commenced. While the Clinton/Lewinsky scandal had the recognizable elements of the democratic scandal narrative, Watergate gave us a "new mythology about the virtue of lawyers, reporters, and investigators."[42] Consequently, political commentators compared Nixon to Clinton. Even Nixon, prior to his death in 1994, favorably compared himself to Clinton. Nixon said that they both came from humble beginnings, lost elections only to come back stronger than ever, and had both "gutted it out" during their scandals.[43] Clinton and his supporters, however, dismissed any comparisons.[44] In terms of his invocation of executive privilege, Clinton claimed that the "facts are quite different in this case" as compared to Nixon's.[45]

Moreover, while both Nixon and Clinton engaged in misconduct and attempted to cover up their actions, the reasons behind the impeachment varied greatly: Nixon lied about illegal political espionage; Clinton lied about sex. Some maintained that the underlying crimes were incomparable while others maintained that a lie is a lie regardless of what it concerned. There was, however, one key difference: people did not know prior to Watergate the extreme extent of Nixon's penchant for unscrupulous politics. One of the first things people knew about Clinton was his rumored infidelity; thus the story of the Clinton/Lewinsky scandal was an all too familiar one.

As with Teapot Dome and Watergate, the Clinton/Lewinsky scandal was a "political drama," but in the genre of a "southern novel."[46] As in the previous scandals, people knew instinctively what was happening. Gore Vidal claimed, "I had a sense that I had, somehow, been through something like this before."[47] In response to accusations of Clinton's infidelity, Democrats remarked, "What we're finding out is that there's nothing new under the sun."[48] In addition, the massive news coverage early on gave "a strong hint of what news editors believe."[49] The same sentiment revolved around the political rhetoric. One editorialist noted, the "impeachment saga will thunder on, perhaps for months, as blood sport for partisans."[50] Another claimed it is "human nature" that the extremist conservatives are taking pleasure in Clinton's public difficulties.[51] Famed Clinton consultant James Carville believed "this could be the most-talked-about [controversy] in modern political history."[52]

While many intuitively knew how the Clinton/Lewinsky scandal would play out, Republicans, Democrats, and Clinton had learned much from the history of modern scandals and revised their roles. Congressional Republicans learned to keep silent for fear of politicizing what they believed to be an investigation headed by a nonpolitical prosecutor.[53] An internal Republican memo advised that members not comment on the scandal. If they did, the note warned, "you will take a non-partisan, non-political situation and make it both partisan and political."[54] As *Time* magazine explained, "Early on, the Republican leadership spread the word to members not to comment or get involved in the scandal lest they lend credence to the idea that this is just another Republican attack."[55] However, the public saw Starr as more political than as an independent prosecutor.

Democrats also learned to keep quiet as they had done in Iran-Contra.[56] A Democratic congressman said the one thing his party should not do was what Republicans did during Watergate: "defend the president until we go down with him."[57] Also, the lack of political rhetoric, which was commonplace in Teapot Dome and Watergate, demonstrated that the public wanted more than just denials. As the *Washington Post* reported,

Clinton advisers inside and outside the White House acknowledged how unlikely these clipped answers are to satisfy the public's demand for reassurance that Clinton and Jordan [one of Clinton's unofficial advisors] did nothing improper. And, uncharacteristically, they made scarcely any effort to play down the severity of their situation.[58]

Clinton also learned and adapted to the scandal narrative. While Clinton eventually conceded the truth, which Fall and Nixon never did, he admitted that the "lie saved me."[59] He believed the day-by-day trickle of information gradually allowed the public to come to terms with the situation. The scandal also taught Clinton that a president has a private life, but sometimes the private person and public chief executive overlap. Campaigning in 1992, then governor Clinton asked a reporter for a private word after the journalist hinted at alleged infidelity. Clinton asked if the "Gary Hart rule was in effect."[60] The reporter replied, "What is that?" to which Clinton explained, "If there's nothing going on contemporaneously, it won't be reported." The reporter replied, "I don't think you can count on that, Governor." Lastly, and perhaps most important, Clinton learned not only to claim that he would cooperate but also to keep his promise.

SCANDAL NARRATIVE

There is a persistent narrative to the political scandal, one that perpetuates and legitimizes the U.S. government's ability to regulate itself, and which limits the typical sovereign agency of "the people." Examining the Teapot Dome, Watergate, Iran-Contra, and Clinton/Lewinsky scandals, the narrative begins in a political context of relative prosperity that is shattered by the press's publicity of misconduct. Politicians then engage in partisan rhetoric that depicts the charges as politically inspired attacks. Shocking evidence and testimony then reinvigorate the public's attention, but the heightened attention is lost as the scandal goes to the courts, where it receives sporadic news coverage and results in little comment by those involved, including the accused. Finally, the scandal concludes with the confirmation of wrongdoing or a vindication of the accused, or in abdication. This is the basic thematic narrative of the scandal.

These thematic elements do not always follow such a linear path; that is, they do not unfold in a strict beginning, middle, and end sequence. That is, while scandals begin with the publicity of wrongdoing and end with confirmation of the allegations, there are exceptions. For example, accusations can occur anywhere throughout the scandal. There can be multiple allegations of wrongdoing that may or may not occur under the umbrella of the major transgression. And one scandal may have multiple instances of scapegoating or mortification. Nevertheless, the basic thematic elements remain.

The thematic narrative that repeats, albeit with variations upon a theme as highlighted in chapter 6, makes those who are involved and passive observers see the unfolding events as a scandal. As Bennett claimed, "It is difficult to watch the development of political issues without experiencing a powerful sense of déjà vu."[61] The seemingly repetitive yet natural evolution of events from beginning to end allows for those involved in the scandal to understand what is happening and presumably what will happen next. Teapot Dome was seen as a model for Watergate, and Watergate for Iran-Contra and Clinton/Lewinsky (and perhaps many more in the future). Watergate, Iran-Contra, and Clinton/Lewinsky were easy comparisons for journalists to make as they unfolded within a thirty-year span. There were journalists and politicians who were involved in each of these scandals, and they carried their experiences with them from one to the next. Comparisons to Teapot Dome were made, but they were infrequent compared to the others. One primary reason was that Teapot Dome happened fifty years prior to the next scandal, Watergate. A generation of reporters and politicians had come and gone.

One of the primary reasons that this book has relied on the four major critical cases is that they are the prime drivers of the scandal narrative. Teapot Dome, Watergate, Iran-Contra, and Clinton/Lewinsky are all distinguished in American politics for their machination. In their quasi-prestigious place in politics, these scandals provide political lessons for what is and is not expected of those who find themselves in the midst of the next scandal. Thus, the scandal narrative instructs the participants on how to respond to potentially scandalous transgressions.

Importantly, this book suggests that it is not just the egregiousness of each scandal, in terms of the transgression, that is the driving influence of events. The very scandal narrative itself demonstrates the political system's ability to inform the public of a transgression, investigate it, and appropriately deal with the transgressor. While there will always be individuals who commit transgressions for the love of money or power, it is the entire scandal narrative that regulates the power of the people and the democratic notions of a free press. As Eric Csapo claimed, "No viable culture relies upon punishment and police functions alone to regulate the behavior of its citizens. Such external regulation is only exceptionally necessary. Far more important is the internal regulation by society's system of beliefs and values which both shape the mind of the individual and create his or her needs and desires."[62] The scandal narrative shapes the mind of the body politic into a shocked yet reassuring passivity that the system that allowed for the transgression can also ameliorate the situation.

Yet there is more to the scandal narrative. The scandal narrative has significant implications for free speech, public discourse, and democracy. As the scandal unfolds, a battle for meaning commences. On the one hand, there is the accused, who engages in several forms of *apologia* to defend him- or herself against the allegations. On the other hand, there is the accuser, who attempts to legitimize and officialize the accusations to rise above the characterization of political rancor. Despite the apparent auspices of officialization, though, the motivation is often partisan.

The battle goes back and forth and thereby creates a crisis of meaning, which is typically settled by a smoking gun. The smoking gun allows for the redefinition of the original misconduct as a major political scandal. The smoking gun, in essence, demonstrates that the accusations are true, but, more importantly, the smoking gun also proves that the accused has lied. To the

official investigators, the main issue of the scandal is not the original misconduct, which may not necessarily be illegal, but the lie, which is obstruction
of justice, an impeachable offense. Redefining the lie as the major scandal
issue empowers Congress, which otherwise would have very little punishment power over the original misconduct, to take action against the accused.

In the end, there is a hero: the accused politician who redeems the political
order through mortification (i.e., resignation) or becoming a scapegoat (i.e.,
being tried and convicted) by the government of which he is a part. The press
is an apparent hero in that they seemingly provided symbolic oversight over
the government, which, in actuality, provides reporters with the information
used in the initial publicity of the misconduct. Members of the electorate,
who are normally agents in a democracy, have their agency limited in the
scandal as the government is able to contend with the accused politician.

This scandal narrative helps us all make sense of what is happening today and potentially what will happen tomorrow. As a case in point, we can
examine an unfolding scandal that has yet to conclude: the Fort Lee/George
Washington Bridge lane closure scandal, also known as Bridgegate.

BRIDGEGATE

The Transgression

September 9, 2013, was the first day of school for schoolchildren in New
Jersey, and workers from Fort Lee were making their daily commute to New
York City across the busiest bridge in the world, the George Washington
Bridge. For those who have not had the experience, normal traffic includes
delays, which range from minimal to substantial. But this day was no normal
delay. Someone had closed off two of the three access lanes from Fort Lee to
the bridge with orange traffic cones. There was catastrophic gridlock. It took
over five hours for the residual morning traffic to be cleared out.

The situation repeated itself every day for a week. One commuter described the situation as the worst traffic delays she had ever seen since twelve
years prior on September 11, 2001. Commuters were furious and inundated
the phones lines of Fort Lee mayor Mark Sokolich, who attempted to get an
explanation from those who control the bridge, the Port Authority of New
York and New Jersey. The only answer was that the Port Authority was con-
ducting a study of bridge traffic. Despite the ongoing chaos on the bridge, the
Port Authority offered no relief or any further explanation.

While traffic studies are not uncommon, they are planned in many high-
level meetings, public notice is given well in advance, and the affected towns,
mayors, police, and others are alerted as well. This was not done. The people

did not know, the police chief did not know, and the mayor did not know. Given the lack of notice and explanation, the seeming ease of moving around some traffic cones to cause gridlock, the busiest bridge in the world at the busiest time of the day, and the vulnerability of the bridge (as well as nearby tunnels) in New York City on the anniversary of the September 11 attacks, people were terrified. Even the most circulated newspaper in the country, the *Wall Street Journal*, reported the traffic jam. This was no normal traffic jam. This was the beginning of a scandal.

Political or Criminal Transgression?

While some commuters were angry and others scared, Mayor Sokolich had a hunch about why this was happening.[63] In an interview for the local paper, the mayor speculated, "I thought we had a good relationship [with the Port Authority]. Now I'm beginning to wonder if there's something I did wrong. Am I being sent some sort of message?"[64]

The mayor was not the only one. *The Record* also noted that there was an equal number of people who called to figure out what was happening as "conspiracy theorists who insisted that the Port was punishing Sokolich—either for failing to endorse Governor Christie's election bid or for pushing through a $500 million, 47-story high-rise housing development near the bridge, or for failing to support the Port's last toll hike."[65]

The makeup of the Port Authority added more speculation to the quickly emerging political overtones. The Port Authority is controlled by a board of twelve individuals (six from New York and six from New Jersey), who are appointed by the governors of the respective states, and one executive director. In 2013, the executive director was Patrick Foye, who was appointed by Democratic New York governor Andrew Cuomo. After four days of an apparent traffic study, Foye opened all the lanes and two weeks later was quoted, "I believe this hasty and ill-advised decision violates federal law and the law of both states."[66] What seemed to be a little thing, two lanes shut down for a study, had started to become a very big thing.

First Officialization

After six weeks had passed since the lanes were closed, the Democratic chairman of the New Jersey legislature's Transportation Committee and the Port Authority announced they would both be investigating the lane closures. The timing seemed partisan. Republican governor Chris Christie was campaigning for reelection against state senator Barbara Buono, who needed all the help she could get against the perennial Garden State favorite. Buono herself tried to make the matter a campaign issue but failed to do so. Like other political candidates such as George McGovern, who attempted to tie a controversy to the opposing political candidate in an election, the accusations and concerns were easily dismissed as a failing political candidate vying for voters.

Christie went on to win the November 5 election, and the Transportation Committee began holding hearings on November 25. The election was over, and thus any such investigations would not be dismissed as tactics to influence the campaign.

Up first was deputy executive director and Chris Christie's first appointee to the board, Bill Baroni, who admitted that the Port Authority failed to communicate the closing and gave no reason for why such a failure took place. Baroni identified David Wildstein, Christie's second appointee, as the person who ordered the study, which was to examine why Fort Lee residents, who make up 4.5 percent of George Washington Bridge traffic have exclusive access to 25 percent of the access roads to the bridge. Slyly, Baroni then recited the percentage of people from each committee member's district and asked, "Shouldn't the people in your district have as much access to the bridge as Fort Lee?"[67] The committee chairman John Wisniewski did not bite and kept pushing on the how and why questions of the gridlock.

Up next was Executive Director Patrick Foye, who testified on December 9, 2013. Foye confirmed that Wildstein ordered the study and that the Christie appointee had instructed the bridge manager and all others involved not to notify the Fort Lee city administration and police. Moreover, Foye believed that if Wildstein had been a New York appointee, he would have been fired immediately for ordering the study and the silence. That was a clear message to Christie.

Dismissal of Investigations as Political and Partisan Attacks

The New Jersey governor did not miss the cue. As the Transportation Committee's inquiry began, Christie quickly described the investigation as playing politics and said that those who are leading it "really have nothing to do."[68] At a press conference, the governor, who is known for his in-your-face abrasiveness, gave the legislative investigators what they seemingly wanted by saying that he himself was the guy who moved the cones to block traffic. This sarcastic retort goes far beyond what others who have been accused of chicanery have said. In effect, Christie not only said that the whole ordeal was a game but he would have fun and play it too.

Christie's second term is his last due to term limits, but there is tremendous speculation that he will run for president in 2016. Thus, there is still the opportunity for him to dismiss the ordeal as nothing but politics. Consequently,

Christie is dismissing state Democrats but is mindful of Democrats on the national stage, who immediately began using the situation to weaken his national standing. In December 2013, Christie responded with the classic partisan dismissals. He said, "National Democrats will make an issue about everything about me. . . . Get used to the new world, everybody."[69] He continued, "It's not that big a deal, just because the press runs around and writes about it both here and nationally. . . . I know why it is, so do you. Let's not pretend it's because of the gravity of the issue. It's because I am a national figure and anything like this will be written about a lot now."[70]

First Resignations of Bridgegate

The scandal narrative tells us that once a transgression happens and after it has been, to some degree, escalated to the proper levels, a sacrifice must be made. Thus far, all the thematic elements of a scandal were present. There was the transgression, which seemed more than just the normal misstep; the partisan accusations and dismissals; and the proper level of investigation with some partial but not complete disclosures. All in all, the events that unfolded in the wake of the lane closures had all the markings of a scandal—except for the sacrifice. Shortly after the investigations began, Christie's first and second appointees to the Port Authority board resigned. After Baroni identified Wildstein as the individual who ordered the study on November 25, Wildstein resigned from the Port Authority on December 6. He claimed he was planning on resigning next year, but the bridge controversy had become a "distraction."[71] Baroni then resigned a week later. Christie responded that both Baroni and Wildstein had made mistakes, but the situation was not politically motivated and no one in his office was involved.

The scandal narrative demands proper penitence, and the resignations were not enough to satisfy demands. There was too much uncertainty. With the resignations, Christie said it was time "to turn the page."[72] New Jersey's Democratic legislative leaders believed the resignations were right, but there was more to be uncovered. National Democrats did too. The resignations did not address the underlying issue, the traffic study.

In the three months that had passed since the initial lane closings, no details of the traffic study other than its mere existence and quick enactment had appeared. Consequently, U.S. senator Jay Rockefeller, who chairs the Senate Committee on Commerce, Science, and Transportation, began investigating. The senator from West Virginia had upped the officialization status of the controversy. Although a Democrat, Rockefeller had the official position as chairman of a federal committee that had jurisdiction and had the proper temperament. Asked about his investigation, Rockefeller clarified, "You want me to talk about Governor Christie. I don't want to. . . . The press always wants to make the political conclusion first, and we'd rather look at the factual conclusion."[73]

In mid-December 2013, the opinion pages of the area newspapers began discussing whether the controversy had become worthy of the title "Bridge-gate" or if the term was just fanning the flames of scandal. Nevertheless, it was clear, as in all other major scandals that had unfolded in a similar manner, that there was more to come. The resignations were not enough to put an end to the scandal.

The Smoking Gun

The events of the first week of January 2014 exacerbated the scandal. New Jersey assemblyman John Wisniewski stated, "There are documents that we've received that would indicate that there was somebody else who initi-ated this. . . . There are words that are used that would imply an improper motive"[74] Wisniewski was cautious not to imply that Christie was involved. In essence the Democratic chairman found *a* smoking gun but was unsure who fired it. Then on January 8, 2014, *the* smoking gun was released, and it was clear who fired it.

A trove of documents were released that included e-mails from Christie's deputy chief of staff, Bridget Kelly. One of her e-mails to David Wildstein instructed, "Time for some traffic problems in Fort Lee."[75] The rest of the documents make it clear that the lane closures were political punishment for Mayor Sokolich and that members of Christie's staff were involved in the planning and execution.

Christie, who earlier claimed that no one in his administration was in-volved, had to respond. Christie quickly fired Kelly, calling her actions "stu-pid" and "deceitful" and dismissed his campaign and political advisor, Bill Stepien.[76] After his comments, Christie answered questions for two hours. His public face-to-face apology and question-and-answer session far exceeded the vulnerability of Weiner's apology, at least in terms of time.

Afterward, Christie traveled to Fort Lee to meet with the mayor and per-sonally apologized. The governor had ostensibly offered his best attempt at mortification. His press conference remarks were "the most contrite apology of his political career"; he directly engaged the press for a remarkable amount of time and then faced the mayor. Often characterized as a bully, Christie was as vulnerable as he could be. He took responsibility in general but was adamant he was not involved.

Christie's lack of involvement was repeated a week later in his State of the State address. The governor briefly addressed the growing controversy by saying, "Mistakes were clearly made."[77] This "passive-evasive way of acknowledging error while distancing the speaker from responsibility for it" comment carries significant political baggage.[78] In response to a series of scandals, President Ulysses S. Grant said, "Mistakes have been made." As the facts of Watergate came pouring out, White House press secretary Ron Ziegler admitted, "Mistakes were made." Nixon used a variation of the phrase in his farewell address. Reagan's 1987 State of the Union address used the "mistakes were made" line to describe Iran-Contra. Clinton also responded to questionable democratic fund-raising tactics with the same exact phrase. If Christie intended to use the phrase to distance himself from scandal, he could have used a better line.

Second Officialization

The situation became even more serious immediately after the document disclosure. Democrats in the New Jersey Assembly and Senate authorized a committee with subpoena power to investigate the scandal. Gov. Christie hired legal counsel to investigate. The Port Authority had its own investigation. The ultimate officialization came when U.S. Attorney Paul Fishman began reviewing the case to determine what if any federal laws were violated.

Very Reluctant Participation

As the existing investigations continued and new ones began, some, true to the scandal narrative, reluctantly participated. The same day the documents were made public, David Wildstein appeared before the New Jersey legislative committee. He repeatedly asserted his Fifth Amendment right against self-incrimination. Given his resignation after being identified by Baroni and the sudden disclosure of incriminating documents, his silence, as the local news described it, "spoke volumes."[79] However, his lawyer made it clear that he would be more forthcoming if he were given immunity from prosecution.

Mayor Sokolich refused to participate in Christie's internal inquiry. But he made it clear that he would participate in the New Jersey legislature and U.S. attorney's investigations. The political reasons are evident.

Those at the heart of the scandal refused to speak to anyone. Christie's former deputy chief of staff Bridget Kelly and dismissed political advisor Bill Stepien refused to cooperate with Christie's internal investigation. However, this refusal may have been strategic. By not including Kelly and Stepien in the internal investigation, there is more validity to the report's conclusion, which was released at the end of March 2014. The report characterized Kelly and Stepien as "acting like some sort of sleeper cell carrying out a secret plan to close down two approach lanes to the George Washington Bridge, for some inexplicable 'ulterior motive.'"[80] That is, if Kelly and Stepien had participated in the internal inquiry, that very participation would undercut their characterization as working independently of Christie.

Naturally, Kelly and Stepien also refused to work with the legislature. In February, lawyers for the duo advised the initial legislative inquiry headed by Wisniewski that they would not comply with subpoenas to turn over documents. Wisniewski and his New Jersey Senate counterpart, Loretta Weinberg, opted to take them to court to comply.

GOING FORWARD

Scandals often quiet down when they go to the courts, and Bride-gate is no exception. This is because the wheels of justice turn slowly. However, this particular example is slowing down for a slightly different reason. Wisniewski and Weinberg are beginning to slow down their investigation because those they hope to question, such as Kelly and Stepien, are also waiting to testify before the U.S. attorney. The only way Kelly and Stepien can be compelled to give testimony to the legislature is if they are given immunity from prosecution. Thus, for Wisniewski and Weinberg to continue to have their moment in the political spotlight is to cost the U.S. attorney the ability to prosecute any crimes that may have been committed.

This is different from Iran-Contra where Congress's desire for publicity trumped justice; that is, those who testified before Congress were given immunity (and others were later pardoned). Here, it seems that state legislators would prefer justice over publicity. One can speculate about the reasons. The New Jersey legislature effectively has no way to seriously punish Christie. By the time Kelly and Stepien resolve the issue of the legislature's subpoena in the courts, Christie may very well be out of the governor's office. Moreover, even if Christie was involved, it is unlikely that his actions would merit removal from office. However, Christie's ambitions are fairly transparent, at least as of the writing of this book. If he does run for president, the findings, if any, from the U.S. attorney would be far more significant than if they came from the legislature. An indictment from the U.S. attorney would certainly prevent or derail Christie's presidential hopes. If he is not indicted, then Christie has been cleared by a significant officialized source.

As of now, Bridgegate's next scene will prominently feature Paul Fishman who is known for not leaking any information whatsoever. He even goes to great lengths to keep witnesses from being seen as they enter and exit the courthouse. The U.S. attorney has held news conferences but has been reserved with his disclosures. At a news conference, Fishman said,

> As you probably know, I rarely, if ever, comment on ongoing investigations by my office, and I'm not going to comment on that investigation either. I will say this: Reports in the press that purport to describe what I might be thinking or what the people working on that matter might be thinking or contemplating have been almost entirely incorrect.[81]

While it is unclear what will happen next, the scandal narrative tells us that Bridgegate will be over when the right person pays the right price. So far, it seems, that has not happened. Who that person is and what the price will be have not been fully answered. If Christie does not run for president, this scandal may fizzle out. If he does run and if history is any predictor, we will find out during the upcoming campaign season.

Notes

CHAPTER 1:
SCANDALOUS STATE OF THE UNION

1. Joanna Walters, "Obama Team Hit by Corruption Scandal," *The Express*, February 4, 2009, 7.

2. Paul Kane and Carol D. Leonnig, "Ensign Broke Law, Panel Finds," *Washington Post*, May 13, 2011, A1.

3. Paul Kane and Ben Pershing, "Rangel Hit with 13 Ethics Charges," *Washington Post*, July 30, 2010, A1.

4. R. Jeffrey Smith, "DeLay Sentenced to 3 Years in Prison," *Washington Post*, January 11, 2011, A1.

5. Susan Schmidt and James V. Grimaldi, "Ney Sentenced to 30 Months in Prison for Abramoff Deals," *Washington Post*, January 20, 2007, A3.

6. Jennifer Steignhauer, "Senate, for Just the 8th Time, Votes to Oust a Federal Judge," *New York Times*, December 9, 2010, A27.

7. James C, McKinley, "Judge Sentenced to Prison for Lying about Harassment," *New York Times*, May 12, 2009, A15.

8. Jennifer Haberkorn, "Will 'Fight' to 'Last Breath,' Refuses to Step Down over Bribery Charges," *Washington Times*, December 20, 2008, A1; Monica Davey and Emma Graves Fitzsimmons, "A State Unconvinced That Its Culture of Corruption Will Ever Fade," *New York Times*, April 19, 2010, A18.

9. Cindy Rodriguez, "Amid Dispute, Plight of Illegal Workers Revisited," *Boston Globe*, January 10, 2001, A14; J. K. Dineen, "Bush's First Test Cabinet Mess," *New York Daily News*, January 9, 2001, 1.

10. Julie Mason, "Loyalty, Diversity Key to Likely Bush Team," *Houston Chronicle*, December 15, 2000, A1; Andy Geller, "Slick Execs Taken Down—Jurors: Why We Nailed Lying, Disgraceful Duo," *New York Post*, May 26, 2006, 4.

11. Anne E. Kornblut, "Third Journalist Was Paid to Promote Bush Policies," *New York Times*, January 29, 2005, A5; Greg Toppo, "White House Paid Commentator to Promote Law," *USA Today*, January 7, 2005, 1A.

12. Amy Goldstein. "Justice Dept. Recognized Prosecutor's Work on Election Fraud before His Firing," *Washington Post*, March 19, 2007, A4; "Politics and the Corruption Fighter," *New York Times*, January 18, 2007, 26.

13. Eric Lichtblau, "Clinton Aide Pleads Guilty to Taking Secret Papers," *New York Times*, April 2, 2005, A1.

14. Curt Anderson, "Berger Says Document Incident 'Honest Mistake,' but GOP Calls for Answers," *Associated Press*, July 21, 2004.

15. John Garrard, "Scandals: An Overview," in *Scandals in Past and Contemporary Politics*, ed. John Garrard and James L. Newell, 13–29 (New York: Palgrave, 2006), 28.

16. Scott J. Basinger and Brandon Rottinghaus, "Skeletons in White House Closets: A Discussion of Modern Presidential Scandals," *Political Science Quarterly* 127 (2012): 213–239, 217–218.

17. John B. Thompson, *Political Scandal: Power and Visibility in the Media Age* (Malden, MA: Polity Press, 2000), 17–25.

18. Basinger and Rottinghaus, "Skeletons in White House Closets," 217–218.

19. Robert Williams, *Political Scandals in the USA* (Edinburgh: Keele University Press, 1998), 6.

20. If the cover-up is successful, then it is highly doubtful that anyone will know about the initial transgression.

21. Thompson, *Political Scandal*, 17–25.

22. Ibid., 13.

23. Ibid., 17.

24. Carol W. Lewis, *The Ethics Challenge in Public Service: A Problem-Solving Guide* (San Francisco: Jossey-Bass, 1991).

25. Williams, *Political Scandals*, 6.

26. Theodore J. Lowi, foreword to *The Politics of Scandal: Power and Process in Liberal Democracies*, ed. Andrei S. Markovits and Mark Silverstein, vii–xii (New York: Holmes & Meier, 1988), vii.

27. Michael Wines, "Packwood Yields Diaries: Judge Is Told of Revisions," *New York Times*, December 17, 1993, A26.

28. Williams, *Political Scandals*, 123.

29. Paul Kane, "Police Release Audio of Senator's Arrest," *Washington Post*, August 31, 2007, A3.

30. Dan Popkey, "Men's Room Arrest Reopens Questions about Craig," *Idaho Statesman*, August 28, 2007, A1.

31. Dana Milbank, "A Senator's Wide Stance: 'I Am Not Gay,'" *Washington Post*, August 29, 2007, A2.

32. Ronald Kessler, *Inside Congress: The Shocking Scandals, Corruption, and Abuse of Power behind the Scenes on Capitol Hill* (New York: Pocket Books, 1997).

33. Williams, *Political Scandals*, 7.

34. Sidney Blumenthal, "The Cover-Up That Kills: A Sex Scandal in the US Congress Has Republicans Pointing Fingers as Mid-Term Elections Near," *Guardian*, October 5, 2006, 33.

35. Jonathan Weisman and Charles Babington, "GOP Leader Rebuts Hastert on Foley," *Washington Post*, October 5, 2006, A1.

36. Kathleen Hall Jamieson, *Packaging the Presidency: A History and Criticism of Presidential Campaign Advertising* (New York: Oxford University Press, 1996), 329.

37. Williams, *Political Scandals*, 8.

38. Robert Busby, *Reagan and the Iran-Contra Affair: The Politics of Presidential Recovery* (New York: St. Martin's, 1999), 19.

39. Ibid.

40. Kessler, *Inside Congress.*

41. Christopher Lee, "GAO Cites Janet Rehnquist's Lapses," *Washington Post*, June 11, 2003, A33.

42. "The Ted Stevens Scandal," *Wall Street Journal*, April 2, 2009, http://online .wsj.com/news/articles/SB123863051723580701.

43. Emma Brown, "Fierce and Canny Legislator Showered Federal Funds on His Beloved Alaska," August 11, 2010, *Washington Post*, A1.

44. Williams, *Political Scandals*, 1.

45. Vincent Blasi, "The Checking Value in First Amendment Theory," *American Bar Foundation Research Journal* 2 (1977): 521–649.

46. Ibid., 531.

47. Ibid., 533.

48. Rodney A. Smolla, *Smolla and Nimmer on Freedom of Speech* (New York: Clark Boardman Callaghan, 1996), 1–5.

49. Ibid.

50. Blasi, "The Checking Value," 534.

51. Geoffrey R. Stone, Louis M. Seidman, Cass R. Sunstein, Mark V. Tushnet, and Pamela S. Karlan, *The First Amendment: A Reader* (New York: Aspen Publishers, 2003), 4.

52. Ibid.

53. Independent counsels and presidential commissions are differentiated from one another in one respect. A presidential commission's investigation is research focused and does not purposely seek to determine guilt but often does uncover wrongdoing. The independent counsel is specifically designed to determine if wrongdoing occurred. The attorney general first determines if an investigation is warranted; then, if there is a perceived conflict of interest, an independent counsel is appointed by representatives of the judicial branch. Every independent counsel since its initiation in 1978 has investigated members of the executive branch, including aides to the president, members of the cabinet, and the president.

54. Stjepan G. Mestrovic, *Durkheim and Postmodern Culture* (New York: A. de Gruyter, 1992), 95.

55. Robert N. Bellah, "Civil Religion in America," in *American Civil Religion*, ed. Russell E. Richey and Donald G. Jones, 21–44 (New York: Harper & Row, 1974), 21.

56. Ibid., 28.

57. Ibid., 29.

58. Sacvan Bercovitch, *The American Jeremiad* (Madison: University of Wisconsin Press, 1978), 145.

59. Ibid., 141–142.

60. Moreover, July 4 is the only day on which multiple presidents have died (Monroe died in 1831; Coolidge was the only president born on July 4).

61. Bellah, "Civil Religion," 142.

62. Mestrovic, *Durkheim*, 93.

63. Bellah, "Civil Religion," 41.

64. Michael Q. Patton, *Qualitative Research and Evaluation Methods* (Thousand Oaks, CA: Sage, 2002), 243.

65. "Experts Uphold Teapot Dome Lease," *New York Times*, October 23, 1923, 23.

66. Frederick Lewis Allen, *Only Yesterday: An Informal History of the Nineteen-Twenties* (New York: Harper & Brothers, 1957), 137; Stanley Frost, "Yes—But What Are the Facts?," *Outlook*, April 2, 1924, 556.

67. David H. Stratton, *Tempest over Teapot Dome: The Story of Albert B. Fall* (Norman: University of Oklahoma Press, 1998), 5.

68. Michael Nelson, *The Evolving Presidency: Addresses, Cases, Essays, Letters, Reports, Resolutions, Transcripts, and Other Landmark Documents* (Washington, DC: CQ Press, 1999), 104.

69. Ibid., 301.

70. Elizabeth Webber and Mike Feinsilber, *Merriam-Webster's Dictionary of Allusions* (Springfield, MA: Merriam-Webster, 1999), s.v. "Teapot Dome."

71. Harold I. Gullan, *Faith of Our Mothers: The Stories of Presidential Mothers from Mary Washington to Barbara Bush* (Grand Rapids, MI: Eerdmans, 2001), 286.

72. T. R. Reid, "'Koreagate' Emerging as Republicans' No. 1 Campaign Issue," *Washington Post*, July 24, 1977, A16.

73. Andrew Miga, "Washington Watch: 'Rubbergate' Incident Perks Up House Scrutiny," *Boston Herald*, October 7, 1991, 4.

74. Lionel Barber, "Covert Campaign for Democracy 'Led to Irangate,'" *Financial Times*, February 16, 1987, 3.

75. Philip Geyelin, "'Billygate' Won't Wash," *Washington Post*, July 31, 1980, A21.

76. Arti Berman, "Attorneygate in Guam," *Nation*, April 7, 2007, 5–6.

77. Melissa Block, "Attorneys Case Is Least of Gonzales Lapses," *All Things Considered*, NPR, March 28, 2007.

78. Julian Borger, "'Plamegate' Reporter Leaves *New York Times*," *Guardian*, November 10, 2005, 22.

79. Mary Dejevsky, "Bush Backs Nominee Caught Up in 'Nannygate' Row," *Independent*, January 9, 2001, 17.

80. Paul Krugman, "Sweet Little Lies," *New York Times*, April 9, 2007, A17.

81. "Representative Is 'Out of Step,' Clinton Charges," *Arkansas Democrat-Gazette*, August 8, 1974, 7A.

82. Craig A. Smith, "Bill Clinton in Rhetorical Crisis: The Six Stages of Scandal and Impeachment," in *Images, Scandal, and Communication Strategies of the Clinton Presidency*, ed. Robert E. Denton and Rachel L. Holloway, 173–194 (Westport, CT: Praeger, 2003), 174.

83. Norman E. Isaacs, *Untended Gates: The Mismanaged Press* (New York: Columbia University Press, 1986), 234.

84. Williams, *Political Scandals*, 7.

CHAPTER 2:
THE ROLE OF JOURNALISM

1. James L. Aucoin, "The Re-Emergence of American Investigative Journalism, 1960–1975," *Journalism History* 21 (1995): 3–15, 8.

2. Vincent Blasi, "The Checking Value in First Amendment Theory," *American Bar Foundation Research Journal* 2 (1977): 528; Aucoin, "The Re-Emergence of American Investigative Journalism," 8.

3. Blasi, "The Checking Value," 521.

4. Ibid., 520.

5. Ari Adut, *On Scandal: Moral Disturbances in Society, Politics, and Art* (Cambridge: Cambridge University Press, 2008), 13.

6. Edward Jay Epstein, *Between Fact and Fiction: The Problem of Journalism* (New York: Vintage, 1975), 19.

7. Janice Rushing and Tom Frentz, "The Mythic Perspective," in *The Art of Rhetorical Criticism*, ed. Jim A. Kuyper, 241–269 (Boston: Pearson/Allyn & Bacon, 2005), 243.

8. Janice Hocker Rushing and Thomas S. Frentz, *Projecting the Shadow: The Cyborg Hero in American Film* (Chicago: University of Chicago Press, 1995), 46.

9. Richard Slotkin, *Gunfighter Nation* (Norman: University of Oklahoma Press, 1998), 653; Matthew Ehrlich, "Shattered Glass, Movies, and the Free Press Myth," *Journal of Communication Inquiry* 29 (2005): 103.

10. Robert Waterman McChesney and Ben Scott, introduction to *Our Unfree Press: 100 Years of Radical Media Criticism*, ed. Robert Waterman McChesney and Ben Scott, 1–30 (New York: New Press, 2004), 1–2; Ehrlich, "Shattered Glass," 104.

11. Leonard W. Levy, *Freedom of the Press from Zenger to Jefferson* (Durham, NC: Carolina Academic Press, 1996); John Peter Zenger, *A Brief Narrative of the Case and Trial of John Peter Zenger, Printer of the "New York Weekly Journal"* (Cambridge, MA: Belknap Press of Harvard University, 1963).

12. Epstein, *Between Fact and Fiction*, 31.

13. Michael Schudson, *Watergate in American Memory: How We Remember, Forget, and Reconstruct the Past* (New York: Basic Books, 1992), 103–104.

14. Theodore H. White, *Breach of Faith: The Fall of Richard Nixon* (New York: Atheneum Publishers, 1975), 224.

15. Ibid.

16. Schudson, *Watergate in American Memory*, 104; Michael Schudson, "Watergate: A Study in Mythology," *Columbia Journalism Review* 31 (1992): 28–33, 29; Matthew C. Ehrlich, *Journalism in the Movies* (Urbana: University of Illinois Press, 2004), 120.

17. Schudson, *Watergate in American Memory*, 104.

18. Mark Feeney, *Nixon at the Movies: A Book about Belief* (Chicago: University of Chicago Press, 2004), 263.

19. Ibid.

20. Ibid., 259.

21. Ibid., 258.

22. Jonathan Kirshner, "*All the President's Men* (1976)," review of *All the President's Men* (DVD), *Film & History: An Interdisciplinary Journal of Film and Television Studies* 36 (2006): 58.

23. Bob Woodward and Carl Bernstein, *The Secret Man: The Story of Watergate's Deep Throat* (New York: Simon & Schuster, 2005), 120.

24. Stanley I. Kutler, *The Wars of Watergate: The Last Crisis of Richard Nixon* (New York: Knopf, 1990); Schudson, *Watergate in American Memory.*

25. Epstein, *Between Fact and Fiction*, 32.

26. Feeney, *Nixon at the Movies*, 259.

27. Livingston Rutherfurd, *John Peter Zenger, His Press, His Trial and a Bibliography of Zenger Imprints* (New York: Peter Smith, 1941), 34.

28. Leonard W. Levy, *Legacy of Suppression: Freedom of Speech and Press in Early American History* (Cambridge, MA: Belknap Press of Harvard University Press, 1960), 131.

29. Rutherfurd, *John Peter Zenger*, 34.

30. Anthony Lewis, *Freedom for the Thought We Hate* (New York: Basic Books, 2009), 13.

31. Carl Bernstein and Bob Woodward, *All the President's Men* (New York: Simon & Schuster, 1974), 224.

32. Ibid.

33. Schudson, "Watergate: A Study in Mythology," 28.

34. Woodward and Bernstein, *The Secret Man.*

35. Kirshner, "*All the President's Men* (1976)," 57.

36. Barbie Zelizer, "Journalists as Interpretive Communities," *Critical Studies in Media Communication* 10 (1993): 219–237.

37. Ioan M. Lewis, *Ecstatic Religion: A Study of Shamanism and Spirit Possession* (London: Routledge, 2005).

38. Barbie Zelizer, "On Communicative Practice: The 'Other Worlds' of Journalism and Shamanism," *Southern Folklore* 49 (1992): 20.

39. Ibid.

40. Michael Janeway, *Republic of Denial: Press, Politics, and Public Life* (New Haven, CT: Yale University Press, 1999), 103.

41. Zelizer, "On Communicative Practice," 25.

42. Ibid., 25.

43. Woodward and Bernstein, *The Secret Man*, 66.

44. Ibid., 77; Bernstein and Woodward, *All the President's Men*, 135.

45. Carl Bernstein, interview by author, Lawrenceville, NJ, September 11, 2013.

46. Woodward and Bernstein, *The Secret Man*, 107.

47. Leonard Downie, *The New Muckrakers* (Washington, DC: New Republic, 1976), 44.

48. Ibid., 44.

49. Blasi, "The Checking Value," 601.

50. Marvin L. Kalb, *The Rise of the "New News": A Case Study of Two Root Causes of the Modern Scandal Coverage* (Cambridge, MA: Harvard University Press, 1998), 28.

51. Marvin L. Kalb, *One Scandalous Story: Clinton, Lewinsky, and Thirteen Days That Tarnished American Journalism* (New York: Free Press, 2001), 80.

52. Ibid., 69–76; Louis Liebovich, *The Press and the Modern Presidency: Myths and Mindsets from Kennedy to Election 2000* (Westport, CT: Praeger, 2001), 220.

53. Kalb, *One Scandalous Story*, 36.

54. Roger Wilkes, *Scandal: A Scurrilous History of Gossip* (London: Atlantic, 2002), 316.

55. Kalb, *One Scandalous Story*, 150.

56. Alicia C. Shepard, "The Isikoff Factor," *American Journalism Review* 20 (1998): 22.

57. Michael Isikoff, *Uncovering Clinton: A Reporter's Story* (New York: Crown, 1999), 189.

58. Evan Thomas and Michael Thomas, "The White House Blames Clinton's Potential Perjury Problem on the Special Prosecutor. But If There Was a Trap, It Was Set by Women Offstage, Not by Starr," *Newsweek*, November 9, 1998, 30; Adut, *On Scandal*, 216.

59. Isikoff, *Uncovering Clinton*, 286.

60. Ibid., 287.

61. Ibid., 297.

62. Ibid.

63. Ibid., 287.

64. Ibid., 300.

65. Kalb, *One Scandalous Story*, 33; Rich Lowry, *Legacy: Paying the Price for the Clinton Years* (Washington, DC: Regnery, 2003), 184–185.

66. Lowry, *Legacy: Paying the Price for the Clinton Years*, 184–185; Kalb, *One Scandalous Story*, 80.

67. Lowry, *Legacy: Paying the Price for the Clinton Years*, 184–185.

68. Kalb, *The Rise of the "New News,"* 4; Shepard, "The Isikoff Factor," 22.

69. Shepard, "The Isikoff Factor," 22; Lawrence W. Sherman, "The Mobilization of Scandal," in *Political Corruption: A Handbook*, ed. Arnold J. Heidenheimer, Michael Johnston, and Victor T. Le Vine, 887–991 (New Brunswick, NJ: Transaction, 1989), 893.

70. Kirshner, *"All the President's Men* (1976)," 58.

71. Aucoin, "The Re-Emergence of American Investigative Journalism," 12.

72. William Safire, *Safire's Political Dictionary* (Oxford: Oxford University Press, 2008), s.v. "Fourth Estate."

73. Douglass Cater, *The Fourth Branch of Government* (Boston: Houghton Mifflin, 1959), 13.

74. *The Encyclopedia of Religion* (New York: Macmillan, 1987), s.v. "Shamanism," by Mircea Eliade and Charles J. Adams, 8269.

75. Frederick Lewis Allen, *Only Yesterday: An Informal History of the Nineteen-Twenties* (New York: Harper & Brothers, 1957), 156.

76. Laton McCartney, *The Teapot Dome Scandal: How Big Oil Bought the Harding White House and Tried to Steal the Country* (New York: Random House, 2008), 260; Paul Y. Anderson, "Many Obstacles Met in Discovering Disposition of Continental Bonds," *Editor & Publisher*, 1929, 10.

77. Paul H. Giddens, *Standard Oil Company: Oil Pioneer of the Middle West* (New York: Appleton-Century-Crofts, 1955), 374.

78. Giddens, *Standard Oil Company*, 373; see transcript of U.S. v. Robert W. Stewart, Supreme Court of the District of Columbia, IV (1928), 667, 673, 675, 676.

79. "Rockefeller Aids Efforts of Senate to Bare Oil Deal," *New York Times*, February 9, 1928, A1.

80. Edmund B. Lambeth, "The Lost Career of Paul Y. Anderson," *Journalism Quarterly* 60 (1983): 401.

81. Ibid., 403.

82. C. D. Stelzer, "'Just a Newspaper Hack on the Side of the Angels': Crusading Reporter Paul Y. Anderson," *St. Louis Journalism Review*, July 2008, 20; Lambeth, "The Lost Career of Paul Y. Anderson," 406.

83. Marquis W. Childs, *Witness to Power* (New York: McGraw-Hill, 1975), 39; Clark R Mollenhoff, *Investigative Reporting: From Courthouse to White House* (London: Collier Macmillan, 1981), 59; Lambeth, "The Lost Career of Paul Y. Anderson," 402.

84. William L. Rivers, *The Adversaries: Politics and the Press* (Boston: Beacon, 1970), 24.

85. Ibid.

86. Donald A. Ritchie, *Reporting from Washington: The History of the Washington Press Corps* (Oxford: Oxford University Press, 2006), 1; Cater, *The Fourth Branch of Government*, 93.

87. Cater, *The Fourth Branch of Government*, 93.

88. M. R. Werner and John Starr, *Teapot Dome* (New York: Viking, 1959), 195; David H. Stratton, *Tempest over Teapot Dome: The Story of Albert B. Fall* (Norman: University of Oklahoma Press, 1998), 280–281.

89. Freda Kirchwey, Oswald G. Villard, and Marguerite Young, *Where Is There Another? A Memorial to Paul Y. Anderson: Death of a Fighter* (Norman, OK: Cooperative Books, 1939), 12.

90. Stelzer, "'Just a Newspaper Hack on the Side of the Angels,'" 21; Lambeth, "The Lost Career of Paul Y. Anderson," 406.

91. Anderson, "Many Obstacles," 10.

92. Ibid.

93. *Encyclopedia of Television*, ed. Horace Newcomb, Cary O'Dell, and Noelle Watson (Chicago: Fitzroy Dearborn Publishers, 1997), s.v. "24 Hour News"; *Encyclopedia of American Journalism*, ed. Stephen L. Vaughn (New York: Routledge, 2008), s.v. "Cable News Network."

94. *Encyclopedia of Television*, s.v. "24 Hour News"; *Encyclopedia of American Journalism*, s.v. "Cable News Network."

95. Steve Michael Barkin, *American Television News: The Media Marketplace and the Public Interest* (Armonk, NY: M. E. Sharpe, 2003), 105; Patricia Leavy, *Iconic Events: Media, Politics, and Power in Retelling History* (Lanham, MD: Lexington Books, 2007), 3; *Encyclopedia of American Journalism*, s.v. "Cable News Network."

96. *Encyclopedia of American Journalism*, s.v. "Cable News Network"; *Encyclopedia of Television*, s.v. "24 Hour News."

97. John William Tebbel and Sarah Miles Watts, *The Press and the Presidency: From George Washington to Ronald Reagan* (New York: Oxford University Press, 1985), 531; Liebovich, *The Press and the Modern Presidency*, 127–128.

98. Michael Schudson and Elliot King, "The Illusion of Ronald Reagan's Popularity," in *The Power of News*, ed. Michael Schudson, 124–141 (Cambridge, MA: Harvard University Press, 1995), 132.

99. Ibid.; David E. Kyvig, *The Age of Impeachment: American Constitutional Culture since 1960* (Lawrence: University Press of Kansas, 2008), 232.

100. Mark Hertsgaard, *On Bended Knee: The Press and the Reagan Presidency* (New York: Farrar, Straus & Giroux, 1988), 302.

101. Leslie H. Gelb, "U.S. Said to Aid Iranian Exiles in Combat and Political Units," *New York Times*, March 7, 1982, A1; Leslie H. Gelb, "Iran Said to Get Large-Scale Arms from Israel, Soviet and Europeans," *New York Times*, March 8, 1982, A1; Ed Magnuson, "Iran: Arms for the Ayatullah," *Time*, July 25, 1983, 26–28.

102. Hertsgaard, *On Bended Knee*, 302.

103. Ihsan A. Hijazi, "Hostage's Release Is Linked to Shift in Iranian Policy," *New York Times*, November 4, 1986, A1.

104. Schudson and King, "The Illusion of Ronald Reagan's Popularity," 124.

105. Theodore Draper, *A Very Thin Line: The Iran-Contra Affairs* (New York: Hill & Wang, 1991), 452.

106. Ibid., 457.

107. "Iran Held McFarlane 5 Days After He Arrived in Disguise: Tehran Says Reagan Sent Cake, Bible," *Los Angeles Times*, http://articles.latimes.com/1986-11-04/news/mn-16213_1_tehran (accessed July 4, 2014).

108. Gerald M. Boyd, "U.S. Looks at Ways to Free Hostages," *New York Times*, November 6, 1986, A10.

109. Eleanor Randolph, "Press Blunders; How Newshounds Blew the Iran-Contra Story," *Washington Post*, November 15, 1987, C1.

110. Hertsgaard, *On Bended Knee*, 302.

111. Epstein, *Between Fact and Fiction*, 21.

112. Schudson, "Watergate: A Study in Mythology," 29; Epstein, *Between Fact and Fiction*, 25–27.

113. Epstein, *Between Fact and Fiction*, 20.

114. Schudson, *Watergate in American Memory*, 108.

115. Blasi, "The Checking Value," 552.

CHAPTER 3:
PARTISAN DISCOURSE
PRIOR TO THE SMOKING GUN

1. Hugh Rawson and Margaret Miner, *The Oxford Dictionary of American Quotations* (Oxford: Oxford University Press, 2006), s.v. "Watergate."

2. Cass R. Sunstein, *Democracy and the Problem of Free Speech* (New York: Simon & Schuster, 1995), 268.

3. Certainly, on the other hand, rhetoric can promulgate an exigence; one can make this argument about the press who, while as the previous chapter addressed may not discover the scandal, can certainly draw the public's attention to an act.

4. Lloyd Bitzer, "The Rhetorical Situation," *Philosophy and Rhetoric* 1 (1968): 6–7.

5. Barry Brummett, "Presidential Substance: The Address of August 15, 1973," *Western Journal of Communication* 48 (1975): 257.

6. Bitzer, "The Rhetorical Situation"; Richard E. Vatz, "The Myth of the Rhetorical Situation," *Philosophy & Rhetoric* 6 (1968): 154–161.

7. Halford Ross Ryan, "Kategoria and Apologia: On Their Rhetorical Criticism as a Speech Set," *Quarterly Journal of Speech* 68 (1982): 254–261.

8. Halford Ross Ryan, *Oratorical Encounters: Selected Studies and Sources of Twentieth-Century Political Accusations and Apologies* (New York: Greenwood Press, 1988), xviii.

9. Robert Busby, *Reagan and the Iran-Contra Affair: The Politics of Presidential Recovery* (New York: St. Martin's, 1999), 19.

10. Ryan, "Kategoria and Apologia," 255.

11. Benjamin Ginsberg and Martin Shefter, *Politics by Other Means: Politicians, Prosecutors, and the Press from Watergate to Whitewater* (New York: Norton, 1999), 28–30.

12. Ryan, *Oratorical Encounters.*

13. Ibid.

14. Eric Charles White, *Kaironomia: On the Will-to-Invent* (Ithaca, NY: Cornell University Press, 1987), 13.

15. Busby, *Reagan and the Iran-Contra Affair*, 18.

16. Two scandals (Watergate and Iran-Contra) followed record-breaking landslide victories of the president. Moreover, Presidents Ulysses S. Grant and Harry Truman both opted not to run for a constitutionally valid third term after their respective major scandals.

17. David H. Stratton, *Tempest over Teapot Dome: The Story of Albert B. Fall* (Norman: University of Oklahoma Press, 1998), 323.

18. John Poulakos, *Sophistical Rhetoric in Classical Greece* (Columbia: University of South Carolina Press, 1995), 61.

19. Bruce Gronbeck, "The Rhetoric of Political Corruption," *Quarterly Journal of Speech* 64 (1978): 157.

20. Ibid., 162.

21. Ibid., 162.

22. Allan J. Lichtman, *The Keys to the White House: A Surefire Guide to Predicting the Next President* (Lanham, MD: Rowman & Littlefield, 2008), 40.

23. Gronbeck, "The Rhetoric of Political Corruption," 162.

24. Ibid., 165.

25. Ibid., 162.

26. William L. Benoit, *Accounts, Excuses, and Apologies: A Theory of Image Restoration Strategies* (Albany: State University of New York Press, 1995).

27. Joseph R. Blaney and William L. Benoit, *The Clinton Scandals and the Politics of Image Restoration* (Westport, CT: Praeger, 2001), 5.

28. David H. Stratton, "Two Western Senators and Teapot Dome: Thomas J. Walsh and Albert B. Fall," *Pacific Northwest Quarterly* 65 (1974): 62.

29. John F, Harris, *The Survivor: Bill Clinton in the White House* (New York: Random House, 2005), 309.

30. Rich Lowry, *Legacy: Paying the Price for the Clinton Years* (Washington, DC: Regnery, 2003), 392.

31. B. L. Ware and Wil A. Linkugel, "They Spoke in Defense of Themselves: On the Generic Criticism of *Apologia*," *Quarterly Journal of Speech* 59 (1973): 277.

32. "Teapot Claims Cost Sinclair $1,000,000," *Wall Street Journal*, October 25, 1922, 6.

33. William L. Bennoit, "Richard M. Nixon's Rhetorical Strategies in His Public Statements on Watergate," *Southern Speech Communication Journal* 47 (1982): 198.

34. William L. Benoit, Paul Gullifor, and Daniel A. Panici, "President Reagan's Defensive Discourse on the Iran-Contra Affair," *Communication Studies* 42 (1991): 279–281.

35. Benoit, *Accounts, Excuses, and Apologies*, 77.

36. Ibid., 15.

37. Benoit, Gullifor, and Panici, "President Reagan's Defensive Discourse," 291.

38. Bennoit, "Richard M. Nixon's Rhetorical Strategies," 280.

39. Blaney and Benoit, *The Clinton Scandals*, 94.

40. M. R. Werner and John Starr, *Teapot Dome* (New York: Viking, 1959), 195; Stratton, *Tempest over Teapot Dome*, 232.

41. Bennoit, "Richard M. Nixon's Rhetorical Strategies," 197.

42. Craig A. Smith and Kathy B. Smith, *The White House Speaks: Presidential Leadership as Persuasion* (Westport, CT: Praeger, 1994), 215–219.

43. Michael Lynch and David Bogen, *The Spectacle of History: Speech, Text, and Memory at the Iran-Contra Hearings* (Durham, NC: Duke University Press, 1996), 220.

44. Blaney and Benoit, *The Clinton Scandals*, 87.

45. "Fall Prefers Court Hearing," *Los Angeles Times*, March 22, 1928, 5. Herman B. Weisner, *The Politics of Justice: A. B. Fall and the Teapot Dome Scandal; A New Perspective* (Albuquerque, NM: Creative Designs, 1994), 132.

46. Bennoit, "Richard M. Nixon's Rhetorical Strategies," 196–197. Fred Emery, *Watergate: The Corruption of American Politics and the Fall of Richard Nixon* (New York: Times Books, 1994), 378.

47. Mary E. Stuckey, *Strategic Failures in the Modern Presidency* (Cresskill, NJ: Hampton Press, 1997), 46.

48. Blaney and Benoit, *The Clinton Scandals*, 81.

49. Ibid., 88.

50. Louis Liebovich, *The Press and the Modern Presidency Myths and Mindsets from Kennedy to Election 2000* (Westport, CT: Praeger, 2001), 60–61.

51. Margaret Ann Blanchard, *Revolutionary Sparks Freedom of Expression in Modern America* (New York: Oxford University Press, 1992), 419.

52. Richard M. Pious, *Why Presidents Fail* (Lanham, MD: Rowman & Littlefield, 2008), 131.

53. Jon Margolis, "No 'Ransom,' President Says," *Chicago Tribune*, November 14, 1986.

54. Frederick Lewis Allen, *Only Yesterday: An Informal History of the Nineteen-Twenties* (New York: Harper & Brothers, 1957), 154.

55. Gronbeck, "The Rhetoric of Political Corruption," 165.

56. Theodore J. Lowi, foreword to *The Politics of Scandal: Power and Process in Liberal Democracies*, ed. Andrei S. Markovits and Mark Silverstein, vii–xii (New York: Holmes & Meier, 1988), viii.

57. Robert Williams, *Political Scandals in the USA* (Edinburgh: Keele University Press, 1998), 106.

58. Lowi, foreword, x.

59. Kenneth L. Hacker, "Interpersonal Communication and the Construction of Candidate Images," in *Candidate Images in Presidential Elections*, ed. Kenneth L. Hacker, 65–82 (Westport, CT: Praeger, 1995), 75.

60. Comer Vann Woodward, *Responses of the Presidents to Charges of Misconduct* (New York: Dell, 1974), xiii.

61. Busby, *Reagan and the Iran-Contra Affair*, 10.

62. Øyvind Ihlen, "On Berger: A Social Constructionist Perspective on Public Relations and Crisis Communication," in *Public Relations and Social Theory: Key Figures and Concepts*, ed. Øyvind Ihlen, Magnus Fredriksson, and Betteke van Ruler, 43–61 (New York: Routledge, 2009), 44.

63. Robert Williams, "Political Scandals and Political Development in the United States," in *Scandals in Past and Contemporary Politics*, ed. John Garrard and James L. Newell, 46–58 (New York: Palgrave, 2006), 47.

64. Ihlen, "On Berger," 46.

65. John B. Thompson, *Political Scandal: Power and Visibility in the Media Age* (Cambridge: Polity Press, 2000).

66. Alan Jay Zaremba, *Crisis Communication: Theory and Practice* (Armonk, NY: M. E. Sharpe, 2010), 111.

67. Ibid., 27.

68. Ihlen, "On Berger," 54.

69. Ibid., 50.

70. Busby, *Reagan and the Iran-Contra Affair*, 10.

71. Stratton, *Tempest over Teapot Dome*, 281; "Fall Resents Attack by Gifford Pinochet," *New York Times*, March 7, 1922, 2.

72. "Fall Resents Attack by Gifford Pinochet," 2.

73. Don Lawson, *Famous Presidential Scandals* (Hillside, NJ: Enslow, 1990): 56.

74. Stratton, *Tempest over Teapot Dome*, 281.

75. Ibid.

76. "Sinclair Declares Oil Inquiry Is 'Politics,'" *New York Times*, January 23, 1924, 1.

77. Allen, *Only Yesterday*, 154.

78. Ibid., 154–155.

79. "Mudgunning in the Senate," *Current Opinion*, April 1924, 393.

80. "Stanley Frost, "Capping the Mud Gusher," *Outlook*, April 16, 1924, 647.

81. J. Leonard Bates, "The Teapot Dome Scandal and the Election of 1924," *American Historical Review* 60 (1955): 305. The scandals included the Newberry scandal, the Daugherty scandal, the Bureau of Engraving scandal, the Goldstein scandal, the ship subsidy and sales scandal, the Veteran's Bureau scandal, the sugar profiteering scandal, the reclamation service scandal, the income tax bureau scandal, the packers and stockyard scandal, the Tolbert scandal, the Slemp scandal, and one in the tariff commission. Many of these smaller scandals "can be traced" to backroom deals in Chicago's Blackstone Hotel in June 1920, which secured Harding's nomination. See "A Business Administration," *Nation*, February 27, 1924, 220.

82. Stanley Frost, "Oil, Mud, and Tom-Toms," *Outlook*, March 12, 1924, 424–425.

83. Bates, "The Teapot Dome Scandal and the Election of 1924," 304.

84. Carl Solberg, *Oil Power* (New York: New American Library, 1976), 98.

85. "Democrats Attack Fall on Oil Leases as a New Ballinger," *New York Times*, January 21, 1924, 1.

86. "Hull Says Scandals Are Campaign Issue," *New York Times*, January 27, 1924, 1.

87. Joseph L. Morrison, *Josephus Daniels: The Small-d Democrat* (Chapel Hill: University of North Carolina Press, 1996), 147.

88. "Sinclair Dodges Newspapermen," *New York Times*, January 28, 1924, 2.

89. "Political Aspects of Teapot Dome," *Wall Street Journal*, January 30, 1924, 10; Morrison, *Josephus Daniels*, 147.

90. "A Teapot Gusher of Scandal," *Current Opinion*, March 1, 1924, 270.

91. "Fall, Benby, Daugherty, Roosevelt, and Coolidge," *Nation*, February 6, 1924, 130; "Daughtery Also Assailed," *New York Times*, January 29, 1924, 1; Werner and Starr, *Teapot Dome*, 142.

92. "Political Aspects of Teapot Dome," 10.

93. "M'Adoo Got $250,000 Gregory Got $2,000 as Fees, Doheny Says," *Washington Post*, February 2, 1924, 1.

94. "Oil and Conservation," *Outlook*, February 13, 1924, 251.

95. "Many Scaldings from Teapot Dome," *Literary Digest*, February 16, 1924, 15.

96. Bates, "The Teapot Dome Scandal and the Election of 1924," 313.

97. Frost, "Oil, Mud, and Tom-Toms," 423.

98. Charles Merz, "At the Bottom of the Oil Story," *The Century Magazine*, May 1924, 84.

99. Ibid.

100. "Mudgunning in the Senate," 393.

101. Frost, "Oil, Mud, and Tom-Toms," 423.

102. "Character Lynching in Washington," *Literary Digest*, March 3, 1922, 10.

103. "The Senate on Teapot Dome," *Chicago Daily Tribune*, January 25, 1925, 8.

104. Stratton, *Tempest over Teapot Dome*, 280.

105. "The Senate on Teapot Dome," 8.

106. "The Teapot Dome Indictments," *Literary Digest*, July 19, 1924, 12.

107. "Placing the Guilt for Teapot Dome," *Literary Digest*, June 21, 1924, 14.

108. Ibid.

109. Ibid.

110. "The Teapot Dome Indictments," 12.

111. "This World," *Youth's Companion*, December 1927, 101.

112. Stanley Frost, "The G.O.P. at the Bar," *Outlook*, March 19, 1924, 472.

113. Allen, *Only Yesterday*, 157.

114. Laurence Stern and Haynes Johnson, "3 Top Nixon Aides, Kleindienst Out; President Accepts Full Responsibility; Richardson Will Conduct New Probe," *Washington Post*, May 1, 1973, A1.

115. Bob Woodward and Carl Bernstein, "Democrats Called in Watergate Case," *Washington Post*, September 6, 1972, A1.

116. Leonard Garment, *In Search of Deep Throat: The Greatest Political Mystery of Our Time* (New York: Basic Books, 2000), 114.

117. "What the President Had to Say Before," *Time*, May 14, 1973, 21.

118. Richard M. Nixon, *The Nixon Presidential Press Conferences* (New York: Earl M. Coleman, 1978), 247.

119. Ibid.

120. Ibid., 248.

121. Ibid., 281.

122. Carl Bernstein and Bob Woodward, "Justice Completes Watergate Probe," *Washington Post*, September 9, 1972, A1, A6.

123. Nixon, *The Nixon Presidential Press Conferences*, 296.

124. Richard M. Nixon, *RN: The Memoirs of Richard Nixon* (New York: Grosset & Dunlap, 1978), 646.

125. Louis Liebovitch, *Richard Nixon, Watergate, and the Press* (Westport, CT: Praeger, 2003), 46.

126. Ernest R. May and Janet Fraser, *Campaign '72: The Managers Speak* (Cambridge, MA: Harvard University Press, 1973), 279.

127. Ibid.

128. H. R. Haldeman, *The Haldeman Diaries* (New York: Putnam, 1994), 449.

129. Ibid., 218; Liebovitch, *Richard Nixon, Watergate, and the Press*, 49.

130. Haldeman, *The Haldeman Diaries*, 219. The wheat sale scandal involved a deal between the Nixon administration and Russia. Nixon would offer a $500 million line of credit to Russia if they agreed to buy $750 million worth of wheat from U.S. farmers over the next three years. The Department of Agriculture did not immediately release the deal, which caused McGovern and other Democrats to claim the Nixon administration was helping top-level investors make money and not the grain farmers. As one might expect in the political rhetoric of scandals, Republicans called McGovern's accusations "gutter tactics." Douglas E. Kneeland, "McGovern Alleges Grain Sale Abuse," *New York Times*, September 10, 1972, 4; James T. Wooten, "G.O.P. Campaign Leader Charges 'Gutter Tactics,'" *New York Times*, October 7, 1972, 18. True to the nature of political rhetoric during scandals, Bill Clinton used the obscure Russian wheat deal scandal as an issue in his failed campaign for U.S. Congress in 1974.

131. Gladys Engel Lang and Kurt Lang, *The Battle for Public Opinion: The President, the Press, and the Polls during Watergate* (New York: Columbia University Press, 1983), 41.

132. William Greider, "McGovern Calls Espionage a Threat to 2-Party Politics," *Washington Post*, September 10, 1972, A4.

133. "The Watergate Tapes," *Time*, September 18, 1972, 18.

134. *Watergate: Chronology of a Crisis*, 2 vols. (Washington, DC: Congressional Quarterly, 1973–1974), 1:12.

135. Bob Greene, *Running* (Chicago: Regnery, 1973), 111.

136. "The Watergate Roils On," *Time*, September 11, 1972, 18.

137. Bob Woodward, "O'Brien Sues GOP Campaign," *Washington Post*, June 21, 1972, A1.

138. Ibid.; Bob Woodward and E. J. Bachinski, "White House Consultant Tied to Bugging Figure," *Washington Post*, June 20, 1972, A1.

139. Carl Bernstein and Bob Woodward, "Judge Wants to Start Watergate Trial," *Washington Post*, August 28, 1972, A7; Bob Woodward and Carl Bernstein, "Banking Panel to Vote on Watergate Probe," *Washington Post*, September 26, 1972, A15.

140. Carl Bernstein and Bob Woodward, "Plea Ties Stans to Bug Suit: GOP Charges 'Political Libel' by Democrats," *Washington Post*, September 12, 1972, A1.

141. Lang and Lang, *The Battle for Public Opinion*, 41.

142. Karlyn Barker and Bob Woodward, "Democrats Step Up Sabotage Charges," *Washington Post*, October 11, 1972, A12.

143. Woodward and Bernstein, "Banking Panel to Vote on Watergate Probe," A15.

144. Bob Woodward, "O'Brien Sues GOP Campaign," *Washington Post*, June 21, 1972, A1, A9; "Moral Novocain," *New Republic*, August 19, 1972, 4.

145. Bob Woodward and Carl Bernstein, "Stans Scathes Report," *Washington Post*, September 14, 1972, A1.

146. "The Watergate Roils On," 18.

147. Carl Bernstein and Bob Woodward, "Lawyer Says He Wouldn't Help GOP Stage Demonstration," *Washington Post*, November 1, 1972, A25.

148. Bob Woodward and Carl Bernstein, "Jury Bares New Details of Break-In," *Washington Post*, September 16, 1972, A10.

149. Bob Woodward and Carl Bernstein, "GOP Loses Bid to Delay Bugging Suit," *Washington Post*, August 12, 1972, A1, A7.

150. John Hughes, "Inching Out of the Iran Mess," *Christian Science Monitor*, December 10, 1986, 20.

151. Busby, *Reagan and the Iran-Contra Affair*, 111.

152. Bernard Gwertzman, "Reagan Stand Criticized by Lawmakers," *New York Times*, November 15, 1986, A5.

153. Bill McAllister, "Staff Actions Called Reagan's Responsibility," *Washington Post*, June 12, 1987, A21.

154. Ibid.

155. Ibid.

156. David Rosenbaum, "Senator Says Reagan Must Face 'Mistake' on Iran," *New York Times*, January 13, 1987, A8.

157. Geoffrey Barker, "Brute or Hero, Handsome Olly North Won't Talk about Iran," *The Advertiser*, December 11, 1986.

158. Bernard Gwertzman, "Shultz Declares He Opposes Giving More Arms to Iran," *New York Times*, November 17, 1986, A1.

159. Ibid.

160. Barker, "Brute or Hero."

161. Thomas J. Craughwell and M. William Phelps, *Failures of the Presidents: From the Whiskey Rebellion and War of 1812 to the Bay of Pigs and War in Iraq* (Beverly, MA: Fair Winds Press, 2008), 268.

162. Alex Brummer, "Democrats Statesmanlike on Irangate," *Guardian*, November 28, 1986, 8; Busby, *Reagan and the Iran-Contra Affair*, 111.

163. Busby, *Reagan and the Iran-Contra Affair*, 111.

164. David P. Thelen, *Becoming Citizens in the Age of Television: How Americans Challenged the Media and Seized Political Initiative during the Iran-Contra Debate* (Chicago: University of Chicago Press, 1996), 41; Barry Sussman, *What Americans Really Think: And Why Our Politicians Pay No Attention* (New York: Pantheon Books, 1988), 246; David Corn, "The Story So Far," *Nation*, June 27, 1987, 874–875.

165. Brummer, "Democrats Statesmanlike on Irangate," 8.

166. David E. Rosenbaum, "Senate to Set Up Iran Inquiry Panel," *New York Times*, January 7, 1987, A8.

167. Ibid.

168. Ibid.

169. Philip Shenon, "Federal Jury on Arms Case to Be Empaneled in Weeks," *New York Times*, January 8, 1987, A10.

170. David S. Broder, "Democrats Agree to Drop Iran-Contra Issue; After a Few Closing Barbs, They Turn to Budget and Foreign Policy Matters," *Washington Post*, August 13, 1987, A18.

171. Ibid.

172. Ibid.

173. Ibid.

174. Ibid.; the two congressional Republicans were Jesse Helms and Lauch Faircloth.

175. Nancy Gibbs, Jay Branegan, Margaret Carlson, et al., "Truth or . . . Consequences," *Time*, February 2, 1998, 18.

176. Nevertheless, a handful of Republicans (e.g., Sen. Trent Lott, Sen. John Ashcroft, Speaker of the House Newt Gingrich, and Republican House Majority Leader Dick Armey) broke the "Republican code of silence" by condemning President Clinton. See Thomas B. Edsall and Terry M. Neal, "GOP Speaks Out against Clinton: Leaders' Criticism Breaks Silence on Allegations," *Washington Post*, January 31, 1998, A1; Lloyd Grove, "Rep. Barr's New Quest: Impeachment," *Washington Post*, February 10, 1998, E1; John F. Harris, "Defending Starr, Republicans Call Leaks Complaints a Ruse," *Washington Post*, February 9, 1998, A8; Karen Tumulty, John F. Dickerson, Michael Duffy, and Michael Weiskopf, "On the Fast Track to Impeach," *Time*, October 12, 1998; Thomas Sowell, "Fallacious Decrial of Inquiry as Partisan," *Washington Times*, October 27, 1998; Richard L. Berke, "G.O.P. Begins Ad Campaign Citing Scandal," *New York Times*, October 28, 1998, A1.

177. Not all Republicans were anti-Clinton. The three major Republican sub-blocs included the libertarians, enterprisers, and moralists. Libertarians sympathized with Clinton due to the government's aggressive invasion into his private life. Enterpris-

ers benefited from the booming economy. It was the Republican moralists who stood firmly against Clinton, which, in turn, made them the target of Clinton. Alongside the moralists, reporters, pundits, and prosecutors were all after Clinton. Unlike Watergate in which Nixon used the CIA, FBI, and IRS against investigators, "this time, the roles are reversed: a president's political enemies are using scary police-state tactics to destroy *him* [emphasis in original]." See James M. McPherson, "Starr Chamber," *New Republic*, February 16, 1998, 6.

178. Thomas Sowell, "Fallacious Decrial of Inquiry as Partisan," *Washington Times*, October 27, 1998, 15.

179. Juliet Eilperin, "Armey Steps Up Attack on Clinton's Character," *Washington Post*, April 8, 1998, A14.

180. Bernard Weinraub, "Hustler behind Sex Story," *New York Times*, December 19, 1998, B3.

181. Nancy Gibbs, Margaret Carlson, Michael Duffy, et al., "This Is a Battle," *Time*, February 9, 1998, 26.

182. Adam Cohen and Andrea Sachs, "Is the Prosecutor Running a Starr Chamber?," *Time*, February 2, 1998, 58.

183. Ibid.

184. Robert G. Kaiser and Ira Chinoy, "Scaife: Funding Father of the Right," *Washington Post*, May 2, 1999, A1. Scaife claimed he had no knowledge of Starr's selection as dean.

185. Marc Fisher, "Starr Warriors," *Washington Post*, February 3, 1998, B1.

186. Sunstein, *Democracy and the Problem of Free Speech*, 268.

187. Ibid., 82.

188. Robert C. McFarlane and Zofia Smardz, *Special Trust* (New York: Cadell & Davies, 1994), 89.

189. Ibid., 281.

190. Bernstein and Woodward, "Justice Completes Watergate Probe," A1, A6.

191. President Bill Clinton, interview with Jim Lehrer, *The NewsHour with Jim Lehrer*, PBS, January 21, 1998.

192. President Bill Clinton, "Remarks on the After-School Child Care Initiative," January 26, 1998.

193. Busby, *Reagan and the Iran-Contra Affair*, 151.

194. Liebovitch, *Richard Nixon, Watergate, and the Press*, 55; J. Anthony Lukas, *Nightmare: The Underside of the Nixon Years* (New York: Viking, 1976), 270.

195. Liebovitch, *Richard Nixon, Watergate, and the Press*, 55.

196. Ibid., 5.

197. Charlotte Saikowski, "White House Tries to Keep to Agenda in Face of Hearings," *Christian Science Monitor*, May 11, 1987, 3.

CHAPTER 4:
FROM SMOKING GUN TO IMPEACHMENT

1. William Safire, *Safire's Political Dictionary* (Oxford: Oxford University Press, 2008), s.v. "Smoking Gun."

2. Richard K. Neumann, "The Revival of Impeachment as a Partisan Political Weapon," *Hastings Constitutional Law Quarterly* 34 (2007): 326.

3. The "*the*" scandal problem, as the chapter will explain, points to the fact that the original misconduct is usually not a problem/crime and is therefore moot, but the cover-up, which is an obstruction of justice, is a serious crime and is an impeachable offense. So the cover-up is not worse than the crime; the cover-up is the only crime that Congress can prosecute.

4. Henry G. Liddell and Robert Scott, *A Lexicon: Abridged from Liddell & Scott's Greek-English Lexicon* (New York: Economy Book House, 1901), 637.

5. Safire, *Safire's Political Dictionary*, s.v. "Smoking Gun."

6. Ibid.

7. Michael Billig and Katie MacMillan, "Metaphor, Idiom and Ideology: The Search for 'No Smoking Guns' across Time," *Discourse & Society* 16 (2005): 459–480, 466.

8. Ibid., 465.

9. Øyvind Ihlen, "On Berger: A Social Constructionist Perspective on Public Relations and Crisis Communication," in *Public Relations and Social Theory: Key Figures and Concepts*, ed. Øyvind Ihlen, Magnus Fredriksson, and Betteke van Ruler, 43–61 (New York: Routledge, 2009), 44.

10. W. Lance Bennett, "Political Scenarios and the Nature of Politics," *Philosophy & Rhetoric* 8 (1975): 23.

11. Billig and MacMillan, "Metaphor, Idiom and Ideology." The term, however, had been used in Watergate before Conable. For example, see Roger Wilkins, "The Evidence for Impeachment; Indicators of a State of Mind," *New York Times*, July 14, 1974, 169.

12. James S. Fleming, *Window on Congress: A Congressional Biography of Barber B. Conable* (Rochester, NY: University of Rochester Press, 2004), 176.

13. Billig and MacMillan, "Metaphor, Idiom and Ideology," 471.

14. Ibid., 468.

15. Ibid., 459–460. George Lakoff and Mark Johnson, *Metaphors We Live By* (Chicago: University of Chicago Press, 1980).

16. Billig and MacMillan, "Metaphor, Idiom and Ideology," 468.

17. Ibid., 472.

18. Ibid., 471.

19. Philip Geyelin, "The Smoking Shredder," *Washington Post*, July 7, 1987, A15.

20. David Hoffman, "Reagan Says No 'Smoking Gun' Exists in Scandal," *Washington Post*, July 17, 1987, A1.

21. Chester L. Karrass, *Give and Take: The Complete Guide to Negotiating Strategies and Tactics* (New York: Thomas Y. Crowell, 1974), 50–51.

22. James L. Heap, "Constructionism in the Rhetoric and Practice of Fourth Generation Evaluation," *Evaluation and Program Planning* 18 (1995): 54.

23. Ibid.

24. Ibid.

25. Lawrence W. Sherman, *Scandal and Reform: Controlling Police Corruption* (Berkeley: University of California Press, 1978), 64.

26. "Doheny Lent Fall $100,000 in Cash . . . ," *New York Times*, January 25, 1924, 1.

27. Michael R. Kramer and Kathryn M. Olson, "The Strategic Potential of Sequencing Apologia Stases: President Clinton's Self-Defense in the Monica Lewinsky Scandal," *Western Journal of Communication* 66 (2002): 365.

28. Ibid.

29. The Supreme Court has stated, "The privilege against self-incrimination would be reduced to a hollow mockery if its exercise could be taken as equivalent either to a confession of guilt or a conclusive presumption of perjury." Slochower v. Board of Higher Education, 350 U.S. 551 (1956).

30. Stefan H. Krieger, "A Time to Keep Silent and a Time to Speak: The Functions of Silence in the Lawyering Process," *Oregon Law Review* 80 (2001): 202.

31. Barry Brummett, "Towards a Theory of Silence as a Political Strategy," *Quarterly Journal of Speech* 66 (1980): 297.

32. Krieger, "A Time to Keep Silent," 202.

33. Richard L. Johannesen, "The Functions of Silence: A Plea for Communication Research," *Western Speech* 38 (1974). Robert L. Heath, "A Time for Silence: Booker T. Washington in Atlanta," *Quarterly Journal of Speech* 64 (1978).

34. Ari Adut, *On Scandal: Moral Disturbances in Society, Politics, and Art* (Cambridge: Cambridge University Press, 2008), 299.

35. Ibid.

36. Krieger, "A Time to Keep Silent," 202.

37. Brummett, "Towards a Theory of Silence as a Political Strategy."

38. Luke M. Milligan, "The 'Ongoing Criminal Investigation' Constraint: Getting Away with Silence," *William & Mary Bill of Rights Journal* 16 (2008): 758.

39. Brummett, "Towards a Theory of Silence as a Political Strategy," 290.

40. Melani Schröter, *Silence and Concealment in Political Discourse* (Amsterdam: Benjamins, 2013), 137.

41. Karen Rasmussen, "Nixon and the Strategy of Avoidance," *Central States Speech Journal* 27 (1973): 198.

42. Brummett, "Towards a Theory of Silence as a Political Strategy," 293.

43. Milligan, "The 'Ongoing Criminal Investigation' Constraint," 747.

44. Ibid., 754.

45. Schröter, *Silence and Concealment*, 137.

46. Theodore J. Lowi, foreword to *The Politics of Scandal: Power and Process in Liberal Democracies*, ed. Andrei S. Markovits and Mark Silverstein, vii–xii (New York: Holmes & Meier, 1988), viii.

47. While the substantial element precedes a procedural element in terms of order of happening, rhetorically, the procedural element often leads to the discovery (or a fuller understanding) of the substantial element of the scandal.

48. David H. Stratton, "Two Western Senators and Teapot Dome: Thomas J. Walsh and Albert B. Fall," *Pacific Northwest Quarterly* 65 (1974): 62.

49. Charles J. Cooper, "A Perjurer in the White House? The Constitutional Case for Perjury and Obstruction of Justice as High Crimes and Misdemeanors," *Harvard Journal of Law & Public Policy* 22 (1999).

50. Charles L. Black, *Impeachment: A Handbook* (New Haven, CT: Yale University Press, 1998), 39.

202 Notes to Pages 86–91

51. Ibid.

52. Kenneth Burke, *A Grammar of Motives* (Berkeley: University of California Press, 1969), 16.

53. Bennett, "Political Scenarios," 32.

54. Bruce E. Gronbeck, "The Rhetoric of Political Corruption: Sociolinguistic, Dialectical, and Ceremonial Processes," *Quarterly Journal of Speech* 64 (1978): 162.

55. Marbury v. Madison, 5 U.S. 137 (1803).

56. Bennett, "Political Scenarios," 27. Bertrand de Jouvenel, *The Pure Theory of Politics* (New Haven, CT: Yale University Press, 1963), 207.

57. Bennett, "Political Scenarios," 27–28.

58. Ibid., 28.

59. Henry George Liddell and Robert Scott, *A Greek-English Lexicon* (Oxford: Oxford University Press, 1940).

60. Bennett, "Political Scenarios," 28.

61. Walter L. Nixon v. United States, 506 U.S. 224 (1993).

62. Black, *Impeachment*, 10.

63. Andrew Johnson, B. F. Wade, Charles Sumner, and William Lawrence, *Proceedings in the Trial of Andrew Johnson President of the United States* (Washington, DC: F & J. Rives & G. A. Bailey, 1868), 249.

64. H. Lowell Brown, *High Crimes and Misdemeanors in Presidential Impeachment* (New York: Palgrave Macmillan, 2010), 85.

65. Peter W. Rodino, *Impeachment of Richard M. Nixon, President of the United States: The Final Report of the Committee on the Judiciary, House of Representatives* (Toronto: Bantam, 1975).

66. Ibid.

67. Bennett, "Political Scenarios," 36.

68. Ibid., 24.

69. W. Lance Bennett, *The Political Mind and the Political Environment: An Investigation of Public Opinion and Political Consciousness* (Lexington, MA: Lexington Books, 1975), 65.

70. "Oil Inquiry Turns to Fall's Finances," *Wall Street Journal*, December 1, 1923, 3; M. R. Werner and John Starr, *Teapot Dome* (New York: Viking, 1959), 3.

71. "Teapot Dome Hearing," *Wall Street Journal*, December 5, 1923, 12.

72. Frederick Lewis Allen, *Only Yesterday: An Informal History of the Nineteen-Twenties* (New York: Harper & Brothers, 1957), 144.

73. "Roosevelt Quits Sinclair over Teapot Dome Deal," *Los Angeles Times*, January 22, 1924, 3; "Roosevelt Kicks Off Lid," *Chicago Daily Tribune*, January 22, 1924, 1.

74. "Sinclair Names Mammoth Holders," *Wall Street Journal*, December 28, 1923, 9.

75. "Fall Denies Charges," *Wall Street Journal*, January 18, 1924, 8; "Fall Terms Charges Malicious and Untrue," *New York Times*, January 18, 1924, 21.

76. William Hard, "Mr. Fall's $100,000," *Nation*, January 30, 1924, 108.

77. "Palmer Explains Loan of $100,000 to Albert B. Fall," *Washington Post*, January 2, 1924, 1.

78. "M'Lean Tells Story of Loan and Fall Substantiates It," *Washington Post*, January 12, 1924, 1.

79. "The Oil Leases," *Washington Post*, January 25, 1925, 6.

80. "Doheny Lent Fall $100,000 in Cash . . . ," *New York Times*, January 25, 1924, 1.

81. "Doheny Explains Why He Lent $100,000 to Fall," *Los Angeles Times*, January 25, 1924, 1.

82. Francis X. Busch, *Enemies of the State: An Account of the Trials of the Mary Eugenia Surratt Case, the Teapot Dome Cases, the Alphonse Capone Case, and the Rosenberg Case* (London: Arco Publications, 1957), 112.

83. "Teapot Dome Casts a Broad Shadow," *New York Times*, January 27, 1924, XX1.

84. Paul Y. Anderson, "The Scandal in Oil," *New Republic*, February 6, 1924, 277.

85. William Hard, "Mr. Fall's $100,000," *Nation*, January 30, 1924, 107.

86. David H. Stratton, *Tempest over Teapot Dome: The Story of Albert B. Fall* (Norman: University of Oklahoma Press, 1998), 5.

87. Stanley Frost, "That Teapot Alarm Clock," *Outlook*, March 5, 1924, 396.

88. Herman B. Weisner, *The Politics of Justice: A. B. Fall and the Teapot Dome Scandal; A New Perspective* (Albuquerque, NM: Creative Designs, 1994), 132.

89. This partisan rhetoric was the use of "bombastic language, sophistic word tricks, and deceptive speech" to fight one another in an attempt at gaining power. Lloyd F. Bitzer, "Political Rhetoric," in *Landmark Essays on Contemporary Rhetoric*, ed. T. B. Farrell, 1–22 (Mahwah, NJ: Lawrence Erlbaum, 1981/1998), 1.

90. "Fall Expresses Confidence," *New York Times*, June 20, 1925, 2.

91. "Court Action Gratifies Sinclair," *New York Times*, March 14, 1924, 3.

92. "Congress to Attack Fall's Oil Leases," *New York Times*, January 20, 1924, 1.

93. "Fall Obeys Subpoena," *New York Times*, January 23, 1924, 2.

94. "Fall Prefers Court Hearing," *Los Angeles Times*, March 22, 1928, 5.

95. "Fall, Ill, Ready to 'Tell All' of Teapot Story," *Chicago Daily Tribune*, March 22, 1928, 1.

96. Busch, *Enemies of the State*, 116.

97. "Fall Cries 'Unfair,'" *Los Angeles Times*, April 2, 1928, 3.

98. Allen, *Only Yesterday*, 144.

99. Busch, *Enemies of the State*, 113.

100. "Fall Obeys Subpoena," 2; "Fall Expresses Confidence," *New York Times*, June 20, 1925, 2.

101. "Teapot Dome Act Defended," *Los Angeles Times*, October 25, 1923, 13.

102. "Fall Denies Hiding in Palm Beach Stay," *New York Times*, January 13, 1924, 10.

103. "The Oil Leases," *Washington Post*, January 25, 1925, 6.

104. "Find the Villain," *Independent*, February 2, 1924, 65.

105. "Abolishing Lame Ducks," *Los Angeles Times*, January 26, 1928, A4.

106. "Sinclair Goes Free," *Literary Digest*, May 5, 1928, 1.

107. "The Indictments That Failed," *Literary Digest*, April 18, 1925, 9.

108. Werner and Starr, *Teapot Dome*, 232.

109. Ibid.

110. "Sinclair Goes Free," 1.

111. Lang and Lang, *The Battle for Public Opinion*, 51.

112. *Watergate: Chronology of a Crisis*, 2 vols. (Washington, DC: Congressional Quarterly, 1973–1974), 1:9.

113. Louis Liebovitch, *Richard Nixon, Watergate, and the Press* (Westport, CT: Praeger, 2003), 71.

114. Lang and Lang, *The Battle for Public Opinion*, 62.

115. Ibid., 74; Schudson, *Watergate in American Memory: How We Remember, Forget, and Reconstruct the Past* (New York: Basic Books, 1992), 18.

116. Bob Woodward and Carl Bernstein, "Dean: Nixon Asked IRS to Stop Audits," *Washington Post*, June 20, 1973, A1.

117. Liebovitch, *Richard Nixon, Watergate, and the Press*, 85.

118. *Watergate: Chronology of a Crisis*, 1:163.

119. Carl Bernstein and Bob Woodward, "Dean Alleges Nixon Knew of Cover-Up Plan," *Washington Post*, June 3, 1973, A1.

120. John W. Dean, *Blind Ambition: The White House Years* (New York: Simon & Schuster, 1976), 288.

121. *Watergate: Chronology of a Crisis*, 1:39.

122. Ibid., 1:194.

123. L. H. LaRue, *Political Discourse: A Case Study of the Watergate Affair* (Athens: University of Georgia Press, 1988), 19–20.

124. Lang and Lang, *The Battle for Public Opinion*, 96.

125. "Seven Tumultuous Days," *Time*, November 5, 1973, 18.

126. Ibid.

127. John G. McKnight and Mark R. Weiss, "Flutter Analysis for Identifying Tape Recorders," *Quarterly Journal of the Audio Engineering Society* 24 (1976): 728.

128. "Report on a Technical Investigation Conducted for the U.S. District Court for the District of Columbia by the Advisory Panel on White House Tapes," May 31, 1974, http://www.aes.org/aeshc/docs/forensic.audio/watergate.tapes.report.pdf.

129. *Public Papers of the President of the United States*, Richard M. Nixon, 1973, 956.

130. Liebovitch, *Richard Nixon, Watergate, and the Press*, 101.

131. Ibid.

132. *Public Papers of the President of the United States*, Richard M. Nixon, 1974, 390.

133. United States v. Richard Nixon, 418 U.S. 683 (1974).

134. John R. Labovitz, *Presidential Impeachment* (New Haven, CT: Yale University Press, 1978), 210.

135. "Iran Arms Profits Were Diverted to Contras," *Washington Post*, November 26, 1986, A1.

136. Mary McGrory, "A Presidency Gutted," *Washington Post*, November 27, 1986, A2.

137. Howard Kurtz, "Meese's Dual Role in Iran-Contra Affair Becomes Focus of Criticism," *Washington Post*, January 6, 1987, A15.

138. Sara Fritz and Maura Dolan, "Low Arms Prices May Have Been Deliberate," *Sydney Morning Herald*, December 19, 1986, 5.

139. Robert Williams, *Political Scandals in the USA* (Edinburgh: Keele University Press, 1998), 44.

140. David E. Kyvig, *The Age of Impeachment: American Constitutional Culture since 1960* (Lawrence: University Press of Kansas, 2008), 251.

141. Steven V. Roberts, "The Tower Reports Inquiry Finds Reagan and Chief Advisers Responsible for 'Chaos' in Iran Arms Deals," *New York Times*, February 27, 1987, A1.

142. Ibid.

143. Bob Woodward and David Hoffman, "Baker Orders Preparation of Iran-Contra Defense," *Washington Post*, March 8, 1987, A1.

144. Ibid.

145. Peter Grier and Peter Osterlund, "New Phase for 'the Hearings,'" *Christian Science Monitor*, July 21, 1987, 1.

146. Thomas J. Craughwell and M. William Phelps, *Failures of the Presidents: From the Whiskey Rebellion and War of 1812 to the Bay of Pigs and War in Iraq* (Beverly, MA: Fair Winds Press, 2008), 270.

147. Fox Butterfield, "White House Cast Wide Net in Seeking Aid for Contras," *New York Times*, February 27, 1987, A1.

148. United States, *Report of the Congressional Committees Investigating the Iran-Contra Affair with Supplemental, Minority, and Additional Views* (Washington, DC: U.S. House of Representatives Select Committee to Investigate Covert Arms Transactions with Iran, 1987), 21.

149. Robert Busby, *Defending the American Presidency* (New York: Palgrave, 2001), 149.

150. "Reports of the Iran-Contra Committees: Excerpts from the Minority View," *New York Times*, November 17, 1987, A6.

151. Ibid.

152. Ibid.

153. Kyvig, *The Age of Impeachment*, 259.

154. "Jury Finds North Guilty on 3 Counts in Scandal," *St. Louis Post-Dispatch*, May 5, 1989, 1A.

155. David Johnston, "Poindexter Is Found Guilty of All 5 Criminal Charges for Iran-Contra Cover-Up," *New York Times*, April 8, 1990, 1.

156. United States v. Oliver North, 902 F.2d 940 (D.C. Cir. 1990); United States v. John Poindexter, 951 F.2d 369 (D.C. Cir. 1991); "The Three Iran-Contra Investigations," *St. Petersburg Times*, August 13, 1987, 18A.

157. David Johnston, "Walsh Criticizes Reagan and Bush over Iran-Contra," *New York Times*, January 19, 1994, A1.

158. David E. Rosenbaum, "The Iran-Contra Report: News Analysis; The Inquiry That Couldn't," *New York Times*, January 19, 1994, A1.

159. Johnston, "Walsh Criticizes Reagan and Bush over Iran-Contra," A1.

160. Neal Devins and Louis Fisher, *The Democratic Constitution* (Oxford: Oxford University Press, 2004), 99; Frederick M. Kaiser and Walter J. Oleszek, "Congressional Oversight Manual," in *Congress of the United States: Oversight, Processes and Procedures*, ed. Carol S. Plesser, 1–131 (New York: Nova Science Publishers, 2007), 89.

161. Nancy Gibbs, Cathy Booth, Jay Branegan, et al., "No Deal," *Time*, May 11, 1998, 26–30; Susan Schmidt and Peter Baker, "Starr Rejects Deal on Lewinsky Testimony," *Washington Post*, February 5, 1998, A1; Peter Baker and Susan Schmidt, "Lewinsky Gets Immunity for Her Testimony," *Washington Post*, July 29, 1998, A1.

162. Nancy Gibbs, Margaret Carlson, Michael Duffy, et al., "This Is a Battle," *Time*, February 9, 1998, 26.

163. Peter Baker and Susan Schmidt, "Clinton Agrees to Testify on Videotape for Starr," *Washington Post*, July 30, 1998, A1.

164. Ibid.

165. Peter Baker and Susan Schmidt, "Clinton Pledges to Testify 'Truthfully,'" *Washington Post*, August 1, 1998, A1.

166. Juliet Eilperin and Peter Baker, "Bickering Forces Delay of Tape Release," *Washington Post*, September 18, 1998, A1.

167. Howard Fineman and Daniel Klaidman, "Race to the Bottom," *Newsweek*, March 3, 1998.

168. Howard Fineman, Debra Rosenberg, Mark Hosenball, and Matthew Cooper, "Enough Already," *Newsweek*, October 10, 1998; Richard Lacayo, "Cover That Keyhole," *Time*, October 5, 1998, 40.

169. Busby, *Defending the American Presidency*, 78.

170. President Bill Clinton, "Address to the Nation on Testimony before the Independent Counsel's Grand Jury," August 17, 1998.

171. Ibid.

172. "And Now I Would Say Let's Don't Have Spin . . . Let's Deal with the Facts," *Washington Times*, April 3, 1998, 10; Caryn James, "A Self-Proclaimed Joe Friday Just Plays It Straight," *New York Times*, November 20, 1998, A27.

173. President Bill Clinton, interview with Jim Lehrer, *The NewsHour with Jim Lehrer*, PBS, September 26, 1998.

174. David Stout, "Lewinsky's Lawyer Sees 'Prosecutorial Abuse,'" *New York Times*, May 28, 1998, A24.

175. Dan Balz, "President Imperiled as Never Before," *Washington Post*, January 22, 1998, A13.

176. Gibbs, Carlson, Duffy, et al., "This Is a Battle," 26.

177. President Bill Clinton, interview with Jim Lehrer, *The NewsHour with Jim Lehrer*, PBS, January 21, 1998.

178. "Clinton: 'There Is No Improper Relationship,'" *Washington Post*, January 22, 1998, A13.

179. Peter Baker, "Clinton May Drop Privilege Appeal," *Washington Post*, June 1, 1998, A1.

180. The White House also developed a special department to handle the accusations, which reinforced the image that the attacks were relatively unimportant. The creation of a separate department demonstrated that the accusations were numerous enough to merit attention but not important enough for the existing White House administration, who, like the president, had more "official" business to conduct.

181. "Tell the Full Story, Mr. President," *New York Times*, January 23, 1998, A20.

182. Hillary Rodham Clinton, "Hillary Rodham Clinton Discusses Allegations against Her Husband, Child Care, and State of the Union Address," interview with Matt Lauer, *The Today Show*, NBC, January 27, 1998.

183. John Herbers, "Tapes Released," *New York Times*, August 6, 1974, A1, 15.

CHAPTER 5:
POLITICAL MARTYRDOM

1. Kenneth Burke, *Attitudes toward History* (Boston: Beacon, 1961), 39.

2. Brian L. Ott and Eric Aoki, "The Politics of Negotiating Public Tragedy: Media Framing of the Matthew Shepard Murder," *Rhetoric & Public Affairs* 5 (2002): 483–505, 493.

3. Ibid., 495; Kenneth Burke, *The Rhetoric of Religion* (Boston: Beacon, 1961), 4.

4. Kenneth Burke, *The Philosophy of Literary Form: Studies in Symbolic Action* (Baton Rouge: Louisiana State University Press, 1967), 16.

5. Kenneth Burke, *A Grammar of Motives* (Berkeley: University of California Press, 1969), 406.

6. Ibid.

7. Ibid., xx; Burke equates hero with agent, but not all agents are heroes as will be described.

8. Burke defines the agent as the one "who did it." See Burke, *A Grammar of Motives*, xvii. For the purposes of this book, the accused is the primary political agent, but he is not the only one involved. Burke distinguishes three types of nonheroic agents. One who inspires the agent's motivation is a superagent. A co-agent is a friend, whereas a counteragent is an enemy to an agent. In context of the scandal, the distinction between the co- and counteragent typically depends on political affiliation, which creates opposition that is seen during the construction of meaning following the initial allegations of misconduct. For example, Republican senator Trent Lott was a co-agent of the Republican Nixon, but by demanding Democratic Clinton's impeachment, Lott was a counteragent. The discovery of sensational evidence typically dissolves the party line distinction between co- and counteragent. For example, Democratic senator Joseph Lieberman admonished the president after Clinton admitted to lying, and Republicans no longer supported Nixon after the contents of the tapes became public. The role of the superagent, however, is critical, for it demonstrates the origin of the hero's agency. For example, many presidents have refused to continue into a third term, which is a tradition credited to George Washington, and all but Franklin Roosevelt have followed. The motivation for self-imposed term limits (until formally established by the Twenty-Second Amendment) is to allow the periodic rebirth of power so that no one individual will ever rule over the United States for any extended period.

9. James Leonard Bates, *The Origins of Teapot Dome: Progressives, Parties and Petroleum, 1909–1921* (Urbana: University of Illinois Press, 1963), 237.

10. Burke, *Attitudes toward History*, 36; Burke, *The Rhetoric of Religion*, 228.

11. Burke, *A Grammar of Motives*, xx.

12. Ibid., xxi.

13. Ibid.

14. Adrienne E. Christiansen and Jeremy J. Hanson, "Comedy as Cure for Tragedy: ACT UP and the Rhetoric of AIDS," *Quarterly Journal of Speech* 82 (1996): 157–170, 159.

15. Bill Clinton and Hillary Rodham Clinton, "Governor and Mrs. Bill Clinton Discuss Adultery Accusations," interview with Steve Kroft, *60 Minutes*, January 26, 1992; "Doheny Explains Why He Lent $100,000 to Fall," *Los Angeles Times*, January 25, 1924, 1; "Text of the President's Address after Impeachment," *New York Times*, December 20, 1998, 31.

16. Lou Cannon, "Reagan Acknowledges Arms-for-Hostages Swap; President Tells Nation Deals with Iran Were a Mistake, but Address Does Not Include an Apology," *Washington Post*, March 5, 1987, A1.

17. John Ehrman and Michael W. Flamm, *Debating the Reagan Presidency* (Lanham, MD: Rowman & Littlefield, 2009), 153.

18. Burke, *The Rhetoric of Religion*, 191.

19. Ibid.

20. Ibid., 190.

21. Arthur G. Neal, *National Trauma and Collective Memory* (Armonk, NY: M. E. Sharpe, 1998), 139.

22. Fall had been longtime friends with the two oilmen, who loaned Fall the money a year before and after the leases. Moreover, one of the oilmen foreclosed on Fall's house for failure to repay the "bribe."

23. Stephen Engelberg, "Aide Says North Was to Take Blame," *New York Times*, August 28, 1987, A3.

24. Oliver North and William Novak, *Under Fire: An American Story* (New York: HarperCollins, 1992), 8.

25. Robin Anderson, "Oliver North and the News," in *Journalism and Popular Culture*, ed. Peter Dahlgren and Colin Sparks, 171–189 (London: Sage, 1992), 173.

26. Anderson, "Oliver North and the News," 183; Philip Shenon, "The Patriotism Defense: Sometimes It Works, Sometimes It Doesn't," *New York Times*, May 29, 1987, B8.

27. Terry Ashe, "Ollie Takes the Hill," *Newsweek*, July 20, 1987, 12; Jonathan Alter, "Ollie Enters Folklore," *Newsweek*, July 20, 1987, 19.

28. Michael C. McGee, "In Search of the 'People': A Rhetorical Alternative," *Quarterly Journal of Speech* 61 (1975): 235–249, 241–242.

29. Carol Corbin, *Rhetoric in Postmodern America: Conversations with Michael Calvin McGee* (New York: Guilford, 1998), 124.

30. Ronald Lee and Matthew H. Barton, "Clinton's Rhetoric of Contrition," in *Images, Scandal, and Communication Strategies of the Clinton Presidency*, ed. R. E. Denton and R. L. Holloway, 219–246 (Westport, CT: Praeger, 2003), 236.

31. "So the Public May Know," *Denver Post*, April 15, 1922, A1.

32. Robert Jewett and John Shelton Lawrence, *The American Monomyth* (Garden City, NY: Anchor, 1977), 210–211.

33. Chiara Bottici, *A Philosophy of Political Myth* (New York: Cambridge University Press, 2007), 99.

34. Burke, *A Grammar of Motives*, 406.

35. Burke, *A Rhetoric of Religion*, 4.

36. Jewett and Lawrence, *The American Monomyth*, 210–211.

37. Burke, *A Rhetoric of Religion*, 20.

38. Kenneth Burke, *Language as Symbolic Action: Essays on Life, Literature, and Method* (Berkeley: University of California Press, 1966), 301.

39. Thomas S. Frentz, "Memory, Myth, and Rhetoric in Plato's *Phaedrus*," *Rhetoric Society Quarterly* 36 (2006): 243–262, 260.

40. Stjepan G. Mestrovic, *Durkheim and Postmodern Culture* (New York: A. de Gruyter, 1992), 93.

41. Burke claims, "Every brilliant doctor hides a murderer." This example shows the paradox that the health-minded physician (i.e., hero) also has the power to kill (i.e., villain). See Burke, *A Grammar of Motives*, 407.

42. Burke, *A Rhetoric of Religion*, 58.

43. W. Lance Bennett, "Myth, Ritual, and Political Control," *Journal of Communication* 30 (1980): 166–179, 17.

44. David R. Gergen, *Eyewitness to Power: The Essence of Leadership, Nixon to Clinton* (New York: Simon & Schuster, 2000), 76.

45. Ibid.

46. Nixon and Ehrlichman, Oval Office conversation, July 19, 1972.

47. United States, *Report of the Congressional Committees Investigating the Iran-Contra Affair: With Supplemental, Minority, and Additional Views* (Washington, DC: U.S. House of Representatives Select Committee to Investigate Covert Arms Transactions), 561.

48. Ken Bode, "Clinton and the Press," in *The Clinton Riddle: Perspectives on the Forty-Second President*, ed. Todd G. Shields, Jeannine M. Whayne, and Donald R. Kelley, 23–46 (Fayetteville: University of Arkansas Press, 2004), 44.

49. Robert M. Eisinger, *The Evolution of Presidential Polling* (Cambridge: Cambridge University Press, 2003), 173.

50. Linda Denise Oakley, "All We Had to Do Was Rationalize the Sex," in *Aftermath: The Clinton Impeachment and the Presidency in the Age of Political Spectacle*, ed. L. V. Kaplan and B. I. Moran, 186–198 (New York: New York University Press, 2001), 188.

51. John F. Harris and Dan Balz, "Aides Debate What Else Clinton Can Do to Sway House Vote," *Washington Post*, December 8, 1998, A1.

52. Dennis Thompson, *Political Ethics and Public Office* (Cambridge, MA: Harvard University Press, 1987), 11.

53. "First Blood in the Oil Fight," *Literary Digest*, June 13, 1925, 13.

54. Francis X. Busch, *Enemies of the State: An Account of the Trials of the Mary Eugenia Surratt Case, the Teapot Dome Cases, the Alphonse Capone Case, and the Rosenberg Case* (London: Arco Publications, 1957), 91.

55. "Whitewashing the Oil Spots," *Independent*, July 4, 1925, 1.

56. "First Blood in the Oil Fight," 13.

57. Busch, *Enemies of the State*, 156.

58. Paul Y. Anderson, "The Fall-Sinclair Mistrial," *Literary Digest*, November 19, 1927, 8.

59. M. R. Werner and John Starr, *Teapot Dome* (New York: Viking, 1959), 212.

60. "Acquit Sinclair; Fall Next?" *Chicago Daily Tribune*, April 22, 1928, 1.

61. "Doheny Interests Act to Evict Fall," *Los Angeles Times*, August 16, 1935, 1; "Fall Loses Eviction Plea," *New York Times*, December 3, 1936, 10.

62. "Fall Gets Year in Prison, $100,000 Fine . . . ," *New York Times*, November 2, 1929, 1.

63. Gerald Ford is the only president to have never been voted into office; the only electorate Ford appeared in front of was Michigan's Fifth Congressional District.

64. Michael Schudson, *Watergate in American Memory: How We Remember, Forget, and Reconstruct the Past* (New York: Basic Books, 1992), 108–109.

65. Ibid., 12.

66. Les Evans and Allen Myers, *Watergate and the Myth of American Democracy* (New York: Pathfinder Press, 1974), 57–58.

67. Robin Andersen, "Oliver North and the News," in *Journalism and Popular Culture*, ed. Peter Dahlgren and Colin Sparks, 171–189 (London: Sage, 1992), 172.

68. Walter Pincus and George Lardner Jr., "Prosecutors Seek to Show Coverup Plot," *Washington Post*, June 18, 1992, A1.

69. North and Novak, *Under Fire*, 21.

70. Woody Klein, *All the Presidents' Spokesmen: Spinning the News, White House Press Secretaries from Franklin D. Roosevelt to George W. Bush* (Westport, CT: Praeger, 2008), 14.

71. Ann Wroe, *Lives, Lies and the Iran-Contra Affair* (London: I. B. Tauris, 1991), 152.

72. Charles Stafford, "Reagan: Private Aid for Contras My Idea," *St. Petersburg Times*, May 16, 1987, 1A.

73. "Excerpts from President's Meeting with Editors," *New York Times*, May 16, 1987, 6.

74. "A Time for Reflection, and Forgetfulness," *Economist*, May 16, 1987, 33.

75. Robert Busby, *Reagan and the Iran-Contra Affair: The Politics of Presidential Recovery* (New York: St. Martin's, 1999), 165; Lou Cannon, "A Widening Credibility Gap," *Washington Post*, July 27, 1987, A2.

76. Cannon, "A Widening Credibility Gap," A2; Busby, *Reagan and the Iran-Contra Affair*, 165.

77. Busby, *Reagan and the Iran-Contra Affair*, 180.

78. Tom Blanton, "Where George Was; What North's Diaries Tell Us about Bush's Iran-Contra Role," *Washington Post*, June 10, 1990, C1.

79. Lawrence E. Walsh, *Firewall: The Iran-Contra Conspiracy and Cover-Up* (New York: Norton, 1997), 8.

80. "Walsh on the President: 'The Horror of It,'" *Newsweek*, January 4, 1993, 16.

81. "The Best Case for the Pardons," *New York Times*, December 29, 1992, A14.

82. Susan Schmidt and Peter Baker, "President Lied and Obstructed Justice, Impeachment Report Contends," *Washington Post*, September 11, 1998, A1.

83. Howard Kurtz, "With a Heavy Topic, Nation's Newspapers Weigh In," *Washington Post*, September 13, 1998, A31.

84. Ibid.

85. Bob Woodward, *Shadow: Five Presidents and the Legacy of Watergate* (New York: Simon & Schuster, 1999), 464.

86. Richard Lacayo, "Cover That Keyhole," *Time*, October 5, 1998, 40.

87. President Bill Clinton, "Address to the Nation on Testimony before the Independent Counsel's Grand Jury," August 17, 1998.

88. Ibid.

89. While there was very little polling during Teapot Dome, news organizations frequently reported poll findings during the Clinton/Lewinsky scandal. Clinton himself relied nearly wholeheartedly on poll results to decide how to react to developments in the scandal. Often his responses came late because he waited for a variety of poll reports.

90. President Bill Clinton, "Remarks at a Breakfast with Religious Leaders," September 11, 1998.

91. John M. Broder, "Clinton Says He Is 'Very Sorry' after Senator's Harsh Criticism," *New York Times*, September 5, 1998, A1.

92. John F. Harris, "Defenders Optimistic as Battle Moves to Political Realm," *Washington Post*, September 25, 1998, A18.

93. Bill Carter, "3 Networks Offer Stations Soap Operas and Debate," *New York Times*, December 19, 1998, B5.

94. Michael G. Gartner, "How the Monica Story Played in Mid-America," *Columbia Journalism Review*, May 1999, 34.

95. Kenneth L. Hacker, Maury Giles, and Aja Guerrero, "The Political Image Management Dynamics of President Bill Clinton," in *Images, Scandal, and Communication Strategies of the Clinton Presidency*, ed. Robert E. Denton and Rachel L. Holloway, 1–38 (Westport, CT: Praeger, 2003), 26.

96. Bob Woodward, "Gerald Ford," in *Profiles in Courage for Our Time*, ed. Caroline Kennedy, 293–318 (New York: Hyperion, 2002), 26.

97. Advisory Panel on the White House Tapes, "Report to Chief Judge John J. Sirica, January 15, 1974," in *Watergate: A Brief History with Documents*, Stanley I. Kutler, 163–165 (Chichester, UK: Wiley-Blackwell, 2010); Mitchell K. Hall, *Historical Dictionary of the Nixon-Ford Era* (Lanham, MD: Scarecrow Press, 2008), s.v. "White House Tapes."

98. W. Lance Bennett, "Myth, Ritual, and Political Control," *Journal of Communication* 30 (1980): 166–179, 166.

CHAPTER 6:
CONTEMPORARY ISSUES AND SCANDALS

1. John Garrard, "Scandals: An Overview," in *Scandals in Past and Contemporary Politics*, ed. John Garrard and James L. Newell, 13–29 (New York: Palgrave, 2006), 23.

2. Amanda Munoz-Temple, "The Man behind Weiner's Resignation," *National Journal*, June 11, 2011, http://www.nationaljournal.com/the-man-behind-weiner-s-resignation-20110616.

3. Jonathan Allen and Ben Smith, "Anthony Weiner: Hackers Posted Lewd Photos on Twitter," *Politico*, March 28, 2011, http://www.politico.com/news/stories/0511/55877.html#ixzz3Af11oFek.

4. "Congressman: A Hacker Placed Lewd Photo on Twitter Account," CNN.com, May 31, 2011, http://www.cnn.com/2011/POLITICS/05/30/weiner.photo.

5. Dan Amira, "Anthony Weiner Not Sure If That's His Wiener," *New York Magazine*, June 1, 2011, http://nymag.com/daily/intelligencer/2011/06/anthony_weiner_not_sure_if_tha.html.

6. Reuven Blau and Corky Siemaszko, "Anthony Weiner Has a Defender: Rep. Charles Rangel Lends Support to Sext-Scandal Colleague," *New York Daily News*, June 10, 2011, http://www.nydailynews.com/news/politics/anthony-weiner-defender-rep-charles-rangel-lends-support-sext-scandal-colleague-article-1.126474.

7. Aaron Blake, "Weiner: Women May Come Forward with More E-Mails, Photos," *Washington Post*, May 23, 2013, http://www.washingtonpost.com/blogs/post-politics/wp/2013/05/23/weiner-women-may-come-forward-with-more-e-mails-photos.

8. Abby Phillip, "Anthony Weiner Says Sexting Continued after Resignation, Now 'Entirely behind Me,'" ABC News, July 23, 2013, http://abcnews.go.com/Politics/anthony-weiner-sexting-continued-resignation-now/story?id=19750923.

9. Don Lawson, *Famous Presidential Scandals* (Hillside, NJ: Enslow, 1990), 46.

10. Herman B. Weisner, *The Politics of Justice: A. B. Fall and the Teapot Dome Scandal; A New Perspective* (Albuquerque, NM: Creative Designs, 1994), 2.

11. Helen Thomas, *Watchdogs of Democracy? The Waning Washington Press Corps and How It Has Failed the Public* (New York: Scribner, 2006), 13.

12. James A. Capo, "Network Watergate Coverage Patterns in Late 1972 and Early 1973," *Journalism Quarterly* 60 (1983): 595–602.

13. "The Dynamic Duo," *Newsweek*, October 30, 1972, 76.

14. Weisner, *The Politics of Justice*, 2.

15. E. J. Dionne Jr., "Gary Hart: The Elusive Frontrunner," *New York Times*, May 3, 1987, http://www.nytimes.com/1987/05/03/magazine/garry-hart-the-elusive-front-runner.html?pagewanted=all&src=pm.

16. "Bob Dole's Affair—1996," *Washington Post*, http://www.washingtonpost.com/wp-srv/politics/special/clinton/frenzy/dole.htm; Susan Paterno, "An Affair to Ignore," *American Journalism Review*, January/February 1997, http://www.ajr.org/article.asp?id=1485.

17. Larry Sabato, Mark Stencel, and S. Robert Lichter, *Peepshow: Media and Politics in an Age of Scandal* (Lanham, MD: Rowman & Littlefield, 2000), 220.

18. Benjamin Ginsberg and Martin Shefter, *Politics by Other Means: Politicians, Prosecutors, and the Press from Watergate to Whitewater* (New York: Norton, 1999), 28–29.

19. David Johnston, "Partisan Anger in House Brings Lockout of Committee Republicans," *Washington Post*, October 23, 2009, 5.

20. Mary Ann Akers, "Monday in a GOP Takeover," *Washington Post*, July 12, 2009, 13; Ruth Marcus, "Wednesday Annoyer in Chief," *Washington Post*, October 27, 2010, 23; Mark Leibovich, "Congressman Emerges as Obama's Annoyer-in-Chief," *Washington Post*, July 7, 2010, 1.

21. Ruth Marcus, "Wednesday Annoyer in Chief," 23.

22. Ibid.

23. Bill Adair and Wes Allison, "He Wants to Revive Congress' Scrutiny," *St. Petersburg Times*, November 13, 2006, 1A.

24. Philip Shenon, "As New 'Cop on the Beat,' Congressman Starts Patrol," *New York Times*, February 6, 2007, 18.

25. Jack Anderson and Jan Moller, "Retirement Splits an Odd Couple in House," *Washington Post*, December 5, 1996, B13.

26. Mary McGrory, "Blessed in Their Enemies," *Washington Post*, May 14, 1998, A3.

27. Ruth Marcus, "Clinton Faces Floodgate of Probes," *Washington Post*, November 7, 1996, A28.

28. "Will the House Do It Again?," *Washington Post*, June 26, 1997, A18.

29. David Rohde, "Committees and Policy Formulation," *Institutions of American Democracy: The Legislative Branch*, ed. Paul J. Quirk and Sarah Binder, 201–223 (Oxford: University of Oxford Press, 2005), 217.

30. Ruth Marcus, "Annoyer in Chief: Two Darrell Issas, One Oversight Panel," *Washington Post*, October 27, 2010, A23.

31. "Our View: House GOP's Lawsuit Is More Likely to Backfire than Succeed," *Baltimore Sun*, August 1, 2014, 16A.

32. Richard Nixon v. A. Ernest Fitzgerald, 457 U.S. 731 (1982), 762.

33. Ibid., 757.

34. William Jefferson Clinton v. Paula Corbin Jones, 520 U.S. 681 (1997).

35. Jeremy W. Peters, "House Votes to Sue Obama for Overstepping Powers," *New York Times*, July 31, 2014, A15.

36. Alan Fram, "House Approves Lawsuit against Obama," *NewsHour*, PBS, July 30, 2014, http://www.pbs.org/newshour/rundown/house-approves-lawsuit-obama.

37. Evan Lehmann, "Rewriting History under the Dome," *Lowell Sun*, January 27, 2006, http://www.lowellsun.com/ci_3444567.

38. Yuki Noguchi, "Wikipedia's Help from the Hill," *Washington Post*, February 9, 2006, A21.

39. Ibid.

40. Andy Myer, "Rewriting History with the Click of a Mouse," *Philadelphia Inquirer*, February 16, 2006, A23.

41. Derek Willis, "With Twitter's Help, Watch Congress Edit Wikipedia," *New York Times*, July 14, 2014, http://www.nytimes.com/2014/07/15/upshot/twitter -wikipedia-and-a-closer-eye-on-congress.html.

42. Mark Berman, "President Obama and the Horse Mask Person," *Washington Post*, July 9, 2014, http://www.washingtonpost.com/news/post-nation/wp/2014/07/09/ president-obama-and-the-horse-mask-person-an-investigation-involving-data-and -charts.

43. Sophia Rosenbaum, "Congress Punished for Wiki 'Tweaks,'" *New York Post*, July 29, 2014, 3.

44. "Five Pillars," Wikipedia, August 15, 2014, http://en.wikipedia.org/wiki/Wikipedia:Five_pillars.

45. Ryan Gorman, "Someone within the US Senate Edited Edward Snowden's Wikipedia Page," *Daily Mail*, August 13, 2013, http://www.dailymail.co.uk/news/article-2384188/Edward-Snowdens-Wikipedia-page-edited-dissident-traitor-US-Senate.html.

46. "Twitter Watchdog Keeps Tabs on Wikipedia Edits from Congress," NBC News, July 15, 2014, http://www.nbcnews.com/tech/social-media/twitter-watchdog-keeps-tabs-wikipedia-edits-congress-n156391; Gregg Levine, "Those Who Do Not Learn History Are Doomed to Retweet It," Al Jazeera, July 11, 2014, http://america.aljazeera.com/blogs/scrutineer/2014/7/11/those-who-do-notlearnhistoryaredoomedtoretweetit.html.

47. "Politwoops," http://politwoops.sunlightfoundation.com.

48. "Excerpts from the House's Final Debate on Impeaching President Clinton," *New York Times*, December 20, 1998, 35.

49. Lee Davidson, "Rocky, Kucinich, Others Attack Bush in House Forum."

50. Davidson, "Rocky, Kucinich, Others Attack Bush in House Forum."

51. Peters, "House Votes to Sue Obama for Overstepping Powers," A15.

52. Dana Milbank, "Priorities, like Wisdom and Understanding, in Short Supply," *Washington Post*, July 31, 2014, A2.

53. Dana Milbank, "Kinda Sorta Impeaching the President," *Washington Post*, July 26, 2008, A3.

54. Adam Clayton Powell, Jr. v. John William McCormack et al., 395 U.S. 486 (1969).

55. Charles V. Hamilton, *Adam Clayton Powell, Jr.: The Political Biography of an American Dilemma* (New York: Atheneum, 1991), 408.

56. Christopher Lee, "Rangel's Pet Cause Bears His Own Name," *Washington Post*, July 15, 2008, A1.

57. Christopher Lee and Lyndsey Layton, "Rangel Insists Ethics Tumult Will Pass," *Washington Post*, September 28, 2008, A2.

58. N. R. Kleinfield, "Amid Routine Business, History and Humiliation," *New York Times*, December 3, 2010, A28.

59. Ibid.

60. Ibid.

61. John Eligon and Michael Schwirtz, "In Rapes, Candidate Says, Body Can Block Pregnancy," *New York Times*, August 20, 2012, 13.

62. Jennifer Brooks and Rachel Stassen-Berger, "'Uncle Thomas' Tweet Ripped," *Star Tribune*, June 26, 2013, 1B.

63. Michael McNutt, "Oklahoma Lawmaker Apologizes for Ethnic Slur," *The Oklahoman*, April 13, 2013, http://newsok.com/oklahoma-lawmaker-apologizes-for-ethnic-slur/article/3787207.

64. Lloyd F. Bitzer, "Political Rhetoric," in *Landmark Essays on Contemporary Rhetoric*, ed. Thomas B. Farrell, 1–22 (Mahwah, NJ: Lawrence Erlbaum, 1981/1998).

65. During the 1988 presidential election, Gary Hart stated in the *New York Times*, "Follow me around. I don't care. I'm serious. If anybody wants to put a tail on me, go ahead. They'll be very bored." The *Miami Herald* took up Hart's request and reported his infidelity on the same day, May 3, 1987, that the *Times* reported Hart's dare.

CHAPTER 7:
YESTERDAY, TODAY, AND TOMORROW

1. Albert B. Fall, *The Memoirs of Albert B. Fall* (El Paso: Texas Western Press, 1966), 4; David H. Stratton, "Behind Teapot Dome: Some Personal Insights," *Business History Review* 31 (1957): 385–402, 385.

2. Frost, "That Teapot Alarm Clock," 396. "The Cast of Characters," *New York Times*, February 3, 1924, xxi; "The Highlights of the Drama," *New York Times*, February 3, 1924, xxi.

3. Burl Noogle, "The Origins of Teapot Dome Investigation," *Mississippi Valley Historical Review* 44 (1957): 237–266, 261.

4. David H. Stratton, *Tempest over Teapot Dome: The Story of Albert B. Fall* (Norman: University of Oklahoma Press, 1998), 398.

5. Ibid., 290.

6. Ibid.

7. M. R. Werner and John Starr, *Teapot Dome* (New York: Viking, 1959), 258.

8. "Guns of Democrats Ready as Inquiry on Teapot Dome Begins," *Washington Post*, October 9, 1923, 1.

9. Ibid.

10. Ibid.

11. Bruce Bliven, "Oil-Driven Politics," *New Republic*, February 13, 1924, 303.

12. "The Teapot Dome Naval Oil Scandal," *Literary Digest*, February 9, 1924, 8.

13. "The Counter-Attack on Oil," *New Republic*, March 26, 1924, 114.

14. "Capers: Operation Watergate," *Newsweek*, July 3, 1972, 18.

15. Louis Liebovitch, *Richard Nixon, Watergate, and the Press* (Westport, CT: Praeger, 2003), 78.

16. Ibid.

17. Bob Woodward and Carl Bernstein, *The Secret Man* (New York: Simon & Schuster, 2005), 2.

18. Nixon and Dean, Oval Office conversation, Nixon Tapes, April 17, 1973.

19. Nixon and Ehrlichman, Oval Office conversation, Nixon Tapes, July 19, 1972.

20. Haynes Johnson, "The Report and the GOP Split," *Washington Post*, November 20, 1987, A2.

21. Robert Busby, *Reagan and the Iran-Contra Affair: The Politics of Presidential Recovery* (New York: St. Martin's, 1999), 2.

22. Eleanor Randolph, "The Scamgate Name Stakes: A Lively Effort to Tag the Troubles," *Washington Post*, December 17, 1986, G1.

23. George C. Kohn, *The New Encyclopedia of American Scandal* (New York: Facts on File, 2001), 200.

24. David P. Thelen, *Becoming Citizens in the Age of Television: How Americans Challenged the Media and Seized Political Initiative during the Iran-Contra Debate* (Chicago: University of Chicago Press, 1996), 37.

25. Robin Anderson, "Oliver North and the News," in *Journalism and Popular Culture*, ed. Peter Dahlgren and Colin Sparks, 171–189 (London: Sage, 1992), 172.

26. Thelen, *Becoming Citizens in the Age of Television*, 33.

27. Thomas J. Craughwell and M. William Phelps, *Failures of the Presidents: From the Whiskey Rebellion and War of 1812 to the Bay of Pigs and War in Iraq* (Beverly, MA: Fair Winds Press, 2008), 268.

28. Ann Wroe, *Lives, Lies and the Iran-Contra Affair* (London: I. B. Tauris, 1991), 48.

29. Ibid.

30. Ibid. United States, John G. Tower, Edmund S. Muskie, and Brent Scowcroft, *The Tower Commission Report: The Full Text of the President's Special Review Board* (New York: Bantam, 1987), B64.

31. Wroe, *Lives, Lies and the Iran-Contra Affair*, 48.

32. Gary Thatcher, "Iran-Contra Affair Back in the Spotlight," *Christian Science Monitor*, November 17, 1987, 1.

33. Busby, *Reagan and the Iran-Contra Affair*, 77.

34. Jonathan Alter, "Will There Be a Backlash?," *Newsweek*, December 15, 1986, 40.

35. Mark Hertsgaard, *On Bended Knee: The Press and the Reagan Presidency* (New York: Farrar, Straus & Giroux, 1988), 325.

36. Alex S. Jones, "The White House Crisis: Fairness Stressed by Nation's Press," *New York Times*, December 5, 1986, A13.

37. Hertsgaard, *On Bended Knee*, 325–326.

38. John Hughes, "Inching Out of the Iran Mess," *Christian Science Monitor*, December 10, 1986, 20.

39. Amy Fried, *Muffled Echoes: Oliver North and the Politics of Public Opinion* (New York: Columbia University Press, 1997), 104.

40. David Ignatius, "Ollie's Last Laugh; Congress Is Stalking Reagan with a Popgun," *Washington Post*, July 12, 1987, C1.

41. Peter Baker, "Lewinsky Testifies before Grand Jury," *Washington Post*, August 7, 1998, A1.

42. Howard Fineman and Daniel Klaidman, "Race to the Bottom," *Newsweek*, March 9, 1998.

43. Stanley A. Renshon, *High Hopes: The Clinton Presidency and The Politics of Ambition* (New York: New York University Press, 1996), 117.

44. John J. Pitney Jr., "Clinton and the Republican Party," in *The Post-Modern Presidency: Bill Clinton's Legacy in Politics*, ed. Steven E. Schiecer, 167–182 (Pittsburgh: University of Pittsburgh Press, 2000), 181.

45. James Bennet, "Clinton Dismisses Parallels to Nixon Case," *New York Times*, May 7, 1998, A1. Starr took advantage of the constant equivocation of Nixon and Clinton by claiming that he was proud to follow the path of Leon Jaworski, who became the special prosecutor of Watergate in the wake of the Saturday Night Massacre. Neil A. Lewis, "Starr's Speech Invokes Days of Watergate," *New York Times*, May 2, 1998, A9.

46. Robert Busby, *Defending the American Presidency* (New York: Palgrave, 2001), 71; Marvin L. Kalb, *One Scandalous Story: Clinton, Lewinsky, and Thirteen Days That Tarnished American Journalism* (New York: Free Press, 2001), 15.

47. Gore Vidal, "Coup de Starr," *Nation*, October 26, 1998, 6.

48. Andrew Phillips, "The Clinton Paradox," *Maclean's*, January 31, 1998, 30.

49. Timothy Noah, "Scandalized," *New Republic*, February 23, 1998, 12.

50. William Greider, "Clinton and Character," *Rolling Stone*, Issue 798, October 29, 1998, 31.

51. "Are You a Right-Wing Conspirator," *National Review*, February 2, 1998, 63.

52. John F. Harris, "Clinton Denies Alleged Affair," *Washington Post*, January 22, 1998, A1.

53. James Bennet and Alison Mitchell, "Ghosts of Watergate Haunt Impeachment Debate," *New York Times*, October 1, 1998, A28.

54. Busby, *Defending the American Presidency*, 105.

55. Nancy Gibbs, Jay Branegan, Margaret Carlson, et al., "Truth or . . . Consequences," *Time*, February 2, 1998, 18.

56. James Benner and Adam Nagourney, "White House's Familiar Battle Plan: Keep Silent, Strike Often and Soldier On," *New York Times*, January 30, 1998, A13.

57. "Ironic Triangle," *New Republic*, February 19, 1998, 14.

58. John F. Harris, "Clinton Denies Alleged Affair," *Washington Post*, January 22, 1998, A1.

59. John F. Harris, *The Survivor: Bill Clinton in the White House* (New York: Random House, 2005), 342.

60. Ken Bode, "Clinton and the Press," in *The Clinton Riddle: Perspectives on the Forty-Second President*, ed. Todd G. Shields, Jeannie M. Whayne, and Donald R. Kelley, 23–46 (Fayetteville: University of Arkansas Press, 2004), 32.

61. W. Lance Bennett, "Myth, Ritual, and Political Control," *Journal of Communication* 30 (1980), 166–179, 166.

62. Eric Csapo, *Theories of Mythology* (Malden, MA: Blackwell, 2005), 263.

63. Shawn Boburg, "Agency Still Silent on Tie-Up at GWB," *The Record*, September 19, 2013, A8.

64. John Cichowski, "Closed Tollbooths a Commuting Disaster," *The Record*, September 13, 2013, L01.

65. Ibid.

66. John Cichowski, "Chokehold Ends at GWB Tollbooths," *The Record*, September 14, 2013, L1.

67. John Cichowski, "PA 'Show' Obscures New Road Decisions," *The Record*, November 27, 2013, L1.

68. Michael Phillis, "Christie Says GWB Hearings Are Dems Playing Politics," *The Record*, December 3, 2013, A3.

69. Charles Stile, "Christie Won't Easily Shake GWB Flap," *The Record*, December 14, 2013, A6.

70. Melissa Hayes, "Christie Says Politics Played a Role in Flap," *The Record*, December 20, 2013, A10.

71. Shawn Boburg, "Criticized Port Official Quits," *The Record*, December 7, 2013, A1.

72. Shawn Boburg and John Reitmeyer, "Shake-Up at the Port Authority," *The Record*, December 14, 2013, A1.

73. Herb Jackson, "Closures at GWB May Shake Agencies across U.S.," *The Record*, December 18, 2013, A1.

74. Mike Kelly, "Higher-Ups Suspected in GWB Mess," *The Record*, January 2, 2014, A01.

75. Shawn Bob, "Stuck in a Jam," *The Record*, January 9, 2014, A1.

76. "Full Transcript: N.J. Gov. Chris Christie's Jan. 9 News Conference on George Washington Bridge Scandal," *Washington Post*, January 9, 2014, http://www.washingtonpost.com/politics/transcript-chris-christies-news-conference-on-george-washington-bridge-scandal/2014/01/09/d0f4711c-7944-11e3-8963-b4b654bcc9b2_story.html.

77. "Full Text of New Jersey Gov. Chris Christie's 2014 State of the State Speech," *Washington Post*, January 14, 2014, http://www.washingtonpost.com/politics/full-text-of-new-jersey-gov-chris-christies-2014-state-of-the-state-speech/2014/01/14/8fd12f08-7d55-11e3-9556-4a4bf7bcbd84_story.html.

78. William Safire, *Safire's Political Dictionary* (Oxford: Oxford University Press, 2008), s.v. "Mistakes Were Made."

79. Shawn Boburg, John Reitmeyer, and Stephanie Akin, "Lawmakers Charge Contempt as Wildstein Refuses to Testify," *The Record*, January 10, 2014, A1.

80. Charles Stile, "Christie Unscathed by Report," *The Record*, March 28, 2014, A1.

81. Kate Zernike, "Lawmakers Press Christie Aide on Her Texts about Lane Closings," *New York Times*, July 18, 2014, 16.

Bibliography

Adut, Ari. *On Scandal: Moral Disturbances in Society, Politics, and Art.* Cambridge: Cambridge University Press, 2008.

Advisory Panel on the White House Tapes. "Report to Chief Judge John J. Sirica, January 15, 1974." In *Watergate: A Brief History with Documents*, edited by Stanley I. Kutler, 163–165. Chichester, UK: Wiley-Blackwell, 2010.

Allen, Frederick Lewis. *Only Yesterday: An Informal History of the Nineteen-Twenties.* New York: Harper, 1957.

Anderson, Robin. "Oliver North and the News." In *Journalism and Popular Culture*, edited by Peter Dahlgren and Colin Sparks, 171–189. London: Sage, 1992.

Aucoin, James L. "The Re-Emergence of American Investigative Journalism, 1960–1975." *Journalism History* 21 (1995): 3–15.

Barkin, Steve Michael. *American Television News: The Media Marketplace and the Public Interest.* Armonk, NY: M. E. Sharpe, 2003.

Basinger, Scott J., and Brandon Rottinghaus. "Skeletons in White House Closets: A Discussion of Modern Presidential Scandals." *Political Science Quarterly* 127 (2012): 213–239.

Bellah, Robert N. "Civil Religion in America." In *American Civil Religion*, edited by Russell E. Richey and Donald G. Jones, 21–44. New York: Harper & Row, 1974.

Bennett, W. Lance. "Myth, Ritual, and Political Control." *Journal of Communication* 30 (1980): 166–179.

———. "Political Scenarios and the Nature of Politics." *Philosophy & Rhetoric* 8 (1985): 23–42.

Bennoit, William L. *Accounts, Excuses, and Apologies: A Theory of Image Restoration Strategies.* Albany: State University of New York Press, 1995.

———. "Richard M. Nixon's Rhetorical Strategies in His Public Statements on Watergate." *Southern Speech Communication Journal* 47 (1982): 192–211.

Bennoit, William L., Paul Gullifor, and Daniel A. Panici. "President Reagan's Defensive Discourse on the Iran-Contra Affair." *Communication Studies* 42 (1991): 272–294.

Bercovitch, Sacvan. *The American Jeremiad*. Madison: University of Wisconsin Press, 1978.

Bernstein, Carl, and Bob Woodward. *All the President's Men*. New York, Simon & Schuster, 1974.

Billig, Michael, and Katie MacMillan. "Metaphor, Idiom and Ideology: The Search for 'No Smoking Guns' across Time." *Discourse & Society* 16 (2005): 459–480.

Bitzer, Lloyd. "The Rhetorical Situation." *Philosophy and Rhetoric* 1 (1968): 1–14.

Bitzer, Lloyd F. "Political Rhetoric." In *Landmark Essays on Contemporary Rhetoric*, edited by Thomas B. Farrell, 1–22. Mahwah, NJ: Lawrence Erlbaum, 1981/1998.

Blanchard, Margaret Ann. *Revolutionary Sparks Freedom of Expression in Modern America*. New York: Oxford University Press, 1992.

Blaney, Joseph R., and William L. Benoit. *The Clinton Scandals and the Politics of Image Restoration*. Westport, CT: Praeger, 2001.

Blasi, Vincent. "The Checking Value in First Amendment Theory." *American Bar Foundation Research Journal* 2 (1977): 521–649.

Bode, Ken. "Clinton and the Press." In *The Clinton Riddle: Perspectives on the Forty-Second President*, edited by Todd G. Shields, Jeannine M. Whayne, and Donald R. Kelley, 23–46. Fayetteville: University of Arkansas Press, 2004.

Bottici, Chiara. *A Philosophy of Political Myth*. New York: Cambridge University Press, 2007.

Brummett, Barry. "Presidential Substance: The Address of August 15, 1973." *Western Journal of Communication* 48 (1975): 249–259.

———. "Towards a Theory of Silence as a Political Strategy." *Quarterly Journal of Speech* 66 (1980): 289–303.

Burke, Kenneth. *Attitudes toward History*. Boston: Beacon Press, 1961.

———. *A Grammar of Motives*. Berkeley: University of California Press, 1969.

———. *Language as Symbolic Action: Essays on Life, Literature, and Method*. Berkeley: University of California Press, 1966.

———. *The Philosophy of Literary Form: Studies in Symbolic Action*. Baton Rouge: Louisiana State University Press, 1967.

———. *The Rhetoric of Religion*. Boston: Beacon Press, 1961.

Busby, Robert. *Defending the American Presidency*. New York: Palgrave, 2001.

———. *Reagan and the Iran-Contra Affair: The Politics of Presidential Recovery*. New York: St. Martin's, 1999.

Capo, James A. "Network Watergate Coverage Patterns in Late 1972 and Early 1973." *Journalism Quarterly* 60 (1983): 595–602.

Cater, Douglas. *The Fourth Branch of Government*. Boston: Houghton Mifflin, 1959.

Childs, Marquis W. *Witness to Power*. New York: McGraw-Hill, 1975.

Cooper, Charles J. "A Perjurer in the White House? The Constitutional Case for Perjury and Obstruction of Justice as High Crimes and Misdemeanors." *Harvard Journal of Law & Public Policy* 22 (1999): 619–646.

Corbin, Carol. *Rhetoric in Postmodern America: Conversations with Michael Calvin McGee*. New York: Guilford Press, 1998.

Craughwell, Thomas J., and M. William Phelps. *Failures of the Presidents: From the Whiskey Rebellion and War of 1812 to the Bay of Pigs and War in Iraq*. Beverly, MA: Fair Winds Press, 2008.

Csapo, Eric. *Theories of Mythology*. Malden, MA: Blackwell, 2005.

Dean, John W. *Blind Ambition: The White House Years*. New York: Simon & Schuster, 1976.

Downie, Leonard. *The New Muckrakers*. Washington, DC: New Republic, 1976.

Draper, Theodore. *A Very Thin Line: The Iran-Contra Affairs*. New York: Hill & Wang, 1991.

Ehrlich, Matthew. "Shattered Glass, Movies, and the Free Press Myth." *Journal of Communication Inquiry* 29 (2005): 103–118.

Ehrlich, Matthew C. *Journalism in the Movies*. Urbana: University of Illinois Press, 2004.

Eisinger, Robert M. *The Evolution of Presidential Polling*. Cambridge: Cambridge University Press, 2003.

Eliade, Mircea, and Charles J. Adams. *The Encyclopedia of Religion*. New York: Macmillan, 1987.

Emery, Fred. *Watergate: The Corruption of American Politics and the Fall of Richard Nixon*. New York: Times Books, 1994.

Epstein, Edward Jay. *Between Fact and Fiction: The Problem of Journalism*. New York: Vintage, 1975.

Evans, Les, and Allen Myers. *Watergate and the Myth of American Democracy*. New York: Pathfinder Press, 1974.

Fall, Albert B. *The Memoirs of Albert B. Fall*. El Paso: Texas Western Press, 1966.

Feeney, Mark. *Nixon at the Movies: A Book about Belief*. Chicago: University of Chicago Press, 2004.

Fleming, James S. *Window on Congress: A Congressional Biography of Barber B. Conable*. Rochester, NY: University of Rochester Press, 2004.

Frentz, Thomas S. "Memory, Myth, and Rhetoric in Plato's *Phaedrus*." *Rhetoric Society Quarterly* 36 (2006): 243–262.

Fried, Amy. *Muffled Echoes: Oliver North and the Politics of Public Opinion*. New York: Columbia University Press, 1997.

Garment, Leonard. *In Search of Deep Throat: The Greatest Political Mystery of Our Time*. New York: Basic Books, 2000.

Garrard, John. "Scandals: An Overview." In *Scandals in Past and Contemporary Politics*, edited by John Garrard and James L. Newell, 13–29. New York: Palgrave, 2006.

Gergen, David R. *Eyewitness to Power: The Essence of Leadership, Nixon to Clinton*. New York: Simon & Schuster, 2000.

Giddens, Paul H. *Standard Oil Company: Oil Pioneer of the Middle West*. New York: Appleton-Century-Crofts, 1955.

Ginsberg, Benjamin, and Martin Shefter. *Politics by Other Means: Politicians, Prosecutors, and the Press from Watergate to Whitewater*. New York: Norton, 1999.

Greene, Bob. *Running*. Chicago: Regnery, 1973.

Gronbeck, Bruce. "The Rhetoric of Political Corruption." *Quarterly Journal of Speech* 64 (1978): 155–172.

Gullan, Harold I. *Faith of Our Mothers: The Stories of Presidential Mothers from Mary Washington to Barbara Bush*. Grand Rapids, MI: Eerdmans, 2001.

Hacker, Kenneth L. "Interpersonal Communication and the Construction of Candidate Images." In *Candidate Images in Presidential Elections,* edited by Kenneth L. Hacker, 65–82. Westport, CT: Praeger, 1995.

Hacker, Kenneth L., Maury Giles, and Aja Guerrero. "The Political Image Management Dynamics of President Bill Clinton." In *Images, Scandal, and Communication Strategies of the Clinton Presidency,* edited by Robert E. Denton and Rachel L. Holloway, 1–38. Westport, CT: Praeger, 2003.

Haldeman, H. R. *The Haldeman Diaries.* New York: Putnam, 1994.

Hall, Mitchell K. *Historical Dictionary of the Nixon-Ford Era.* Lanham, MD: Scarecrow Press, 2008.

Hamilton, Charles V. *Adam Clayton Powell, Jr.: The Political Biography of an American Dilemma.* New York: Atheneum, 1991.

Harris, John F. *The Survivor: Bill Clinton in the White House.* New York: Random House, 2005.

Heap, James L. "Constructionism in the Rhetoric and Practice of Fourth Generation Evaluation." *Evaluation and Program Planning* 18 (1995): 51–61.

Heath, Robert L. "A Time for Silence: Booker T. Washington in Atlanta." *Quarterly Journal of Speech* 64 (1978): 385–399.

Hertsgaard, Mark. *On Bended Knee: The Press and the Reagan Presidency.* New York: Farrar, Straus & Giroux, 1988.

Ihlen, Øyvind. "On Berger: A Social Constructionist Perspective on Public Relations and Crisis Communication." In *Public Relations and Social Theory: Key Figures and Concepts,* edited by Øyvind Ihlen, Magnus Fredriksson, and Betteke van Ruler, 43–61. New York: Routledge, 2009.

Isaacs, Norman E. *Untended Gates: The Mismanaged Press.* New York: Columbia University Press, 1986.

Isikoff, Michael. *Uncovering Clinton: A Reporter's Story.* New York: Crown, 1999.

Jamieson, Kathleen Hall. *Packaging the Presidency: A History and Criticism of Presidential Campaign Advertising.* New York: Oxford University Press, 1996.

Janeway, Michael. *Republic of Denial: Press, Politics, and Public Life.* New Haven, CT: Yale University Press, 1999.

Jewett, Robert, and John Shelton Lawrence. *The American Monomyth.* Garden City, NY: Anchor.

Johannesen, Richard L. "The Functions of Silence: A Plea for Communication Research." *Western Speech* 38 (1974): 25–35.

Johnson, Andrew, B. F. Wade, Charles Sumner, and William Lawrence. *Proceedings in the Trial of Andrew Johnson President of the United States.* Washington, DC: F & J. Rives & G. A. Bailey, 1868.

Jouvenel, Bertrand de. *The Pure Theory of Politics.* New Haven, CT: Yale University Press, 1963.

Kaiser, Frederick M., and Walter J. Oleszek. "Congressional Oversight Manual." In *Congress of the United States: Oversight, Processes and Procedures,* edited by Carol S. Plesser, 1–131. New York: Nova Science Publishers, 2007.

Kalb, Marvin L. *One Scandalous Story: Clinton, Lewinsky, and Thirteen Days That Tarnished American Journalism.* New York: Free Press, 2001.

————. *The Rise of the "New News": A Case Study of Two Root Causes of the Modern Scandal Coverage.* Cambridge, MA: Harvard University Press, 1998.

Karrass, Chester L. *Give and Take: The Complete Guide to Negotiating Strategies and Tactics.* New York: Thomas Y. Crowell, 1974.

Kessler, Ronald. *Inside Congress: The Shocking Scandals, Corruption, and Abuse of Power behind the Scenes on Capitol Hill.* New York: Pocket Books, 1997.

Kirchwey, Freda, Oswald G. Villard, and Marguerite Young, *Where Is There Another? A Memorial to Paul Y. Anderson: Death of a Fighter.* Norman, OK: Cooperative Books, 1939.

Kirshner, Jonathan. "All the President's Men (1976)." *Film & History: An Interdisciplinary Journal of Film and Television Studies* 36 (2006): 57–58.

Klein, Woody. *All the Presidents' Spokesmen: Spinning the News, White House Press Secretaries from Franklin D. Roosevelt to George W. Bush.* Westport, CT: Praeger, 2008.

Kohn, George C. *The New Encyclopedia of American Scandal.* New York: Facts on File, 2001.

Kramer, Michael R., and Kathryn M. Olson. "The Strategic Potential of Sequencing Apologia Stases: President Clinton's Self-Defense in the Monica Lewinsky Scandal." *Western Journal of Communication* 66 (2002): 347–368.

Krieger, Stefan H. "A Time to Keep Silent and a Time to Speak: The Functions of Silence in the Lawyering Process." *Oregon Law Review* 80 (2001): 199–266.

Kutler, Stanley I. *The Wars of Watergate: The Last Crisis of Richard Nixon.* New York: Knopf, 1990.

Kyvig, David E. *The Age of Impeachment: American Constitutional Culture since 1960.* Lawrence: University Press of Kansas, 2008.

Lakoff, George, and Mark Johnson. *Metaphors We Live By.* Chicago: University of Chicago Press, 1980.

Lambeth, Edmund B. "The Lost Career of Paul Y. Anderson." *Journalism Quarterly* 60 (1983): 401–406.

Lang, Gladys Engel, and Kurt Lang. *The Battle for Public Opinion: The President, the Press, and the Polls during Watergate.* New York: Columbia University Press, 1983.

LaRue, L. H. *Political Discourse: A Case Study of the Watergate Affair.* Athens: University of Georgia Press, 1988.

Lawson, Don. *Famous Presidential Scandals.* Hillside, NJ: Enslow, 1990.

Leavy, Patricia. *Iconic Events: Media, Politics, and Power in Retelling History.* Lanham, MD: Lexington Books, 2007.

Lee, Ronald, and Matthew H. Barton. "Clinton's Rhetoric of Contrition." In *Images, Scandal, and Communication Strategies of the Clinton Presidency*, edited by R. E. Denton and R. L. Holloway, 219–246. Westport, CT: Praeger, 2003.

Levy, Leonard W. *Freedom of the Press from Zenger to Jefferson.* Durham, NC: Carolina Academic Press, 1996.

————. *Legacy of Suppression: Freedom of Speech and Press in Early American History.* Cambridge, MA: Belknap Press of Harvard University Press, 1960.

Lewis, Anthony. *Freedom for the Thought We Hate.* New York: Basic Books, 2009.

Lewis, Carol W. *The Ethics Challenge in Public Service: A Problem-Solving Guide.* San Francisco: Jossey-Bass, 1991.

Lewis, Ioan M. *Ecstatic Religion: A Study of Shamanism and Spirit Possession.* London: Routledge, 2005.

Lichtman, Allan J. *The Keys to the White House: A Surefire Guide to Predicting the Next President.* Lanham, MD: Rowman & Littlefield, 2008.

Liddell, Henry G., and Robert Scott. *A Lexicon: Abridged from Liddell & Scott's Greek-English Lexicon.* New York: Economy Book House, 1901.

Liddell, Henry George, and Robert Scott. *A Greek-English Lexicon.* Oxford: Oxford University Press, 1940.

Liebovich, Louis. *The Press and the Modern Presidency: Myths and Mindsets from Kennedy to Election 2000.* Westport, CT: Praeger, 2000.

———. *Richard Nixon, Watergate, and the Press.* Westport, CT: Praeger, 2003.

Lowi, Theodore J. Foreword to *The Politics of Scandal: Power and Process in Liberal Democracies,* edited by Andrei S. Markovits and Mark Silverstein, vii–xii. New York: Holmes & Meier, 1988.

Lowry, Rich. *Legacy: Paying the Price for the Clinton Years.* Washington, DC: Regnery, 2003.

Lukas, J. Anthony. *Nightmare: The Underside of the Nixon Years.* New York: Viking, 1976.

Lynch, Michael, and David Bogen. *The Spectacle of History: Speech, Text, and Memory at the Iran-Contra Hearings.* Durham, NC: Duke University Press, 1996.

May, Ernest R., and Janet Fraser. *Campaign '72: The Managers Speak.* Cambridge, MA: Harvard University Press, 1973.

McCartney, Laton. *The Teapot Dome Scandal: How Big Oil Bought the Harding White House and Tried to Steal the Country.* New York: Random House, 2008.

McChesney, Robert Waterman, and Ben Scott. Introduction to *Our Unfree Press: 100 Years of Radical Media Criticism,* edited by Robert Waterman McChesney and Ben Scott, 1–30. New York: New Press, 2004.

McFarlane, Robert C., and Zofia Smardz. *Special Trust.* New York: Cadell & Davies, 1994.

McGee, Michael C. "In Search of the 'People': A Rhetorical Alternative." *Quarterly Journal of Speech* 61 (1975): 235–249.

Mestrovic, Stjepan G. *Durkheim and Postmodern Culture.* New York: A. de Gruyter, 1992.

Milligan, Luke M. "The 'Ongoing Criminal Investigation' Constraint: Getting Away with Silence." *William & Mary Bill of Rights Journal* 16 (2008): 747–807.

Mollenhoff, Clark R. *Investigative Reporting: From Courthouse to White House.* London: Collier Macmillan, 1981.

Morrison, Joseph L. *Josephus Daniels: The Small-d Democrat.* Chapel Hill: University of North Carolina Press, 1966.

Neal, Arthur G. *National Trauma and Collective Memory.* Armonk, NY: M. E. Sharpe, 1998.

Nelson, Michael. *The Evolving Presidency: Addresses, Cases, Essays, Letters, Reports, Resolutions, Transcripts, and Other Landmark Documents.* Washington, DC: CQ Press, 1999.

Neumann, Richard K. "The Revival of Impeachment as a Partisan Political Weapon." *Hastings Constitutional Law Quarterly* 34 (2007): 161–327.

Newcomb, Horace, Cary O'Dell, and Noelle Watson. *Encyclopedia of Television.* Chicago: Fitzroy Dearborn Publishers, 1997.

Nixon, Richard M. *The Nixon Presidential Press Conferences.* New York: Earl M. Coleman, 1978.

———. *RN: The Memoirs of Richard Nixon.* New York: Grosset & Dunlap, 1978.

Noogle, Burl. "The Origins of Teapot Dome Investigation." *Mississippi Valley Historical Review* 44 (1957): 237–266.

North, Oliver, and William Novak. *Under Fire: An American Story.* New York: HarperCollins, 1992.

Oakley, Linda Denise. "All We Had to Do Was Rationalize the Sex." In *Aftermath: The Clinton Impeachment and the Presidency in the Age of Political Spectacle*, edited by L. V. Kaplan and B. I. Moran, 186–198. New York: New York University Press, 2001.

Ott, Brian, and Eric Aoki. "The Politics of Negotiating Public Tragedy: Media Framing of the Matthew Shepard Murder." *Rhetoric & Public Affairs* 5 (2002): 483–505.

Patton, Michael Q. *Qualitative Research and Evaluation Methods.* Thousand Oaks, CA: Sage, 2002.

Pious, Richard M. *Why Presidents Fail.* Lanham, MD: Rowman & Littlefield, 2008.

Pitney, John J., Jr. "Clinton and the Republican Party." In *The Post-Modern Presidency: Bill Clinton's Legacy in Politics*, edited by Steven E. Schiecer, 167–182. Pittsburgh: University of Pittsburgh Press, 2000.

Poulakos, John. *Sophistical Rhetoric in Classical Greece.* Columbia: University of South Carolina Press, 1995.

Rasmussen, Karen. "Nixon and the Strategy of Avoidance." *Central States Speech Journal* 27 (1973): 193–202.

Rawson, Hugh, and Margaret Miner. *The Oxford Dictionary of American Quotations.* Oxford: Oxford University Press, 2006.

Renshon, Stanley A. *High Hopes: The Clinton Presidency and the Politics of Ambition.* New York: New York University Press, 1996.

Ritchie, Donald A. *Reporting from Washington: The History of the Washington Press Corps.* Oxford: Oxford University Press, 2006.

Rivers, William L. *The Adversaries: Politics and the Press.* Boston: Beacon Press, 1970.

Rodino, Peter W. *Impeachment of Richard M. Nixon, President of the United States: The Final Report of the Committee on the Judiciary, House of Representatives.* Toronto: Bantam, 1975.

Rohde, David. "Committees and Policy Formulation." In *Institutions of American Democracy: The Legislative Branch*, edited by Paul J. Quirk and Sarah Binder, 201–223. Oxford: University of Oxford Press, 2005.

Ryan, Halford Ross. "Kategoria and Apologia: On Their Rhetorical Criticism as a Speech Set." *Quarterly Journal of Speech* 68 (1982): 254–261.

———. *Oratorical Encounters: Selected Studies and Sources of Twentieth-Century Political Accusations and Apologies.* New York: Greenwood Press, 1988.

Rushing, Janice, and Tom Frentz. "The Mythic Perspective." In *The Art of Rhetorical Criticism*, edited by Jim A. Kuyper, 241–269. Boston: Pearson/Allyn & Bacon, 2005.

Rushing, Janice Hocker, and Thomas S. Frentz, *Projecting the Shadow: The Cyborg Hero in American Film.* Chicago: University Of Chicago Press.

Rutherfurd, Livingston. *John Peter Zenger, His Press, His Trial and a Bibliography of Zenger Imprints.* New York: Peter Smith, 1941.

Sabato, Larry, Mark Stencel, and S. Robert Lichter. *Peepshow: Media and Politics in an Age of Scandal.* Lanham, MD: Rowman & Littlefield, 2000.

Safire, William. *Safire's Political Dictionary.* Oxford: Oxford University Press, 2008.

Schröter, Melani. *Silence and Concealment in Political Discourse.* Amsterdam: Benjamins, 2013.

Schudson, Michael. "Watergate: A Study in Mythology." *Columbia Journalism Review* 31 (1992): 28–33.

———. *Watergate in American Memory: How We Remember, Forget, and Reconstruct the Past.* New York: Basic Books, 1992.

Schudson, Michael, and Elliott King. "The Illusion of Ronald Reagan's Popularity." In *The Power of News*, edited by Michael Schudson, 124–141. Cambridge, MA: Harvard University Press.

Sherman, Lawrence W. "The Mobilization of Scandal." In *Political Corruption: A Handbook*, edited by Arnold J. Heidenheimer, Michael Johnston, and Victor T. Le Vine, 887–911. New Brunswick, NJ: Transaction, 1989.

———. *Scandal and Reform: Controlling Police Corruption.* Berkeley: University of California Press, 1978.

Slotkin, Richard. *Gunfighter Nation.* Norman: University of Oklahoma Press, 1998.

Smith, Craig A. "Bill Clinton in Rhetorical Crisis: The Six Stages of Scandal and Impeachment." In *Images, Scandal, and Communication Strategies of the Clinton Presidency*, edited by Robert E. Denton and Rachel L. Holloway, 173–194. Westport, CT: Praeger, 2003.

Smith, Craig A., and Kathy B. Smith. *The White House Speaks: Presidential Leadership as Persuasion.* Westport, CT: Praeger, 1994.

Smolla, Rodney A. *Smolla and Nimmer on Freedom of Speech.* New York: Clark Boardman Callaghan, 1996.

Solberg, Carl. *Oil Power.* New York: New American Library, 1976.

Stone, Geoffrey R., Louis M. Seidman, Cass R. Sunstein, Mark V. Tushnet, and Pamela S. Karlan. *The First Amendment: A Reader.* New York: Aspen, 2003.

———. *Tempest over Teapot Dome: The Story of Albert B. Fall.* Norman: University of Oklahoma Press, 1998.

———. "Two Western Senators and Teapot Dome: Thomas J. Walsh and Albert B. Fall." *Pacific Northwest Quarterly* 65 (1974): 57–65.

Stratton, David H. "Behind Teapot Dome: Some Personal Insights." *Business History Review* 31 (1957): 385–402.

Stuckey, Mary E. *Strategic Failures in the Modern Presidency*. Cresskill, NJ: Hampton Press, 1997.

Sunstein, Cass R. *Democracy and the Problem of Free Speech*. New York: Free Press, 1995.

Sussman, Barry. *What Americans Really Think: And Why Our Politicians Pay No Attention*. New York: Pantheon Books, 1988.

Tebbel, John William, and Sarah Miles Watts. *The Press and the Presidency: From George Washington to Ronald Reagan*. New York: Oxford University Press, 1985.

Thelen, David P. *Becoming Citizens in the Age of Television: How Americans Challenged the Media and Seized Political Initiative during the Iran-Contra Debate*. Chicago: University of Chicago Press, 1996.

Thomas, Helen. *Watchdogs of Democracy? The Waning Washington Press Corps and How It Has Failed the Public*. New York: Scribner, 2006.

Thompson, Dennis. *Political Ethics and Public Office*. Cambridge, MA: Harvard University Press, 1987.

Thompson, John B. *Political Scandal: Power and Visibility in the Media Age*. Malden, MA: Polity Press, 2000.

United States, John G. Tower, Edmund S. Muskie, and Brent Scowcroft. *The Tower Commission Report: The Full Text of the President's Special Review Board*. New York: Bantam, 1987.

Vatz, Richard E. "The Myth of the Rhetorical Situation." *Philosophy & Rhetoric* 6 (1968): 154–161.

Vaughn, Stephen L. *Encyclopedia of American Journalism*. New York: Routledge, 2008.

Walsh, Lawrence E. *Firewall: The Iran-Contra Conspiracy and Cover-Up*. New York: Norton, 1997.

Ware, B. L., and Wil A. Linkugel. "They Spoke in Defense of Themselves: On the Generic Criticism of *Apologia*." *Quarterly Journal of Speech* 59 (1973): 273–283.

Webber, Elizabeth, and Mike Feinsilber. *Merriam-Webster's Dictionary of Allusions*. Springfield, MA: Merriam-Webster, 1999.

Weisner, Herman B. *The Politics of Justice: A. B. Fall and the Teapot Dome Scandal; A New Perspective*. Albuquerque, NM: Creative Designs, 1994.

Werner, M. R., and John Starr. *Teapot Dome*. New York: Viking, 1959.

White, Eric Charles. *Kaironomia: On the Will-to-Invent*. Ithaca, NY: Cornell University Press, 1987.

White, Theodore H. *Breach of Faith: The Fall of Richard Nixon*. New York: Atheneum Publishers, 1975.

Wilkes, Roger. *Scandal: A Scurrilous History of Gossip*. London: Atlantic, 2002.

Williams, Robert. "Political Scandals and Political Development in the United States." In *Scandals in Past and Contemporary Politics*, edited by John Garrard and James L. Newell, 46–58. New York: Palgrave, 2006.

———. *Political Scandals in the USA*. Edinburgh: Keele University Press, 1998.

Woodward, Bob. "Gerald Ford." In *Profiles in Courage for Our Time*, edited by Caroline Kennedy, 293–218. New York: Hyperion, 2002.

———. *Shadow: Five Presidents and the Legacy of Watergate*. New York: Simon & Schuster, 1999.

Woodward, Bob, and Carl Bernstein. *The Secret Man: The Story of Watergate's Deep Throat*. New York: Simon & Schuster, 2005.

Woodward, Comer Vann. *Responses of the Presidents to Charges of Misconduct*. New York: Dell, 1974.

Wroe, Ann. *Lives, Lies and the Iran-Contra Affair*. London: I. B. Tauris, 1991.

Zaremba, Alan Jay. *Crisis Communication: Theory and Practice*. Armonk, NY: M. E. Sharpe, 2010.

Zenger, John Peter. *A Brief Narrative of the Case and Trial of John Peter Zenger, Printer of the "New York Weekly Journal."* Cambridge, MA: Belknap Press of Harvard University, 1963.

Zelizer, Barbie. "Journalists as Interpretive Communities." *Critical Studies in Media Communication* 10 (1993): 219–237.

———. "On Communicative Practice: The 'Other Worlds' of Journalism and Shamanism." *Southern Folklore* 49 (1992): 19–36.

Index